Kant on Conscience

Studies in Moral Philosophy

VOLUME 11

The titles published in this series are listed at *brill.com/simp*

Kant on Conscience

A Unified Approach to Moral Self-Consciousness

By

Emre Kazim

BRILL

LEIDEN | BOSTON

The Library of Congress Cataloging-in-Publication Data is available online at http://catalog.loc.gov
LC record available at http://lccn.loc.gov/2016054106

Typeface for the Latin, Greek, and Cyrillic scripts: "Brill". See and download: brill.com/brill-typeface.

ISSN 2211-2014
ISBN 978-90-04-34065-7 (hardback)
ISBN 978-90-04-34066-4 (e-book)

Printed by Printforce, the Netherlands

Contents

Acknowledgements

To duly acknowledge influence is a queer task. Indeed, a task that I cannot justly execute in brevity and through the superfluity of words. I must, nonetheless, extend my thanks to John J. Callanan for all of the instruction and patience that he has afforded me throughout the process of completing this work. Thanks are also due to Sorin Baiasu and Jens Timmermann for their careful readings and pertinent feedback. I wish also to extend my gratitude to an anonymous reviewer whose comments proved extremely instructive. Additionally I must acknowledge *Hocam* Ihsan Fazlioglu and Ausaf A. Farooqui. Their erudition has been a great inspiration to me.

This work is dedicated to my dearest and loving parents ... to whom I owe everything.

Dina Muteber Beyazyürek
Kâzım Bekir

After all, I shall assert that honour does not come from one's lineage but rather from knowledge and maturity that come after decency and morality. My conscience impelled me to serve the people, only their praises make me proud. My whole end has been to reveal the honourable Arab lineage of this people and to invite our children to the path of knowledge and civility, so that they will serve humanity. Only God conveys the truth.

Muhammed Emin Galib et-Tavil

Anasının Kuzusu

Key to Abbreviations and Translations of Kant

Apart from references to the *Critique of Pure Reason*, all references to Kant are to the volume and page of the Academy Edition (*Akademie Ausgabe*) of his writings. References to the *Critique of Pure Reason* are to the standard A and B pagination of the first and second editions, respectively. Specific works cited are referenced to by either the full title of the work or an appropriate abbreviation (see below).

First *Critique* A/B	*Critique of Pure Reason*, trans. and ed. P. Guyer and A. W. Wood, Cambridge University Press (2009).
Second *Critique*	*Critique of Practical Reason*, trans. and ed. M. Gregor, Cambridge University Press (2012).
Third *Critique*	*Critique of the Power of Judgement*, trans. P. Guyer and E. Matthews, ed. P. Guyer, Cambridge University Press (2001).
Metaphysics of Morals	*The Metaphysics of Morals*, trans. and ed. M. Gregor, Cambridge University Press (1996).
Groundwork	*Groundwork of the Metaphysics of Morals*, trans. and ed. M. Gregor, Cambridge University Press (2010).
Miscarriage	*On the Miscarriage of All Philosophical Trials in Theodicy*, trans. G. di Giovanni, in *Religion and Rational Theology*, ed. A. W. Wood and G. di Giovanni, Cambridge University Press (2005).
Religion	*Religion within the Boundaries of Mere Reason*, trans. G. di Giovanni, in *Religion and Rational Theology*, ed. A. W. Wood and G. di Giovanni, Cambridge University Press (2005).
Lectures on Ethics	*Lectures on Ethics*, trans. P. Heath, ed. P. Heath and J. B. Schneewind, Cambridge University Press (2001). This text is comprised of notes taken by Kant's students which I directly refer to in each case in the following way: *Herder, Collins, Mrongovius* and *Vigilantius*. I also refer to *Brauer*, which are translated notes taken by a student of Kant, *Lectures on Ethics*, trans. J. Macmurray, Methuen & Co. (1979).
Lectures on Logic	*Lectures on Logic*, trans. and ed. J. M. Young, Cambridge University Press (2009).

Lectures on Religion	*Lectures on the Philosophical Doctrine of Religion*, trans. A. W. Wood, in *Religion and Rational Theology*, ed. A. W. Wood and G. di Giovanni, Cambridge University Press (2005).
Notes on Moral Philosophy	From: *Notes and Fragments*, trans. C. Bowman, P. Guyer and F. Rauscher, ed. P. Guyer, Cambridge University Press (2005).
Prolegomena	*Prolegomena to Any Future Metaphysics*, trans. and ed. G. Hatfield, Cambridge University Press (2007).
Conflict of Faculties	*The Conflict of the Faculties*, trans. M. J. Gregor and R. Anchor, in *Religion and Rational Theology*, ed. A. W. Wood and G. di Giovanni, Cambridge University Press (2005).
The End of All Things	*The End of All Things*, trans. A. W. Wood, in *Religion and Rational Theology*, ed. A. W. Wood and G. di Giovanni, Cambridge University Press (2005).
Lectures on Anthropology	*Lectures on Anthropology*, trans. R. R. Clewis, R. B. Louden, G. F. Munzel and A. W. Wood, ed. R. B. Louden and A. W. Wood, Cambridge University Press (2012).
Observations on the Feeling of the Beautiful and Sublime	*Observations on the Feeling of the Beautiful and Sublime and Other Writings*, trans. P. Guyer, ed. P. Guyer and P. Frierson, Cambridge University Press (2011).
b.	Date of birth.
d.	Date of death.

CHAPTER 1

Introduction

1.1   Introduction

The concept of conscience is a curiously neglected aspect of Kant's practical philosophy. As the first systematic treatment of Kant's theory of conscience in the Anglophone literature, the present study seeks to fill this lacuna.[1] No doubt

---

1   For a selection of studies conducted in other languages see W. Hohlrabe, *Kants Lehre vom Gewissen; historisch-kritisch dargestellt*, Inaugural Dissertation, Leipzig (1880), A. Senser, *Kant und das Gewissen* (Phd diss., University of Bern 1997) and F. Desideri, *L'ascolto della coscienza: una ricerca filosofica*, Feltrinelli Editore (1998). To the best of my knowledge the following is a list of the major treatments of Kant's theory of conscience: D. Moyar, 'Unstable Autonomy: Conscience and Judgment in Kant's Moral Philosophy', *Journal of Moral Philosophy*, 5, (2008), 327–60, A. W. Wood, *Kantian Ethics*, Cambridge University Press (2008), 182–92, J. J. Howard, 'Kant and Moral Imputation: Conscience and the Riddle of the Given', *American Catholic Philosophical Quarterly*, 78, 4, 609–27, J. Timmermann, 'Kant on Conscience, "Indirect" Duty, and Moral Error', *International Philosophical Quarterly*, 46, 3, (2006), 293–308, M. Vujosevic, 'The Judge in the Mirror: Kant on Conscience', *Kantian Review*, 19, 3, (2014), 449–74, T. Hill, *Human Welfare and Moral Worth*, Oxford University Press (2002), 279–307, M. Despland, 'Can Conscience Be Hypocritical? The Contrasting Analyses of Kant and Hegel', *The Harvard Theological Review*, 68, ¾, (1975), 357–70, M. Sticker, 'When the Reflective Watch-Dog Barks: Conscience and Self-Deception in Kant', *Journal of Value Inquiry*, (forthcoming), 1–20, O. Ware, 'The Duty of Self-Knowledge', *Philosophy and Phenomenological Research*, 79, (2009), 671–98, M. Ojakangas, *The Voice of Conscience: A Political Genealogy of Western Ethical Experience*, Bloomsbury Academic Press (2013), 143–63, H. J. Paton, 'Conscience and Kant', *Kant-Studien*, 70, (1979), 239–51, A. M. Esser, 'The Inner Court of Conscience, Moral Self-Knowledge, and the Proper Object of Duty (TL 6:437–444)', in *Kant's "Tugendlehre". A Comprehensive Commentary*, ed. O. Sensen, J. Timmermann and A. Trampota, Walter de Gruyter (2013), 269–91. There are also a number of more minor studies of Kant's theory of conscience, a list of these are as follows: R. Sorabji, *Moral Conscience Through the Ages*, Oxford University Press (2014), 178–83, R. P. Stevens, *Kant on Moral Practice: A Study of Moral Success and Failure*, Mercer University Press (1981), P. Guyer, 'Moral Feelings in the Metaphysics of Morals', in *Kant's Metaphysics of Morals: a Critical Guide*, ed. L. Denis, Cambridge University Press (2010), 143–52, H. D. Kittsteiner, 'Casuistry and Character', in *Conscience and Casuistry in Early Modern Europe,* ed. E. Leites, Cambridge University Press (1988), 185–213, M. G. J. Beets, *Reality and Freedom: Reflections on Kant's Moral Philosophy*, Eburon Press (1988). Interestingly, D. Velleman attempts to reconcile Kant's notion of conscience with Freud's theory of moral development. I do not address Velleman's paper in this study because he does not address Kant's specific writings on conscience but rather explores how Kantian concepts such as

the relative lack of attention to this aspect of Kant's ethics is partly due to the fact that discussions of conscience appear scattered and disconnected within the corpus. This naturally leads to the view that Kant had no unified theory of conscience, a view that is reflected in the secondary literature.² Indeed,

---

duty and autonomy can be viewed in terms of Freudian notions of conscience, D. Velleman, 'The Voice of Conscience', *Proceedings of the Aristotelian Society*, 99, (1999), 57–76. I will also refrain from addressing S. Kahn's forthcoming treatment of conscience as I have not been able to access his text ('Kant's Theory of Conscience', in *Rethinking Kant*, ed. P. Muchnik, O. Thorndike, Cambridge Scholars Publishing, forthcoming). For treatments of Kantian conscience in the German literature see, F. Ishikawa, 'Das Gerichtshof-Modell des Gewissens', *Aufklärung*, 7, 1, (1993), 43–55, T. S. Hoffmann 'Gewissen als praktische Apperzeption: Zur Lehre vom Gewissen in Kants Ethik-Vorlesungen' *Kant-Studien*, 93, (2002), 424–43, G. Funke, 'Gutes Gewissen, falsches Bewußtsein, richtende Vernunft', *Zeitschrift für Philosophische Forschung*, 25, (1971), 226–51, W. Heubült, 'Gewissen bei Kant', *Kant-Studien*, 71, (1980), 445–54, E. Schmidt, D. Schönecker, 'Kants Philosophie des Gewissens. Skizze für eine kommentarische Interpretation', in M. Egger (ed.), *Philosophie nach Kant. Neue Wege zum Verständnis von Kants Transzendental- und Moralphilosophie*, Berlin/Boston: de Gruyter, (2014), 279–312, E. Schmidt, D. Schönecker, 'Vernunft, Herz und Gewissen. Kants Theorie der Urteilskraft zweiter Stufe als Modell für die Medizinische Ethik', in *Gewissen. Dimensionen eines Grundbegriffs medizinischer Ethik*, ed. F.-J. Bormann, V. Wetzstein, Berlin/Boston: de Gruyter, (2014), 229–50, O. Sensen, 'Kants Begriff des Gewissens', in, *Gewissen zwischen Gefühl und Vernunft*, ed. S. Bunke, K. Mihaylova, Würzburg: Königshausen und Neumann, (2015), 126–38, and, G. Lehmann, *Kants Tugenden*, Berlin: Walter de Gruyter, (1980), 27–36.

2   Central themes that run throughout both the more considered and the more minor pieces of secondary literature are the claims that Kant's various discussions of conscience are inconsistent and unsystematic. For example, Ojakangas describes Kant's writings on conscience as 'minimal', as 'remarks [that] are sporadic rather than systematic' and as inconsistently shifting through various works (*The Voice of Conscience*, 149). Sorabji argues that Kant's conception continuously changes throughout his work, exhibiting four different conceptions: an early conception (1762–64) that allows conscience to be 1. 'artificial' and 2. 'erroneous'. A conception found both in the *Metaphysics of Morals* and *Religion* that 3. places error in the faculty of understanding rather than in the judgement of conscience and has conscience in a supervisory role, passing judgements regarding the thoroughness with which an agent examines their actions, and another conception also found in the *Metaphysics of Morals* that 4. conscience addresses the apparent problem of a person being split, in terms of the various faculties within the mind of an agent when in a state of moral deliberation. Paton argues that Kant's conception of conscience can be criticised on the account that his use of the term seems to shift throughout his writings, seemingly committing him to various, imprecise and contradictory position ('Conscience and Kant', 239). Moyar ('Unstable Autonomy, 329) and Esser ('The Inner Court', 270–4) also claim that Kant's assertions regarding conscience shift and are inconsistent. Timmermann offers a limited study (concentrating on a particular dimension of Kantian conscience, namely the notion of an 'indirect duty') which points to differences and contradictions that can be found in Kant's treatment of conscience in

prima facie reasons for thinking that the various treatments of conscience cannot be considered as internally consistent are that his writings on conscience span his entire Critical period, that he talks of conscience both as practical reason and within the context of feelings (*Metaphysics of Morals* 6:399–403), that conscience is discussed in terms of erroneousness (*Collins* 27:353, *Herder* 27:43, *Religion* 6:187) and as non-erring (*Metaphysics of Morals* 6:401, *Miscarriage* 8:268, *Vigilantius* 27:614–5), and that conscience is talked of both in a non-religious sense and as the voice of God (*Metaphysics of Morals* 6:439–40, *Miscarriage* 8:270, *Herder* 27:19, *Collins* 27:296, *Vigilantius* 27:575). Contrary to the dominant view found within the secondary literature I will show that the various treatments and talk of conscience (as a feeling, a power, a judgement, a capacity, a court, as the voice of God, etc.) are philosophically coherent descriptions of the same unified thing. I shall term this the 'Unity Thesis'. I will present Kant's notion of conscience within the various contexts of his Critical thought and philosophically evaluate the coherence of his claims.[3]

Religion and the *Metaphysics of Morals* ('Kant on Conscience', 304fn30, 305fn34). Hill does not make the explicit claim that Kant is inconsistent, although he does explain that his analysis represents only a 'selective endorsement' of what he takes to be plausible claims by Kant and as such his treatment neither attempts to explore, nor makes claims regarding, the consistency of Kant's position (*Human Welfare*, 279–80). Similarly, Howard states that 'my goal [...] is only to defend a particular [...] function of conscience' ('Kant and Moral Imputation', 610). Indeed, both Sticker's and Ware's articles primarily concern conscience and self-deception ('When the Reflective Watch-Dog Barks', 1–20, 'The Duty of Self-Knowledge', 690–8, respectively. Where the latter identifies a shift in the discussion of conscience between *Religion* and the *Metaphysics of Morals*). However, two notable exceptions within the secondary literature that do treat Kant's notion of conscience as a consistent and coherent whole are those of Wood (*Kantian Ethics*, 182–92) and Vujosevic ('The Judge in the Mirror', 449–74). Although Vujosevic attempts to 'join together Kant's views about the natures and activities of conscience into one coherent account' (ibid., 453), she nonetheless omits central elements from her discussion such as the crucially important notion of an erring conscience and the notion of an internal lie (see, ibid., 472fn7). Indeed, both treatments are cursory and differ from the account that I provide in this study.

3   A hermeneutic note is in order regarding the use of Kant's lecture notes (*Lectures on Ethics*). The lecture notes of Kant's students that I will primarily draw upon are those that are translated and contain references to discussions of conscience. These are (where the number proceeding the text's abbreviation represents when the notes were taken): Johann Gottlieb Herder's notes from lectures on Kant's practical philosophy (*Herder* 1762/4), Georg Ludwig Collins's notes from Kant's lectures on moral philosophy (*Collins* 1784/5[?]) and Johann Friedrich Vigilantius's notes from Kant's lectures on the *Metaphysics of Morals* (*Vigilantius* 1793–4). Although the date of *Collins* is given as 1784/5 (in keeping with the date that Collins himself wrote at the beginning of the manuscript), it is far more likely that the notes were

A central aim of this study is philosophical. Locating and reconstructing Kant's claims within his Critical philosophy will provide the preamble to analytical explorations of certain issues raised by his theory of conscience. The analytical approach that I take presents Kantian conscience favourably and sheds light on the importance of conscience to the wider ethical project. It is my contention that a central question that Kant's theory of conscience addresses is moral motivation and imputability. In this study I highlight the motivational efficacy of conscience, how this relates to moral action (Chapter 2), and then connect this to other aspects of conscience (Chapters 3–5). By approaching Kantian conscience in this unified manner, I hope to show that the neglect of other scholars to treat conscience more comprehensively has led to the false view that conscience is of merely marginal importance to Kant's ethics. Indeed, I will demonstrate that conscientious reflection provides an agent with a mechanism for higher-order moral judgement (Chapter 3), for resisting a particular class of self-deception (Chapter 4), and as a crucial aid in moral

---

initially taken in the mid-1770's and then annotated in 1784/5. I also make use of notes taken by Theodor Friederich Brauer (1780/81)—hereafter referred to as *Brauer*. Here I use the page number of the translation rather than the page of the Academy Edition. It is noticeable that Brauer's notes closely parallel *Collins* (with translational differences), as such I read Collins's notes to be at the very least attributable to Kant's lessons in the early 1780's. Important to note is that the former two lecture series were based on two texts by A. G. Baumgarten (*Introduction to Practical First Philosophy* and *Philosophical Ethics*) and as such Kant's own notion of conscience was undoubtedly influenced by this. At various points in this study I will attempt to note where I think this is most apparent. As both texts are yet to be translated, here I am indebted to Dr. Toshiro Osawa's study of Baumgarten, which he has kindly allowed me to utilise ('Perfection and Morality: A Commentary on Baumgarten's *Ethica Philosophica* and its Relevance to Kantian Ethics', PhD Diss. Macquarie University 2014). This study is particularly germane as it reads Baumgarten's ethics within an exploration of its relevance to Kantian Ethics. I should note that Dr. Osawa continues to develop his study and as such any further reference to his work that is based on my use of it here should be done in consultation with Dr. Osawa directly. Additionally, as observed from the dates when these were taken, *Herder* is firmly in the pre-Critical period, *Collins* is from the late pre-Critical/early-Critical period and *Vigilantius* is from the matured Critical period. As these are the notes of Kant's students and because of the scholarly debate concerning the authoritativeness of these sources, throughout this study I primarily rely on Kant's published work and use the *Lectures on Ethics* in a supportive manner. More specifically I do not present arguments that are solely based on the *Lectures on Ethics*. In particular, where appropriate I will justify my use of *Herder* as these notes where taken quite some time before the Critical period. Finally, where relevant I will utilise and footnote discussions, comments and remarks from *Lectures on Religion* (1783–6), Kant's *Notes on Moral Philosophy* (1783–4) and *Conflict of Faculties* (1798).

self-improvement (Chapter 5). It is only when taken as a whole that the significance of conscience to Kant's ethics is understood.

Indeed, in defending the Unity Thesis I will not only bring to the fore the richness of Kant's theory of conscience, but also highlight the concern that Kant himself has for this concept. Moreover, I will show that the concept not only reveals aspects of Kant's thoughts regarding key themes within the corpus, but also shows that conscience itself—its function, activity and cultivation—provides a perspective on the nature of moral practice in Kant generally. My claim is that conscience demonstrates a double movement. Firstly it provides a direct aide in the advancement of moral action through its higher-order moral judgement. Secondly, conscience provides an important *turn inwards*. It directs an agent to show concern for actions that 'I' must undertake. Conscience brings together the (external) practical action with the (internal) concern for morality itself: I must act morally, and such moral actions must be conducted veraciously. More directly, Kantian conscience helps us better understand the ethics as a whole when it is pointed out that it completes the moral picture. Conscience functions at the higher (reflective) level of morality. When Kant discusses conscience, he can be read as doing so *after* laying the foundations of this ethical thought in the *Groundwork* and the Second *Critique*. In these texts the basic concepts of morality and moral action are presented. It is following these that Kant can then discuss moral practice more generally. It is in this broader sense, in explication of the full vocation of moral life, that conscience can be observed as central, and as such, in order to fully appreciate Kant's ethics his notion of conscience must be understood. In other words, conscience completes Kant's account of a fully functioning moral agent (hence why the concept touches on such disparate themes as higher-order moral judgement, subjective certitude, and moral cultivation).

Regarding the Unity Thesis a number of clarifications are in order. By claiming that Kant's various treatments and talk of conscience are philosophically coherent descriptions of the same unified thing, I am not asserting that Kant's notion of conscience remained the same throughout the Critical period. Indeed, that he amends, adds to and changes the emphasis on particular aspects of conscience is entirely compatible with the Unity Thesis. What the Unity Thesis does assert is that the seemingly disparate discussions of conscience do not in themselves evidence entirely novel and discontinuous notions of conscience. As such, this study, if successful, provides an important descriptive account of Kant's notion of conscience. The Unity Thesis will demonstrate that it is possible to read Kant's descriptions of conscience in as disparate terms as 'practical reason' and 'the voice of God' while referring to the same unified concept i.e. internal consistency. Showing how Kant is able to do this will involve a foray into such topics as Kant's theory of judgement, the epistemology of belief, the possibility of self-deception and the notion of moral self-improvement. My methodological approach involves a conceptual reconstruction of Kant's numerous discussions of conscience throughout his Critical period, investigating the coherence of his claims in light of the broader claims of his ethical corpus and locating the various discussions within the appropriate context that he was talking within. Philosophical notions of conscience that were present in the Early Modern period are key to understanding why Kant discusses conscience in various ways. Therefore, it is important that the historical basics are introduced and that what Kant is likely to be referring to and reacting against is historically situated. This will not involve an attempt at full historical reconstruction. Instead I will thematically introduce notions where appropriate at relevant junctures of this study.[4]

Two more general points can be made in support of the Unity Thesis. Firstly, at various points throughout the study I treat the moral feeling of respect as analogous to conscience. Given that the various descriptions of respect and the various contexts within which respect is treated are all referents to one unifying concept, by analogy it is likely that Kant would provide an account of conscience in a similarly (albeit less robust) unified manner. Secondly, a stronger reason in support of the Unity Thesis is the fact that Kant raises and discusses the various disparate notions of conscience *within the same context*. Passages that describe conscience as judgement, as non-erring and as the

---

4 It should be noted that my assumption is that Kant was familiar with the issues that various thinkers had raised even if he had not read all of the works of the philosophers that I will reference. Hence I follow Schneewind in including Pufendorf among Kant's influences although there is no evidence that Kant had read his work. See J. B. Schneewind, *The Invention of Autonomy*, Cambridge University Press (1998), 509. Here I use the selected translation of *The Duty of Man and Citizen* found in J. B. Schneewind, *Moral Philosophy from Montaigne to Kant*, Cambridge University Press (2003), 156–82 (for a full translation see S. Pufendorf, *On the Duty of Man and Citizen According to Natural Law*, ed. J. Tully, Cambridge University Press (1991)). The cited pages are in reference to Schneewind's translations. Aside from specific references to philosophers that Kant may have been responding to there is the more general Protestant-Lutheran tradition to consider. Here I draw from the in-depth treatment of the Lutheran approach to conscience in, B. T. G. Mayes, *Counsel and Conscience, Lutheran Casuistry and Moral Reasoning after the Reformation*, Vandenhoeck & Ruprecht (2011). The most extensive overview and analysis of Kant's historical context that pays attention specifically to the development of his ethical theory is found in Schneewind, *The Invention of Autonomy*. Other important studies include *Conscience and Casuistry in Early Modern Europe*, ed. E. Leites, Cambridge University Press (1988) and S. Darwall, *The British Moralists and the Internal 'Ought' 1640–1740*, Cambridge University Press (1995). For a general overview of the period see T. Irwin, *The Development of Ethics, Vol II*, Oxford University Press (2011).

voice of God, all occur in discussions that follow one another. For example, in the *Metaphysics of Morals* (6:400–1) Kant moves immediately from talk of conscience as constitutive to the non-erring claim and then to the fact that conscience must be cultivated (when the text then returns to the subject of conscience, the discussion naturally correlates to the latter point of the cultivation of conscience via a discussion of the inner judge as ideal other/God (6:438–41)). In *Religion* (6:184–6) Kant begins the section by posing the question of how the judgement of conscience is to be utilised. He follows this with assertions regarding subjective certainty before entering into a discussion of the relationship between conscience and (revealed) religious belief. In *Collins* 27:351–6 he moves from discussing the relationship between conscience and moral judgement, to matters that relate to the analogues of conscience, to the notion of an errant conscience and then to the temporal operation of conscience (before, during and after an action). Similar observations can be made in other discussions (for example see *Vigilantius* 27:614–20 and *Miscarriage* 8:268–70). Although it is also the case that there are more sporadic and piecemeal comments on the subject of conscience throughout the practical corpus, that his notion of conscience can in the main be drawn from specific discussions of conscience strongly suggests that the notion was considered by Kant to be a unified concept (notwithstanding the complex and difficult task—as evidenced by this study—of reconstructing, comparing and evaluating these various treatments).[5]

By neglecting the fact that these various aspects of conscience are discussed together, commentators have either misunderstood or misinterpreted the importance of conscience. For example, the judgement of conscience cannot be understood outside of a discussion on moral improvement, which naturally allays into a discussion of perfection and the divine. Indeed, the non-erring judgement of conscience cannot be understood without contextualising it within a discussion of self-deception. Moreover, given that the subject concerns moral motivation (a fundamental issue within Kant's ethics), it is my contention that conscience is crucial in understanding the moral project as a whole and the development of an agent's character *qua* moral practice. It is only through this sustained treatment of conscience that the centrality of

---

5 Kant distinguishes between the following temporal operations of conscience: conscience before an agent acts, conscience during an action and the voice of conscience that is heard after an action (*Herder* 27:44, *Vigilantius* 27:618–20). Distinctions between the three are to be made (particularly between the latter and the former two) and as such I will discuss issues pertaining to this in the study. However, unless stated otherwise it is to be taken that the temporal operation of conscience that is being discussed is of conscience before an act.

conscience is highlighted. As such, this study will be of particular relevance to those interested in the aforementioned notions and to those who are interested more broadly in Kant's views on the practice of morality. Finally, because Kant's philosophy is situated at the end of the Early Modern period (where conscience is of central importance) readers of this epoch will find Kant's reactions to discussions of conscience within this context particularly informative.

1.2   Outline of Chapters

The study is divided into chapters that treat Kant's assertions regarding conscience thematically. I show that in each seemingly disparate description of conscience he is referring to a particular aspect of the notion. At the end of each chapter I write a brief conclusion that indicates the relevance of the chapter to the overall Unity Thesis.

In Chapter 2 'Conscience and its Judgement', I will concentrate primarily on passages from the *Metaphysics of Morals* (6:399–403) and argue that Kant takes conscience to be a particular manifestation of practical reason which results in a feeling that is produced as a result of its determination. I show that conscience passes a higher-order judgement with respect to whether or not an agent has been diligent in the examination of their actions. In order to forward such claims I begin by introducing the concept of 'moral feeling' within which conscience is discussed and show how this concept relates to moral motivation in general. I then explain that conscience is an activity of practical reason (I denote this as 'intellectual conscience') whose determination affects the capacity of moral feeling. Following this I explicate that the judgement of conscience concerns whether an agent has 'diligently examined' (*Religion* 6:186) their actions. I then explicate that should an agent choose to consult their conscience (which I refer to in terms of 'voluntarism'), a higher-order form of moral imputation upon moral judgement will occur. This chapter constitutes the first stage in the defence of the Unity Thesis by outlining the fundamental nature and function of conscience *qua* the judgement of conscience.

Throughout Kant's various discussions of conscience there is an insistent denial of the possibility of an erring conscience, which in the *Metaphysics of Morals* he calls 'an absurdity' (6:401). Herein this shall be referred to as the 'Absurdity Thesis'. Given the centrality of the Absurdity Thesis to Kant's overall notion of conscience, Chapter 3 'The Errors and Failures of Conscience', concerns the explication of this notion. My central claim in this chapter is that Kant is found to have two expressions of the Absurdity Thesis: one found in *Miscarriage* and *Vigilantius* (Absurdity Thesis$_1$) and another found in the *Metaphysics of Morals* (Absurdity Thesis$_2$). Through textual exegesis I outline these expressions and argue that whereas Absurdity Thesis$_1$ is philosophically coherent, Absurdity Thesis$_2$ is problematic and implausible. I also discuss the relationship between the two expressions. I point out that although Kant is being inconsistent both expressions nonetheless share the notion of a higher-order judgement that concerns subjective belief. I argue that the two expressions are a result of Kant responding to two different questions in the historical context regarding the errors of conscience. Following this I discuss the notion of 'subjective certainty', which is a notion that concerns the propositional subjective *beliefs* that an agent assents to. I then explicate Kant's notion of conscientiousness, showing that a conscientious agent is one that takes a sceptical stance towards their beliefs and the evaluative procedures that are used to substantiate their beliefs, and is thereby always in an active state of re-evaluation. Finally, I discuss further the categories of error and failure that are associated with conscience and highlight in particular their relation to moral judgement. Chapter 3 provides an important step in the defence of the Unity Thesis as it builds upon, and fleshes out further, the explication of the judgement of conscience presented in Chapter 2.

In Chapter 4 'Conscience and Internal Lies' I provide the first exploration that addresses specifically Kant's notion of an internal lie within his discussions of conscience. I argue that Kantian conscience must be viewed as a capacity that can keep self-deception in check and in a roundabout manner facilitate the fundamental duty to oneself, namely to maintain personhood (taken as rational agency). It will also become clear that the analysis presented supports an interpretation that reads Kant's fundamental value as rational self-governance. Central to this chapter will be an explication of Kant's treatment of the 'inner judge' as an 'ideal other', as presented in passages from the *Metaphysics of Morals* (6:429–30, 438–9). In order to interpret these passages I first provide a conceptual analysis of lying, then secondly turn to Kant's discussions of lying in terms of duties. It is only following these treatments that I will be able to fully explicate the above passages. The format of the chapter will be as follows. I begin by providing an analysis of Kant's definition of a lie as an 'intentional untruth' (*Metaphysics of Morals* 6:429–30). I argue that there are four conditions that a lie should satisfy to be considered a lie, these being: i. intention to deceive, ii. belief, iii. background assumptions of beliefs/context of action, and iv. communicability. In arguing for this I challenge the 'semantic' view that language is fundamental to lying by suggesting that the condition of communicability can be fulfilled without the use of language. Following this

I then explicate the distinction between lying as it relates to the duty agents have to others and as it relates to the duty agents have to oneself (this involves discussing lying as it relates to the Doctrine of Right (6:239) and the Doctrine of Virtue (6:429–31)). This will introduce Kant's notions of external and internal lies (6:430), the latter of which I then expand upon. This will involve exploring how internal lies violate the basic duty to oneself to maintain personhood (a duty grounded upon the rational nature of an agent). Finally, via the employment of the notion of 'multiple consciousness', I provide an account of how internal lies are possible and show how this notion fits with Kant's discussion of the internal court of conscience. Chapter 4 is a natural corollary to the discussion of the non-erring judgement of conscience found in Chapter 3, and as such it is a vital step in the defence of the Unity Thesis. Indeed, the notion of subjective certainty provides the foundation upon which Kant can present conscience as a mechanism that resists a particular class of self-deception.

In Chapter 5 'The Cultivation of Conscience and Moral Self-Improvement', I explicate Kant's account of moral self-improvement with respect to the cultivation of conscience, particularly through religious conceptions. I argue that the reason Kant employs rational religious notions in his various treatments of conscience is because he believes that such representations present a more effective means, relative to non-religious rational representation, by which conscience is to be cultivated as an indirect duty. I also argue that Kant's claim is philosophically plausible. In order to achieve this, I begin by outlining that for Kant moral self-improvement involves three notions of perfection, namely i. 'pragmatic perfection' (concerned with the proper use of an agent's capacities), ii. 'agent perfection' (concerned with attaining a disposition of always choosing to act morally) and iii. 'end perfection' (concerned with the notion of the highest good, which is the notion of an idealised world). I then turn to explicating the cultivation of conscience in terms of Kant's warnings against 'bad conscience' (*Herder* 27:43–4, see also *Collins* 27:356–7, *Vigilantius* 27:619–20), which is a conscience that is deficient in terms of practical action. Following this I then explicate the notion of an agent having an 'indirect duty' (*Metaphysics of Morals* 6:401) to cultivate their conscience and explain that such cultivation is through 'rational [religious] representation' (6:400). This involves detailing how the notion of 'holiness' can function as an aspirational ideal that an agent can strive for. Concerning the Unity Thesis, this chapter shows that Kant's views on conscience are firmly situated within his views on moral self-improvement and that conscience must be cultivated in such a manner as to sustain the viability of the internal court that an agent takes authoritatively. Indeed, this highlights that the concept of conscience may contain the notion of divinity, a point that cannot be understood by simply looking at the judgement of conscience (Chapter 2), or the non-erring nature of conscience (Chapter 3), or the fact that conscience resists self-deception (Chapter 4).

I close this study in Chapter 6 with a brief conclusion that evaluates the Unity Thesis and offers suggestions for further inquiries.

Conscience: The Judgement and Its Feeling

2.1 Introduction

Within the historical context there are some philosophers who characterised conscience in terms of a feeling and others who characterised conscience in terms of a rational judgement. In addition to this there were discussions that offered characterisations of conscience in terms of first-order and higher-order moral judgements and reflections. For example, the Natural Law theorists Pufendorf and Grotius,[1] both characterised conscience rationalistically and in terms of a higher-order judgement upon natural law.[2] Similarly, in an

---

1 For detailed analysis of the development of modern natural law see K. Haakonssen, *Natural Law and Moral Philosophy*, Cambridge University Press (1996), T. Hochstrasser, *Natural Law Theories in the Early Enlightenment*, Cambridge University Press (2000), I. Hunter, *Rival Enlightenments: Civil and Metaphysical Philosophy in Early Modern German*, Cambridge University Press (2001), R. Tuck, *The Rights of War and Peace: Political Thought and the International Order from Grotius to Kant*, Oxford University Press (1999), and K. Haakonssen, 'Early Modern Natural Law', in *Routledge Companion to Ethics*, ed. J. Skorupski, Routledge (2010), 76–87.

2 Pufendorf tells us that 'the efficacy of a natural obligation consists principally in the fact that it binds the conscience of a man, or that a man realizes, when he has not fulfilled it, that he is disobeying the will of God, whose law all men recognize that they should obey, just as they are indebted to Him for their very existence' (*The Duty of Man and Citizen*, 156). As such, Pufendorf's notion of conscience is simply the ability of agents to judge actions in terms of laws. Hugo Grotius discusses the notion of conscience in his magnum opus *On the Law of War and Peace* (all quotes taken from Schneewind, *Moral Philosophy from Montaigne to Kant*, 88–110. For a full translation see H. Grotius, *On the Law of War and Peace* A. C. Campbell, Wildside Press (2011)). For a brief overview of Grotius on Conscience see Ojakangas, *The Voice of Conscience*, 101–2). Before explicating his view of conscience Grotius first asserts that humans are endowed with a faculty of 'knowing and of acting in accordance with general principles' (Grotius, *On the Law of War and Peace*, 91). He then explicates his theory of natural law, which is 'the dictate of right reason, which points out that an act, according as it is or is not in conformity with rational nature, has in it a quality of moral baseness or moral necessity; and that in consequence, such an act is either forbidden or enjoined by the author of nature, God' (ibid., 98). For Grotius conscience bears witness to the natural law, he asserts that 'justice brings peace of conscience, while injustice causes torments and anguish' (ibid., 94). In sort, Grotius's notion of conscience is one of a capacity that is able to judge actions and bring about an effect in the agent (in terms of a sense of peace or anguish) in accordance with natural law.

© KONINKLIJKE BRILL NV, LEIDEN, 2017 | DOI 10.1163/9789004340664_003

extended discussion of conscience, Wolff asserts that agents have a 'natural obligation' to pursue 'virtue' and this natural obligation comes from the fact that men are endowed with reason, which coupled with 'understanding', will lead them to fulfil this natural obligation.[3] Espousing a perfectionist view of virtue,[4] Wolff maintains that reason provides an agent with knowledge of what the right thing to do is and through conscience an agent can judge whether or not they have acted in accordance with that which is right to do ('the judgment of whether our actions are good or bad is called conscience').[5] As such, Wolff's notion of conscience is as a higher-order rational moral judgement.[6]

In contrast to these views is the characterisation of conscience as a moral feeling. For example, both Hutcheson's and Shaftesbury's notions of conscience are situated within their perspective formulations of 'moral sense',

---

3   Wolff dedicates an entire chapter to conscience in his text, *Vernüfftige Gedancken von der enschen Thun und Lassen zu Beförderung ihrer Glückseeligkeit* (1736) (trans. Schneewind), *Moral Philosophy from Montaigne to Kant*, 331–50). Quotes from 333–4.

4   Ibid., 334–5.Wolff also argues that observation of the law of nature also makes 'man happy' and thus 'one cannot call happy anyone without virtue' (ibid., 338). Although Wolff discusses happiness within the context of his discussion of conscience, because he takes perfection and happiness to be intractably related, I will not discuss happiness further.

5   Ibid. He expands upon this by stating, '[I]nsofar as man is capable of judging the consequences of his actions as to whether his [...] condition [...is] more perfect, so far he has a conscience' (ibid.). Here the judgement of conscience is the judgement about how the particular action will effect the extent to which an agent is closer to, or further from, their natural condition i.e. perfection.

6   Due to the fact that an agent's pursuit of virtue is to seek perfection, Wolff argues that there are cases when theoretical conscience picks out something as good, but practical conscience picks out something as bad, and in this way 'we take the good for bad' (ibid.) Wolff reduces this down to 'special circumstances', which, it seems would be tantamount to situations where what is theoretically 'good' would practically result in a move away from perfection. Wolff argues that there is a 'teaching/theoretical' conscience that 'judges whether something is good or bad' and that there is a 'moving/practical' conscience that judges 'whether we ought to do it or not' (ibid.). In a much less developed account of conscience, Leibniz argues that there are God given 'instincts' that 'lead, straight away and without reasoning, to part what reason commands', and these instincts are called 'conscience'. This seems to suggest that conscience is a motivational capacity that interacts with rational judgements. Leibniz acknowledges that such instincts can be obstructed by desires and inculcation of immoral customs however he points out that evidence for this instinct can be found by appealing to the apparent respect accorded to this instinct universally i.e. in all traditions. Leibniz argues that such instincts are indispensable in making reason practical, otherwise reason will remain inactive (G. W. Leibniz, *New Essays on Human Understanding*, ed. B. Remmant and J. Bennet, Cambridge University Press (1998), 70, 94, page numbers correspond to the original text).

or the 'moral faculty' that all agents are said to have within themselves.[7] On Shaftesbury's account, moral sense is a feeling that does not occur immediately but rather arises through reflection by an agent with respect to the agent's state.[8] When an agent's state is in harmony with the natural state, or in disharmony with it, moral sense will apprehend this and this will lead to an agent's happiness or unhappiness.[9] Conscience, being part of the moral faculty that moral sense is rooted within, is similarly a result of this reflection. However Shaftesbury introduces conscience after talking of the self-consciousness that is associated with 'several degrees of reflection',[10] thereby suggesting that

---

7   Francis Hutcheson asserts that all agents are born with a moral faculty (*On Human Nature*, ed. T. Mautner, Cambridge University Press (1993), 99–100. This is actually two texts, *Reflections on Our Common Systems of Morality* (96–106), and *On the Social Nature of Man* (124–47). Mautner also provides an extensive overview of Hutcheson's work in this edition). In a discussion of moral motivation Hutcheson argues that there is a 'natural conscience' from which agents can 'see clearly that the vices do not belong to our nature'. He asserts that 'however much the force and power of this sense or conscience may have been reduced, so as often to be incapable of ruling over the lower impulses, it is nevertheless seen to be fit to rule by its very nature' (*On Human Nature*, 131). Elsewhere he also asserts that conscience renders 'internal joyful applause' for right action and 'sorrowful hatred [...] grief and indignation' for wrong action, and that it is the feeling of conscience that motivates an agent to act (*A Short Introduction to Moral Philosophy*, 26, see also 45, 121. For a discussion of Hutcheson's view of the relation between moral sense and moral motivation see Darwall, *British Moralists*, 223). For a discussion on the difference between Shaftesbury and Hutcheson see Darwall, *British Moralists*, 181.

8   Shaftesbury talks of the 'innateness', 'instinct', and 'imprint' of moral sense and conscience interchangeably (Anthony Ashley Cooper, Third Earl of Shaftesbury, *Characteristics of Men, Manners, Opinions, Times*, Cambridge University Press (2000), 325–6, see also 167). He also states that even if agents do not reflect their conscience will still remain (albeit inactively) i.e. moral sense and conscience are constitutive of an agent (ibid., 209). For discussions of Shaftesbury's moral sense theory see R. B. Voitle, 'Shaftesbury's Moral Sense', *Studies in Philology*, 52, 1, (1955), 17–38.

9   Ibid., 167.

10   Ibid., 208–9. Shaftesbury does mention conscience in passing in a number of places. Indeed, within a discussion of the Delphic inscription 'Know Thyself!' Shaftesbury describes how 'A knave, they thought, could never be by himself. Not that his conscience was always sure of giving him disturbance, but he had not, they supposed, so much interest with himself as to exert this generous faculty and raise himself a companion who, being fairly admitted into partnership, would quickly mend his partner and set his affairs on a right foot' (ibid., 77), seemingly assuming that conscience has been activated in this situation (see also ibid., 95). Indeed Shaftesbury talks of 'self-inspection' and 'sincerity' in this context, asserting that 'a rational creature must be horridly offensive and grievous, namely, to have the reflection in this mind of an unjust action or behaviour, which he

conscience occurs at higher-order levels of moral deliberation.[11] Indeed, Rousseau also characterises conscience in non-rational terms.[12] He describes conscience as a constitutive 'moral instinct', that is 'the voice of the soul'.[13] He

knows to be naturally odious and ill-deserving' (ibid., 208). For a discussion that picks up on this higher-order reflectivity of conscience in Shaftsbury see Darwall, *British Moralists*, 178–9.

11   The characterisation of conscience by Crusius is less clear (here I draw from *Anweisung vernünftig zu Leben* (1744), translated by Schneewind as *A Guide to Rational Living*, from *Moral Philosophy from Montaigne to Kant*, 568–85). On the one hand Crusius defines the judgement of the morality of acts as conscience and explains that 'the basic drive to recognise the divine moral law' is that which grounds the 'drive of conscience' (ibid., 574). This is 'a natural sensation of what is right and proper, which does us good service with its quickness in judging moral matters' (ibid., 584). Indeed, in a suggestively similar tone to that of the British Moral Sense theorist Shaftsbury, Crusius claims that 'there is a *natural sensation* of justice and propriety in us that has something more than a mere judgment of the understanding as its ground (emphasis mine)' (ibid.). On the other hand Crusius offers two approaches to proving the universality of the drive of conscience. One method is 'through proofs' and 'clear arguments' (ibid., 575). However, Crusius tells us that these are problematic, evidenced by the fact that 'most scholars do not get very far in doing so'. A second 'shorter path to knowledge of it' is present, and this proof functions by first assuming the 'reality of divine law [and then] a priori [there] must be an innate drive to conscience'. Evidence for this comes from 'experience', which shows that even 'men of moderate understanding' can become 'aware of what is right or wrong, even without being able to give clearly any sufficient grounds for his judgment or even to defend it' (ibid.). This leaves ambiguous what the ontological status of conscience is. An extended discussion would be required to flesh this out and as such I will refrain from doing so here.

12   The most sustained treatment of the concept of conscience by Rousseau appears in *Emile, or On Education* (1762), in a subsection of Book IV entitled 'Profession of Faith on the Savoyard Vicar'. Passages are cited from the readily available and authoritative translation of Allan Bloom, J. J. Rousseau, *Emile, or On Education*, Basic Books (1979). Although I will explicate Rousseau's views on conscience as found in *Emile*, it must be noted that Rousseau does talk of conscience in other writings, notably the *First Discourse*. For a discussion of conscience in Rousseau that takes into account the *First Discourse* see J. Marks, 'The Divine Instinct? Rousseau and Conscience', *The Review of Politics*, 68, (2006), 564–85. A translation of *First Discourse* can be found in *Rousseau, The Discourses and Other Early Political Writings*, ed. V. Gourevitch, Cambridge University Press (1997). For a treatment of Rousseau's view on conscience that takes into consideration his other texts and one that situates it within his broader philosophical project see A. M. Melzer, *The Natural Goodness of Man: On the System of Rousseau's Thought*, University of Chicago Press (1990), 16–7, 30fn1, 146–7, 169, 280.

13   Rousseau, *Emile*, 290 (see also 288), 286. On a number of occasions Rousseau also refers to conscience as 'innate' (ibid., 289, see also 279, which I read as equivalent to the notion of conscience as a moral instinct that an agent possesses), and as an 'innate sentiment'.

implores agents to directly follow their conscience ('conscience never deceives; it is man's true guide') as authoritative over what reason tells them to do ('too often reason deceives us').[14] Rousseau argues that for conscience to be invoked an agent must pay special attention to it and be actively concerned with its evaluative activity ('if you wish to listen to your conscience, countless vain obstacles will disappear at its voice').[15] As such, Rousseau's view of conscience is that it is a constitutive, reliable and immediate sentiment that directs agents towards good.[16]

Although 'sentiment' is a term that seems to shift in meaning depending on the context that Rousseau employs it (ibid., 262, 264, 265, 267, 269, 275, 279, 286, 289, 291, 302–3, 307, 313) he certainly asserts that conscience is constitutive and common to all of humanity (ibid., 288–9) and he goes as far as describing an agent who has no conscience as morally 'dead' (ibid., 264, see also 287).

14   Ibid., 286. In this passage he refers to the instinct that is conscience in relation to the obeying of nature. Rousseau's assertion is that man is corrupted by the interactions of the world (customs, education, authorities etc.) and that if such corruption was not present then naturally man would be moral. It should be noted that this claim is more complex then stated here and requires further unpacking as to how exactly conscience functions with respect to good and bad. For example, on a hermeneutic point Sorabji points out that in Book 1 of *Emile* Rousseau claims that reason teaches agents to know good and evil and conscience makes agents love the one and hate the other (*Moral Conscience Through the Ages*, 177). This seems to suggest that conscience plays a motivational role in determining which action an agent should pursue rather than a determining role in terms of what good and evil actually are. Further discussion of this point will require an analysis that is beyond the remit of this study. See J. N. Shklar, *Men and Citizens: A Study of Rousseau's Social Theory*, Cambridge University Press (1969), 33–74, see also Melzer, *The Natural Goodness of Man*, 15–28. For an extensive discussion of Rousseau's view on natural perfection see J. Marks, *Perfection and Disharmony in the Thought of Jean-Jacques Rousseau*, Cambridge University Press (2011).

15   Ibid., 311. Rousseau refers to the *phenomenology* of conscience as a speaking voice stating 'conscience is the voice of the soul' (ibid., 286) and elsewhere that 'when we are solely occupied with comparing what we have done with what we ought to have done-then the *voice of conscience* will regain its strength and its empire' (emphasis mine, ibid., 282–3). Rousseau also talks about the voice of conscience as an 'inner voice' and an 'inner light' (ibid., 286, see also 269). The morality that remains after all prejudices have been removed and an agent has been truly enlightened is termed by Rousseau as 'natural religion' (ibid., 262, see also 258–9, 293, 296, 298, 300, 304, 310–12).

16   A figure that I have not discussed thus far but who is likely to be relevant within the historical context is Pierre Bayle (b. 1674). The reason for this is two-fold: 1. the majority of his work remains untranslated, 2. there is a lack of consensus among scholars regarding what Bayle's notion of conscience actually is. With respect to the latter point, G. Mori takes a chronological approach and argues that Bayle's position shifts from conscience

In turning to Kant's various discussions of conscience it is noticeable that he describes the notion within the context of moral feelings, as practical reason and as a judgement (*Metaphysics of Morals* 6:399–403). Within even a short passage Kant talks of conscience as an 'unavoidable fact', as an 'internal tribunal' and as a form of 'consciousness' (6:400–401). Indeed, elsewhere in the *Metaphysics of Morals* he discusses conscience as a judgement that takes 'place before a tribunal' (6:438). Due to the various ways in which Kant talks about conscience the question is raised as to what exactly conscience is. Within the secondary literature there are some who argue that Kant's notion of conscience is simply a non-rational disposition, others who assert that it is a feeling, some who argue that it is only practical reason, and others who argue that conscience must be thought of within a framework that maintains both practical reason and feeling.[17]

In this chapter I will concentrate primarily on the passages referred to above from the *Metaphysics of Morals* (6:399–403) and argue that Kant takes conscience to be a particular manifestation of practical reason which results in a feeling that is produced as a result of its determination. I will show that conscience passes a higher-order judgement with respect to whether or not an agent has been diligent in the examination of their actions. In order to forward this claim I will begin by introducing the concept of 'moral feeling' within which conscience is discussed and show how this concept relates to moral motivation in general. I then turn to Kantian conscience specifically

---

being a kind of feeling/perception to conscience being something rational ('Pierre Bayle, the Rights of the Conscience, the Remedy of Toleration', *Ratio Juris*, 10, 1, (1997), 45–60). In contrast R. Fulton takes a syncretic approach and argues for continuity within Bayle's corpus ('Pierre Bayle and Human Rights', *Fifth Annual History Graduate Student Association Conference, Northern Illinois University Selected Conference Papers*, (2012), 60–93). In Chapter 3 I will note the similarity of discussions of conscience by Bayle with Kant's notion of an erring conscience because of the indicated influence on this particular issue. For further discussion of Bayle's notion of conscience see J. Kilcullen, *Sincerity and Truth: Essays on Arnauld, Bayle and Toleration*, Oxford University Press (1988), Sorabji, *Moral Conscience Through the Ages*, 153–9, and for a discussion of the historical influence of Bayle in the Early Modern period see T. M. Lennon, *Reading Bayle*, Toronto University Press (1999), 15.

17 As non-rational disposition see Stevens, *Kant on Moral Practice*, cited in Howard 'Kant and Moral Imputation', 61nfn, as feeling see Howard, 'Kant and Moral Imputation', 627, as practical reason see Timmermann, 'Kant on Conscience', 297, Guyer, 'Moral Feelings in the Metaphysics of Morals', 143, Vujosevic, 'The Judge in the Mirror', 453, and Kittsteiner, 'Casuistry and Character', 185–213, as both practical reason and feeling see Patron, 'Conscience and Kant', 241, Wood, *Kantian Ethics*, 183 and Hill, *Human Welfare*, 301.

by explaining that it is practical reason (I denote this as 'intellectual conscience') whose determination effects the capacity of moral feeling. I will
thereby show that conscience is fundamentally practical reason (thereby agree-
ing with the view that conscience-proper is only practical reason). Following
this I will explicate that the judgement of conscience concerns whether an
agent has 'diligently examined' (*Religion* 6:186) their actions. I will also argue
that the activity of the judgement of conscience is structured disjunctively.[18]
I will then explicate that should an agent choose to consult their conscience
(which I refer to in terms of 'voluntarism'), a higher-order form of moral imputation upon moral judgement will occur. In doing so I will show that Moyar's
account of Kant's notion of conscience as a first-order form of moral imputation is wrong.[19]

2.2   Moral Feelings

The absence of conscience in both the pre-Critical writings and the
Groundwork is noticeable.[20] Indeed, within the *Groundwork* conscience is

---

18   Here, rather than referring to the judgement of conscience in terms of the outcome/
      product of a particular determination, I instead refer to the judgement of conscience in
      terms of an activity/process. By disjunctive, I am referring to the fact that this process is
      structured in a manner that is of the form of a disjunctive syllogism.

19   Moyar, 'Unstable Autonomy', 327–60. Although Ojakangas makes similar claims to Moyar
      (that conscience is first-order and involuntary, *The Voice of Conscience*, 153), Moyar's
      account presents a more robust and sustained defence of the claim and as such I will
      direct my criticism to Moyar's account taking it to be the case that it address Ojakangas
      also.

20   To the best of my knowledge discussion of conscience occurs only twice within Kant's
      pre-Critical works (1744–70). Discussions are found in *Observations on the Nature of
      Beauty and the Sublime* (1764) and Herder's notes from Kant's lectures on practical phi-
      losophy (1762–4). In *Observations on the Nature of Beauty and the Sublime* two mentions
      of conscience occur: In a discussion of the notion of obligation, Kant asserts that the
      concept contains within it the idea of equality between agents (20:158). Kant claims that
      the religion that 'Christ sought to bring to human beings' rests upon this concept. The
      mention of conscience then occurs after he asserts that Jews, whose religion is 'founded
      [...] only on empty concepts', do not experience 'any pangs of conscience' when they 'lie
      and deceive' because to experience such pangs presupposes 'an idea of equality' (20:158),
      which the Jewish religion supposedly lacks. Kant asserts that 'the moral feeling *applied*
      to one's own actions is conscience', following which he states that 'Providence probably
      gave us this feeling for the sake of universal perfection, yet in such a way that the latter is
      not thought of in its greatness, just as we have the sexual drive for reproduction without

only cursorily mentioned twice (4:404, 422).[21] Given that the *Groundwork* is Kant's most important and central ethical work it would seem to follow that the lack of discussion regarding conscience is indicative of the unimportance he ascribes to this notion. A first point to note is that the *Groundwork* is not the text within which Kant should be found to be discussing conscience. As I will discuss below, there Kant is discussing issues regarding moral worth, the grounding of an action and what rational principle is expressed as the moral law. Secondly, when Kant's wider ethical picture and work is taken into consideration it is clear that he discusses conscience throughout the entire Critical period. Discussions of conscience are present in all the *Lectures on Ethics, Religion, Metaphysics of Morals* and the essay *Miscarriage*. Taking these two points together it is clear that the lack of discussion of conscience within the *Groundwork* is not in itself indicative of the importance (or lack of importance) that Kant ascribes to the notion. Indeed, particularly in the *Metaphysics of Morals* he discusses the notion of 'Moral Feelings' (6:399–403) and explains that conscience is one of the key moral feelings.

In this section I outline Kant's account of 'moral feeling' within which conscience is discussed.[22] I explicate how the account of moral feelings *in general* is to be considered within Kant's picture of moral motivation (in the

---

intending it' (20:168). The first of these two mentions appears to be a remark rather than a considered philosophical point. However one interpretation that may be derived from it is the idea that conscience is not constitutive to all human beings but rather comes about through Christian belief. With respect to the second of the two mentions, important and central elements of what Kant will go on to assert about moral feeling in his post-Critical work appear to be present. '[C]onscience as moral feeling applied to one's own action' reads similar to his talk of moral feeling as 'subjective conditions of receptiveness to the concept of duty' (*Metaphysics of Morals* 6:399) and the notion that 'providence probably gave use this feeling' reads as conscience is probably constitutive (which is what Kant asserts in his discussion of moral feelings (6:399–403)). In Herder's notes from Kant's *Lectures on Ethics* conscience is mentioned at greater length and clearly with greater consideration (*Herder* 27:5, 19–22, 42–4). Although these are taken from the pre-Critical period, in this study I will discuss these within the subsequent chapters.

21   Kant states that '[With respect to lying when attempting to borrow money, an agent] would like to make such a promise, but he still has enough conscience to ask himself: is it not forbidden and contrary to duty to help oneself out of need in such a way?' (4:422).

22   On 'moral feeling' in Kant see I. P. D. Morrisson, *Kant and the Role of Pleasure in Moral Action*, Ohio University Press (2008), R. R. McCarty, 'Kantian Motivation and the Feeling of Respect', *Journal of the History of Philosophy*, 31, 3, (1993), 421–35, *Kant on Emotion and Value*, ed. A. Cohen, Palgrave Macmillan (2014), M. MacBeath, 'Kant on Moral Feeling', *Kant-Studien*, 74, (1973), 313 and G. Banham, 'Kantian Respect', *Kant Studies Online*, (2008), 1–14.

subsequent sections of this chapter I will specifically discuss conscience).[23] I will do so in order to introduce key concepts within Kant's account of morality and then relate these to moral feeling. I will show that Kant possesses a strictly rational account of moral worth that does not involve feelings in the determination of a moral judgement. However once moral motivation is taken into account, moral feelings (considered as the feelings of reason) are to be considered within the ethical picture. In doing so I show that moral feeling is a constitutive capacity of an agent that involves the subjective receptiveness of relating an agent to the concept of duty i.e. moral imputation.

In the Kantian account of ethics, explicated most clearly in the *Groundwork*, the criterion for judging whether an agent acts morally concerns whether or not an agent has willed actions that were grounded in reason or in inclination (4:399–400).[24] When an agent's will has been grounded purely on reason then an agent is said to have acted 'autonomously' (4:431–4).[25] When an agent's will has been grounded in inclination then an agent is said to have acted 'heteronomously' (4:441–4).[26] Rationally willed actions are moral because they are said to be 'objectively valid'. By objectively valid what is being referred to is reason providing a grounding for an action that is based upon a universal criterion of morally permissible behaviour. Kant tells us that the criterion is that such action is in accordance to the Categorical Imperative, defined as

---

23   On Kant's theory of moral motivation see McCarty, 'Kantian Motivation' 421–35, M. Timmons, 'Kant on the Possibility of Moral Motivation', *Southern Journal of Philosophy*, 23, (1984), 377–98, D. Guevara, *Kant's Theory of Moral Motivation*, Westview Press (2000), K. Sargentis, 'Moral Motivation in Kant', *Kant Studies Online*, (2012), 93–121, M. Zinkin, 'Respect for the Law and the Use of Dynamical Terms in Kant's Theory of Moral Motivation', *Archiv für Geschichte der Philosophie*, 88, 1, (2006), 31–53, Howard, 'Kant and Moral Imputation', 609–27, and P. Schollmeier, 'Practical Reason and Empirical Principles', *The Pluralist*, 2, 3, (2007), 120–33.

24   For an introduction to Kant's *Groundwork* see S. Sedgwick, *Kant's Groundwork of the Metaphysics of Morals*, Cambridge University Press (2008). For an advanced passage-by-passage commentary on the *Groundwork* see J. Timmermann, *Kant's Groundwork of the Metaphysics of Morals: A Commentary*, Cambridge University Press (2007).

25   For an extensive discussion of Kant's notion of autonomy see A. Reath, *Agency and Autonomy in Kant's Moral Theory*, Oxford University Press (2006).

26   For a discussion of Kant's notion of heteronomy see G. A. Schrader, 'Autonomy, Heteronomy, and Moral Imperatives', *The Journal of Philosophy*, 60, 3, (1963), 65–77.

> Act only in accordance with that maxim through which you can at the same time will that it become a universal law (4:421).[27]

In contrast to this there are heteronomously willed actions that are always based on inclination. These are deemed morally impermissible because they are grounded on a 'subjective criterion' of moral determination. By subjective criterion what is being referred to is criteria that takes an individual's particular empirical states to be a ground for action (4:397–400). Kant states that in doing so an agent is acting not out of pure rationality but is instead acting out of self-love (4:406, 419–20). More broadly, any non-rational grounding for actions are said to be morally impermissible. Hence Kant talks of the impermissibility of grounding morality on non-rational notions such as happiness and perfection (4:410–1, 441–3).[28]

In the Kantian picture of morality what is of interest is not the consequence of the particular action but rather the (rational) nature of the action itself. Judging the consequence of the action and using it as a criterion of moral worth would involve a host of empirical variables: for example, how many people benefitted from the act? What was the quality of the supposed benefit to agents? How can a decision between competing notions of benefit be definitively judged upon?[29] In addition to these concerns, another consequence that could be evaluated, should consequences be taken as a valid criterion of

---

27 Here I have quoted the 'first formula', or the 'Universal Law Formulation of the Categorical Imperative' (for a discussion of the first formula see C. M. Korsgaard, 'Kant's formula of universal law', *Pacific Philosophical Quarterly*, 66, 1–2, (1985), 24–47). However, Kant also formulates the Categorical Imperative in the formula of 'humanity', namely 'so act that you use humanity, whether in your own person or in the person of any other, always at the same time as an end, never merely as a means' (4:429), and the 'kingdom of ends', namely, 'act in accordance with the maxims of a member giving universal laws for a merely possible kingdom of ends' (4:439). Which, if any, of these three are the fundamental formulation and whether these formulations are equivalent expressions of one formula or distinct expressions, is a matter of debate among Kantian scholars. Answers to these questions are not of relevance to this study and as such I will not digress into this debate. For a discussion of Kant's Categorical Imperative see H. J. Paton, *Categorical Imperative: A Study of Kant's Moral Philosophy*, University of Pennsylvania Press (1971), and P. Kitcher, 'Kant's Argument for the Categorical Imperative', *Nous*, 38, 4, (2004), 555–84.

28 For a discussion on Kant's views on happiness see A. Hills, 'Kant on Happiness and Reason', *History of Philosophy Quarterly*, 23, 3, (2006), 243–61.

29 For a discussion of Kant's nuanced views on consequences in moral matters see D. Cummiskey, 'Kantian Consequentialism', *Ethics*, 100, 3, (1990), 586–615.

morally permissible behaviour, is the effect of the action upon the agent themselves i.e. in what emotional state (happiness, sadness etc.) does the particular action generate in an agent as a consequence of their action. Such a judgement would be, as Kant states in the *Metaphysics of Morals*, nothing more than a feeling that could only be of a 'state of contentment and peace of soul in which virtue is its own reward' (6:377). The point that Kant is making with respect to emotions that precede or follow from an action, is that they are not to be the principle of moral judgement with respect to actions that are of *moral worth* for agents.[30]

The Kantian picture of moral worth can thus be said to be strictly rational. Empirical factors and any other grounding principle of action are strictly prohibited. However, what must be made clear is that Kant's strict rationality with respect to morality is in reference to *moral judgements*. By moral judgements what is meant is simply an agent willing according to a maxim that is either morally permissible i.e. rationally grounded, or morally impermissible i.e. grounded in inclination. The reason why this is important is because Kant's overall picture of morality is far more nuanced. For example, with respect to moral development and improvement Kant maintains throughout his corpus discussions of themes such as historical, social, educational and religious factors, which although in some cases involve empirical elements nonetheless feature as important dimensions in an agent's moral development.[31] Indeed, Kant's account of *moral experience* is likewise more nuanced than simply acting out of consideration for the moral law. For example, within this context he discusses such things as moral feelings, deliberation, and reflective judgements.[32]

---

30   Indeed the *Groundwork* is a text where Kant addresses the question of moral worth. See also K. Simmons, 'Kant on Moral Worth', *History of Philosophy Quarterly*, 6, 1, (1989), 85–100, and J. G. Hernandez, 'Impremisibility and Kantian Moral Worth', *Ethical Theory and Moral Practice*, 13, 4, (2010), 403–19.

31   For example see G. F. Munzel, 'Kant on Moral Education, or "Enlightenment" and the Liberal Art', *The Review of Metaphysics*, 57, 1, (2003), 43–73.

32   Throughout the secondary literature there are numerous attempts to show that Kant's views on moral experience, contrary to the view of Kantian morality as 'soulless', is rich, nuanced and embodied. For an in-depth discussion of this see the works of S. M. Shell, *Kant and the Limits of Autonomy*, Harvard University Press (2009), and *The Embodiment of Reason*, University of Chicago Press (1995), as well as J. Grenberg, *Kant's Defense of Common Moral Experience: A Phenomenological Account*, Cambridge University Press (2013).

Indeed, one particular aspect of experience that Kant talks at length about throughout his corpus is that of feelings. Typically Kant talks of feelings as providing a powerful motivation against morally permissible behaviour. For example in the *Groundwork* he discusses an impermissible action that is based on inclination as acting 'in the propensity of feeling' (4:399), and in the *Metaphysics of Morals* he states that

> Impulses of nature, accordingly, involve obstacles within man's mind to his fulfilment of duty and (sometimes powerful) forces opposing it (6:380).

Where impulses of nature i.e. inclination, is to be read as a feeling present within an agent that originates from the agent's sensible self. Indeed, Kant uses the term 'pathological' in a number of places in a manner that is synonymous with 'dependent on an agent's sensible self' (*Groundwork* 4:399, Second *Critique* 5:80, 119, *Lectures on Anthropology* 7:254).

However, Kant's views on feeling are not simply confined to a discussion of the obstacles to moral behaviour that originate in the sensible self. As was noted earlier, feelings here are being denied with respect to the grounding of morally permissible behaviour. However this exclusion does not bracket out feelings *per se* in the wider story of morality. For example, in the *Groundwork* Kant talks of a type of feeling that relates to morally permissible behaviour

> In order for a sensibly affected rational being to will that for which reason alone prescribes the "ought," it is admittedly required that his reason have the capacity to *induce a feeling of pleasure* or of delight in the fulfillment of duty, and thus there is required a causality of reason to determine sensibility in conformity with its principles (4:460).

Here Kant is asserting that a feeling of some sort is induced when an agent acts according to duty. For this reason he develops an account of *moral interest* that is deemed valid. Such an account is Kant presenting a picture of feelings that can be deemed *moral feelings* rather than simply feelings that are not related to morally permissible behavior. Kant provides an account of moral feeling that result, as he states in the Second *Critique*, 'independent of sense' (5:62). At first contact this seems puzzling as it appears to assert that there are types of feeling that are not based on sense, where sense appears to be the domain of feeling *in toto*. Indeed, in the Third *Critique* Kant talks of a type of feeling that is 'a vocation of the mind that entirely oversteps the domain of [nature]' (5:268). In the Kantian picture of the human being, as presented in the *Groundwork*, where an agent is said to have a rational based intelligible self and an inclination based sensible self (4:451–5), the only candidate that remains once the sensible is removed from the equation is the rational aspect of the Self.[33] This is precisely what Kant is characterizing as 'moral feelings' in the *Metaphysics of Morals* (6:399–401).[34] Thus, a distinction is to be made between feelings that relate to the intelligible self (feelings of reason), and feelings that relate to the sensible self (pathological feelings).[35]

Building upon the above, in the following subsection I will explicate Kant's account of the role of moral feeling in moral motivation.

2.2.1   *Moral Feeling and Moral Motivation*

In the *Metaphysics of Morals* Kant expands on the notion of moral feeling under the section titled 'Concepts of What is Presupposed on the Part of Feeling by the Mind's Receptivity to Concepts of Duty as Such' (6:399). He begins by outlining that this section is about 'moral endowments' (6:399). He then goes on to list such concepts as 'moral feeling', 'conscience', 'love of one's neighbour'[36] and '[self] respect' (6:399).[37] The first notion to flesh out is what Kant means by 'moral endowment' (6:399). He claims that

---

33   In *Vigilantius* Kant also refers to these as *homo noumenon* and *homo phenomenon* (27:593). This distinction between an agent's rational self and sensible self is a distinction that Kant can make as a result of his work in the First *Critique*, which distinguishes things-in-themselves and things-as-they-appear (B294–316). However, with respect to an agent's self, how these claims are to be understood is a matter of considerable debate among Kantian scholars. For example contributions to this debate see H. Allison, *Kant's Transcendental Idealism: An Interpretation and Defence*, Yale University Press (2004), 97–156, and P. Guyer, *Kant and the Claims of Knowledge*, Cambridge University Press (1987), 333–70.

34   For a discussion of the interrelation between Kant's discussion of the rational and intelligible self throughout his post-Critical corpus see O. Sensen, *Kant on Human Dignity*, Walter de Gruyter Press (2011). For a generic discussion of such feelings of reason see C. Wellmon, 'Kant and the Feelings of Reason', *Eighteenth-Century Studies*, 42, 4, (2009), 557–80.

35   For a collection of essays on the role of emotion within Kant's ethical system see A. Cohen (ed.), *Kant on Emotion and Value*.

36   For a discussion of this feeling see D. von der Pfordten, 'On the Dignity of Man in Kant', *Philosophy*, 84, 329, (2009), 371–91. As this feeling is not relevant to this study I will not explore it further.

37   Although Kant is talking about respect here, I have added 'self' parenthetically because unlike the discussion of respect in *Groundwork* and *Second Critique*, where respect relates

[A]nyone lacking them [moral feelings] could have no duty to acquire them [...] All of them are natural dispositions of the mind (*praedispositio*) [...] every human being has them—Consciousness of them is not of empirical origin (6:399).

What is meant here can be understood by pointing out that the bracketed Latin term '*praedispositio*' is translatable as *predisposition*. This is important as 'disposition' in itself is ambiguous. An agent can be disposed to react to a particular thing either by an innate capacity or by a capacity that has been developed within the agent over time. For example, it is typically the case that agents close their eyes when a projectile is directed towards them; this is often taken to be a reflex that the agent has no control over. In other cases, such as swimming, it is typically taken to be the case that agents can learn with time how to perform this and various similar activities. Whereas an agent would be disposed to learning how to swim by being healthy and motivated, in the case of the closing of eyes in the face of a projectile, the agent would be predisposed i.e. the agent would simply have this reflex within them on the condition that they are healthy adults. Similarly, moral endowments are predispositions, not dispositions, because they are something a moral agent simply has within them i.e. they are innate, that is to say *constitutive*.[38] In Kant's words 'every man (as a moral being) has [the endowment to moral feeling] in him originally' (6:400). It is necessary to make clear that by this phrase Kant is referring to capacities rather than to phenomenological feelings as such i.e. occurrent feelings (as experienced) are conditioned upon an innate capacity *to be receptive to concepts of duty*. Hence, when Kant states that moral feeling is not of empirical origin he is simply referring to the innateness of the capacity that agents are constituted with. As such, a further and crucial distinction is to be made between the capacities of moral feelings being affected by the concept of duty (see below) and the feelings that are experienced phenomenologically

---

to all duties, within this particular context the primary concern is self-respect and the duties associated with it. I shall not discuss this distinction further. For an exposition of Kant on self-respect see S. J. Massey, 'Kant on Self-Respect', *Journal of the History of Philosophy*, 21, 1, (1983), 57–73.

38   In a similar analysis of the term '*praedispositio*' Guyer takes the concept that is being referred to as a referent to 'preconditions' that are 'necessary conditions of being put under obligation'. Guyer provides this analysis in order to counter any attempt to render what Kant is referring to as 'prejudices', which, as I argued with respect to the notion of 'dispositions', may suggest that such concepts occur through socialisations or inculcations that may bring about such concepts ('Moral Feeling', 137–8).

by an agent.[39] I shall say more about this when fleshing out the capacity of conscience below.

Above I have described moral feelings as constitutive, however, the question still remains: what do moral feelings do? Kant states that moral feelings

> [L]ie at the basis of morality, as subjective conditions of receptiveness to the concept of duty, not as objective conditions of morality [...], for being affected by concepts of duty [...], and it is by virtue of them that he can be put under obligation (6:399).

In order to understand this it is necessary to note that morality (as duty) is determined by and relates to the rational faculty of agents (more strictly, the faculty of understanding, based upon the Categorical Imperative, determines duty in a particular circumstance).[40] Because of this the activity of relating the duty to the agent must *follow* from the generation of duty, or, at the very least presuppose the concept of duty. The picture here is one of moral judgement, which relates to the objective conditions of morality, and one of moral imputation, which relates to the receptivity of the concept of duty (generated by the moral judgement) to the agent i.e. the possibility that an agent can be motivated to actualise the moral judgement.[41] Therefore it can be pointed out that moral feeling involves the subjective relating of rational morality to the agent i.e. the subjective receptiveness that a particular agent has to the said duty. As Kant states in the *Groundwork* 'moral feeling [...] remains [close] to morality and its dignity' (4:442), however moral feelings are not moral judgements (as they fall under the objective conditions of morality). Hence, within

---

39   As Howard succinctly makes the point, '[on Kant's account] conscience denotes our natural propensity for the moral law, that is to say, our affinity for the moral law, whose ontological roots escape conceptual categorisation. We cannot fully explain why human beings are originally responsive to morality. To do so would be to explain the actual genesis of conscience. All investigations into morality must simply begin with this fact' ('Kant and Moral Imputation', 612).

40   For further discussion on the nature of such moral determinations see P. Formosa, 'Is Kant a Moral Constructivist or a Moral Realist?', *European Journal of Philosophy*, 21, 2, (2013), 170–96 and A. W. Wood, *Kant's Ethical Thought*, Cambridge University Press (1999), 156–92. For a broader discussion, that incorporates contemporary ethics, see C. Korsgaard, 'Realism and Constructivism in Twentieth-Century Moral Philosophy', *The Journal of Philosophical Research*, 28, (2003), 99–122.

41   For a discussion on how Kant's theory of moral feelings fit into his picture of moral imputation see C. Wellmon 'Kant and the Feelings of Reason', *Eighteenth-Century Studies*, 42, 4, (2009), 557–80.

this section Kant makes clear that moral feeling is not moral judgement. If moral feeling was involved in any way in determining the moral judgement it would be 'moral sense'.[42] In other words, Kant is not a moral sense theorist.[43]

Thus the constitutive nature of moral feeling can be stated in terms of a capacity that allows for the possibility of receptivity to duty (a capacity that does not make an incursion into the domain of moral judgements but nonetheless allows an agent to be motivated by the moral judgement). This is precisely what Kant is stating in the opening paragraph of his treatment of moral feeling in the *Metaphysics of Morals*

> There is no obligation to have these [...] to have these predispositions cannot be considered a duty [because] it is by virtue of them that he can be put under obligation (6:399).

The importance of this to the Kantian moral picture of agency is that moral feeling provides an account of how an agent can be morally motivated. An agent cannot have a duty to have moral feeling because the possibility of imputing that duty would require a capacity to impute duty, which is exactly what moral feeling is in the first place.

Kant expands upon this in the subsection 'Moral Feeling' by fleshing out that moral feelings are the 'susceptibility to feel pleasure or displeasure merely from being aware that our actions are consistent with or contrary to the law of duty' (6:399). The notion of receptivity to duty (that the capacity of moral feeling accounts for), are feelings of pleasure or displeasure that result as a consequence of an agent's awareness of whether or not their actions are done out of duty. Kant then goes on to describe a picture of moral deliberation where an agent makes a choice to act based on an interest 'in the action or its effect'

---

42 As Kant states "it is inappropriate to call this feeling a moral *sense*, for by the word 'sense' is usually understood a theoretical capacity for perception directed toward an object, whereas moral feeling (like pleasure and displeasure in general) is something merely subjective, which yields no knowledge [...] we no more have a special *sense* for what is (morally) good and evil than for *truth*, although people often speak in this fashion" (6:400).

43 Writings and debates by a number of British moral philosophers in 18th century developed a position that has come to be known as 'moral sense theory' or 'moral sentimentalism'. This position can be situated between two prevalent views of the time, namely, 'egoism', the view that all morality is reducible to self-interest, and 'moral rationalism', the view that morality is based entirely on self-interest. Although moral sense theorists disagreed on many things, common to their view is the claim that *non-selfish moral affection* is central to morality. For an extensive discussion of this tradition see Darwall, *British Moralists* and M. B. Gill, 'Ethics and Sentiment', in *Routledge Companion to Ethics*, 111–2.

> Every determination of choice proceeds *from* the representation of a pos-
> sible action *to* the deed through the feeling of pleasure or displeasure,
> taking an interest in the action or its effect (6:399).

Here the determination of choice proceeds from two possible representations that an agent can choose to act upon (i.e. the deed): a choice between
an action that takes an interest in the action in itself or an action that takes an
interest in the actions effect. Kant explicates very clearly that an action can
be considered to be of genuine moral worth if and only if it is done out of
respect for the moral law (*Groundwork* 4:399–403). Thus, if an agent chooses
to act upon the action that is represented in such a way as to concern only the
interest of the action, the agent's will can be said to be autonomous, whereas
when an agent chooses to act upon the action that is represented in such a way
as to concern only the effect of the action, the agent's will can be said to be
heteronomous. Crucially, the choice between these two possibilities is stated
by Kant in terms of the 'feeling of pleasure or displeasure' (6:399),[44] in doing
so Kant is stating explicitly that *feeling* (moral or pathological) can motivate an
agent either to act autonomously or heteronomously.[45]

   Kant then locates these feelings with respect to time, where pathological
feeling 'precedes the representation of the law' and moral feeling 'can only
follow upon it' (6:399). Here Kant is alluding to the fact that when an agent
is determined to act upon the representation that takes interest in the moral
worth of an action, the moral feeling will follow. In contrast to this, a pathological feeling occurs before an agent is determined to act; the representation
takes interest in the effect of the action. As such the pathological feeling is the
ground for such action.

---

44   Immediately following this passage Kant explicates this difference by pointing to what I
     have denoted as the feelings of reason and pathological feelings. He asserts that 'the state
     of *feeling* [*ästhetische Zustand*] here (the way in which inner sense is affected) is either
     sensibly dependent [pathological feeling] or *moral* [feelings of reason]' (*Metaphysics of
     Morals* 6:399).
45   Indeed, Kant presents the same account of moral motivation in *Mrongovius* where he
     states: 'We now come again upon the feeling, which in another connection we have previ-
     ously rejected [as in the case of pathological feeling]. The moral feeling is a capacity for
     being effected by a moral judgement. When I judge by understanding that the action is
     morally good, I am still very far from doing this action of which I have so judged. But if this
     judgement moves me to do the action, that is the moral feeling. Nobody can or ever will
     comprehend how the understanding should have a motivating power; it can admittedly
     judge, but to give this judgement power so that it becomes a motive able to impel the will
     to performance of an action—to understand this is the philosophers' stone' (27:1428).

In *Mrongovius* Kant explicates how moral feeling can effect moral judge-ments i.e. motivate an agent, in terms of the 'possibility of rules' (27:1428).[46] Here Kant is explicating the fact that moral feelings accord with rules that generate a 'moving force' from the 'pure principle of morality', which is 'internal to its mind in virtue of its nature'. On numerous occasions in the *Groundwork* Kant talks about how, in the words of Andrew Reath, 'the moral law is a law that the rational will in some sense legislates'.[47] For example, Kant states that 'the will of every rational being as a will [...] legislating [the] universal law' (4:341), '[the will is] subject to the law in such a way that it must be regarded also as legislating itself and only on this account as being subject to the law' (4:341), and '[autonomy is] the property of the will through which it is a law to itself (independently of any property of the objects of volition)' (4:440).[48] In these passages, similarly to what he is stating in *Mrongovius*, Kant con-nects the legislating of the moral law (i.e. universal law) with the will and then maintains that the will is autonomous because of the rational nature of the will. The result is of course paradoxical: how can asserting autonomy in terms of the will's rational necessitating of the moral law and the will's freedom, be reconciled? I will not address this problem here.[49] For the present purpose it suffices to state that Kant talks of moral feelings and the rational necessity of the will both as according with law and as autonomous: 'internal to the mind' (*Mrongovius*) and independent from 'any property of the objects in volition' (*Groundwork*). This convergence can be reconciled by recalling that Kant takes moral feelings to be the feelings of reason and therefore the only significant difference in his treatment of moral feeling and willing according to rules (i.e. universal laws) is that in the former he talks of a 'motivating force'. This is a crucial result as it indicates a direct relation between moral judgements and moral motivation *qua* moral feeling.[50]

---

46   'The understanding pays regard to everything that eliminates the possibility of rules; it accepts everything that accords with the use of its rule, and opposes itself to everything that is contrary to that rule. Now since immoral actions are contrary to rules, in that they cannot be made into a universal law, the understanding is resistant to them, because they run counter to the use of its rule. Hence, from a pure principle of morality internal to the mind in virtue of its nature there resides in the understanding a *moving force*' (empha-sis mine, 27:1428).

47   A. Reath, 'Legislating the Moral Law', *Nous*, 28, 4, (1994), 435.

48   See also *Groundwork* 4:342–5, 447, 461.

49   For a well-known attempt to solve this problem see H. Allison, 'Morality and Freedom: Kant's Reciprocity Thesis', *The Philosophical Review*, 95, 3, (1986), 393–425.

50   In *Mrongovius* Kant also discusses the motivating force of moral feeling *in contrast* to the moving forces of pathological feelings (27:1429). For an account of Kantian moral

At this juncture it should also be noted that the notion that *any* feeling can be introduced into Kant's account of morally permissible actions is rejected by many Kantian scholars.[51] The contention is that to include feelings in the picture of Kantian moral action would be to compromise his strictly rationalist account of morality. For example, Wolff argues that 'the introduction of the emotion of reverence is contradictory to the entire thrust of Kant's argument[s, about moral action]'.[52] However, as O'Neill points out, a reason to reject the claim that moral feeling (here being spoken of as the moral feeling of respect) is a claim that relates to pathological feeling is because "to act 'out of reverence for the law' [...] is not to act with any peculiar feeling of reverence or awe [...] pathology, as Kant would have it [pathological feeling] is irrelevant to the moral worth of acts".[53] As such, the problem with the type of account that Wolff presents is that an assumption is made that 'reverence for the law' is a pathological feeling. Due to the fact that Kant takes moral feelings to be the feelings of reason, the inclusion of moral feelings into his picture of moral action does not compromise his strictly rational account of the moral worth of actions.[54]

In the above I have explicated Kant's account of moral feelings as constitutive capacities that function as the mechanism of moral motivation within an agent. The necessary background is now in place from which to turn specifically to the treatment of Kant's conceptualisation of conscience.

---

motivation that rests upon moral feeling but not the moral feelings of respect or conscience, but rather a *sui generis* feeling see Guevara, *Kant's Theory of Moral Motivation*.

51   For example see R. Wolff, *The Autonomy of Reason*, Harper and Row (1973), 83, MacBeath, 'Kant on Moral Feeling', 313, M. Timmons, 'Kant on the Possibility of Moral Motivation', *Southern Journal of Philosophy*, 23, (1984), 377–98, and R. C. S. Walker, *Kant*, Routledge & Kegan Paul (1978), 98. See also S. L. Darwall, 'Kantian Practical Reason Defended', *Ethics*, 96, 1 (1985), 89–99.

52   Wolff, *The Autonomy of Reason*, 83.

53   O. O'Neill, *Acting on Principle*, Columbia University Press (1974), 111 (this quote and the quote from Wolff are quoted in McCarty, 'Kantian Motivation', 424).

54   In addition to the above Kant also introduces a normative element to moral feeling. Kant states that 'Obligation with regard to moral feeling can be only to *cultivate* it and to strengthen it through wonder at its inscrutable source. This comes about by its being shown how it is set apart from any sensibly dependent stimulus and is induced most intensely in its purity by a merely rational representation' (6:399–400). I will not explicate this here as it would take the discussion beyond the remit of this chapter, however in Chapter 5 I will return to this point and explain how the duty to cultivate conscience through rational representation occurs.

2.3   Intellectual Conscience and Moral Feeling

Kant states that moral feeling is 'susceptibility on the part of free choice to be *moved* by pure practical reason (and its law)' (emphasis mine, *Metaphysics of Morals* 6:400). Stated as such, he can be seen as claiming that what motivates an agent is the effect that 'pure practical reason' has on moral feeling. In the case of conscience he makes it very clear that the moral feelings that are associated with conscience come from ('moved by') practical reason doing a particular kind of thing. Indeed, 'conscience is practical reason holding man's duty before him' (6:400). As such, as a point of departure a distinction can be made between:

i.   Consideration of the activity of conscience as a capacity of practical reason.

ii.   Consideration of the feelings that result as a consequence of this capacity being engaged (effecting moral feeling).

In order to flesh out this distinction I denote 'intellectual conscience' (concerning i. above), which is to be differentiated from the effect that the determination of practical reason has on the capacity of moral feeling (concerning ii. above).[55] Intellectual conscience will be seen to relate to the activity of practical reason and what is discussed as the effect on moral feeling will be seen to relate to the experienced feeling that results from the determination of intellectual conscience. It will become clear that intellectual conscience, as an activity of practical reason *is* conscience (conscience proper) and what is discussed as the effect on moral feeling is simply a reference to the phenomenological consequence of intellectual conscience.[56]

---

55   Reath denotes the 'intellectual aspect of respect' as referring to the determination of reason *qua* the moral feeling of respect (*Agency and Autonomy*, 9–14). Indeed, Reath argues that respect exhibits two-aspects (an intellectual determination and an affective motivation). My use of the notion of 'intellectual conscience' is disanalogous to Reath's treatment of respect, insofar as I take intellectual conscience as practical reason (conscience proper) and differentiate this from the affect that the determination of practical reason has (as a reference to the phenomenological consequence of the affect that conscience proper has on the capacity of moral feeling). For an introduction to the various locations within Kant's moral theory that respect can be found see Banham, 'Kantian Respect', 1–14. See also J. DeWitt, 'Respect for the Moral Law: the Emotional Side of Reason', *Philosophy*, 89, 1, (2014), 31–62.

56   In this study I remain agnostic concerning the relation between the intelligible and sensible self of an agent. This is a concern because the question is raised as to how (i.e. what

To begin: it is necessary to point out that Kant affirms that the capacity of conscience is constitutive, 'conscience is not something that can be acquired, and we have no duty to provide ourselves with one; rather, every man, as a moral being, *has* a conscience within him originally' (6:400). Following this Kant explains that the capacity of conscience involves 'recognising duties' (6:400). Here he is speaking about the activity of conscience i.e. by recognising duty conscience is understood to involve moral imputation.[57] As such, a clear distinction must be made between the capacity of conscience *qua* practical reason and the feeling that is experienced by an agent. As Kant states, conscience '*affect*[s] moral feeling by its act [i.e. judgement, determination, intellectual conscience]' (emphasis mine, 6:400).

Although the feelings that occur relate to the voice of the inner judge, how that 'voice' occurs (i.e. the feeling) is the result of a determination. This is clear from the fact that Kant employs the metaphor of the 'internal court' of conscience (I shall expand upon this metaphor below).[58] In the section

---

mechanism) reason *qua* the intelligible self, can affect moral feeling *qua* the sensible self. For discussions on this point see, P. Guyer, *Kant on Freedom, Law, and Happiness*, Cambridge University Press (2000), 292–305 and DeWitt, 'Respect for the Moral Law', 54. See also H. E. Allison, *Kant's Theory of Freedom*, Cambridge University Press (1990), 73–82, P. Kitcher, 'Kant on Self-Identity', *Philosophical Review*, 91, 1, (1982), 515–47, *Self and Nature In Kant's Philosophy*, ed. A. W. Wood, Cornell University Press (1984), S. S. Xie, 'What Is Kant: A Compatibilist Or An Incompatibilist? A New Interpretation of Kant's Solution to the Free Will Problem', *Kant-Studien*, 100, 1, 53–76.

57   In *Collins* (27:351) Kant describes conscience as an instinct that 'directs oneself'. In this same passage Kant states that 'Conscience [...] has a driving force, to summon us against our will before the judgement-seat, in regard to the lawfulness of our actions', which he completes with the assertion that 'it is thus an instinct, and not merely a faculty of judgement'. Such phrases are also found in *Brauer* 129–30. Two notes can be made on these sections of *Collins* and *Brauer*: i. Kant's later writings on conscience drop the characterisation of conscience as an 'instinct' and replace it instead with talk of conscience as a moral endowment (which I have denoted as constitutive), and ii. his characterisation of conscience here does not clearly delineate conscience as passing its own judgement but rather describes it in the more ambiguous terms of 'giving force to the law' (motivational efficacy?). Taken together, it is clear that this notion of conscience is clarified, and in part amended, by a clearer notion of conscience as higher-order judgement in the *Metaphysics of Morals* and *Religion*.

58   For examples of Kant's employment of these metaphors see *Metaphysics of Morals* 6:401, 430, *Collins* 27:295. For a discussion of Kant's notion of the inner court of conscience in the *Metaphysics of Morals* see Esser, 'Inner Court', 269–92, Ishikawa, 'Das Gerichtshof-Modell des Gewissens', 43–55. In chapter 4 and 5 I will expand upon this metaphor further.

entitled 'On a Human Being's Duty to Himself as His Own Innate Judge' in the *Metaphysics of Morals*, he states

[C]onsciousness of an internal court in man (before which his thoughts accuse or excuse one another) is **conscience** (6:438).

Here Kant explicates the notion of an internal court as the domain where an agent's 'thoughts accuse or excuse one another'. The term 'thought' in Kant's corpus is discussed under the notion of 'thinking' in the First *Critique*. For the present purpose it is necessary to simply note that conscience is therefore a *type of thinking* and that, as Kant asserts, thinking is judgement through concepts (A69/B94, B141). In the case of conscience, the judgement i.e. the determination, is of the internal court. *Strictly speaking this is what conscience is*. From this the following distinction can be made:

Intellectual Conscience: the judgement (i.e. determination) of the internal court i.e. conscience proper.

Effect on Moral Feeling: consciousness of this judgement (i.e. the inner voice), which motivates an agent.

The above has expressed intellectual conscience as a judgment. In doing so it becomes possible to understand that intellectual conscience is what Kant is referencing when he states that 'conscience is practical reason'.[59] As such, because the feelings associated with conscience result from the judgement of conscience, conscience is to be taken as *fundamentally practical reason* whose activity results in an agent experiencing feelings. These feelings are simply a result of the effect that the determination of practical reason has on moral feeling. In a further clarification of the notion of conscience proper as practical reason Vujosevic correctly points out that it is more accurate to state that

---

59   This distinction may even be read into Kant's claim in *Herder* that 'Conscience is *logica* [cognitive/moral] in that I am aware of some property; and *moralis*, in that I couple this with my moral feeling (27:42). The conscience described in the above passage as *logica* is intellectual conscience. It can be referred to in such a manner because of the judgement that is intellectual conscience. This is contrasted with what Kant terms *moralis*, which is to be read in terms of the moral feeling that occurs as a result of the judgement of conscience. Of course, this reading requires further elaboration, which I will refrain from doing so here.

conscience is a capacity *of* practical reason 'in performing a specific function'.[60] The distinction that is being made is between conscience proper i.e. the determinate aspect of conscience (intellectual conscience), and the phenomenology of feeling (as a result of the effect on moral feeling).[61]

The above analysis allows firstly for a clear dismissal of the thesis that conscience is a non-rational disposition or simply a feeling, as the notion of a judgement (practical reason) of conscience precludes this.[62] Of the alternative readings of conscience noted in the introduction, that conscience is only practical reason and that conscience must be thought of within a framework that maintains both practical reason and feeling,[63] the above analysis is to be read as defending the former position.[64] The point can be made in an alternative

60   Vujosevic, 'The Judge in the Mirror', 464.

61   Similarly, Esser identifies conscience as 'fundamental status determination' i.e. intellectual conscience, and speaks of 'the phenomenology of conscience' i.e. effect on moral feeling ('Inner Court', 273).

62   See Stevens, *Kant on Moral Practice*, cited in Howard 'Kant and Moral Imputation', 611fn. Moreover it also allows for a dismissal of Howard's position that conscience is 'only a feeling, but it is more than mere subjective feeling' (Howard, 'Kant and Moral Imputation', 627). The reason being that Howard goes as far as claiming that conscience is an 'emotion' that is completely separate from 'practical reason' (ibid.). Howard's position can be dismissed because he grounds his argument on the claim that conscience is an 'evaluative capacity' that is an 'emotional facticity' (ibid.), in making these two claims Howard is confusing the evaluative *capacity* with the emotional *facticity* of conscience by failing to recognise that it is the capacity that generates the facticity (I read facticity as the experience of the feelings associated with of conscience).

63   Regarding the former see Timmermann 'Kant on Conscience', 297, Guyer, 'Moral Feeling', 143 and Vujosevic, 'The Judge in the Mirror', 453, and Kittsteiner, 'Casuistry and Character', 185–213. Regarding the latter see Paton, 'Conscience and Kant', 241, Wood, *Kantian Ethics*, 183 and Hill, *Human Welfare*, 301.

64   For example, with respect to the position that holds that conscience is only practical reason Timmermann states that "[Conscience] affects the faculty of 'moral feeling' by its act, which is why it is discussed in what might be called the 'aesthetic' of the 'Metaphysical Principles of the Doctrine of Virtue.'" ('Kant on Conscience', 297). The central point here is that the experience of moral feeling is a resultant rather than conscience itself. Similarly, Guyer asserts that, '[A]lthough conscience is being included among the aesthetic preconditions of receptivity to duty, it is not itself a feeling. However, it causes or stimulates— "affects"—some moral feeling [...] though not a feeling, conscience must be an empirical phenomenon, an empirical awareness of moral law' ('Moral Feeling', 143). Indeed, when Guyer states that conscience is an 'empirical phenomenon, an empirical awareness of the moral law', he is not claiming that the capacity of conscience is empirical, rather he is claiming that the phenomenological consequence of the activity of conscience is empirical i.e. felt in the sensible realm (ibid.). Again, there is no contradiction between the

manner: conscience proper can be thought *of as one capacity that effects another distinct capacity* (practical reason-moral feeling).[65]

Thus far I have argued that intellectual conscience is conscience proper. Its determination results in the experience of feelings that are a result of the effect that practical reason has on the capacity of moral feeling.[66] By stating that the determination of conscience proper results in an effect on moral feeling the question is raised concerning the nature of that feeling. On the one hand, by 'effect on moral feeling' what may be read is something akin to a generic claim i.e. there is moral feeling *per se* and in the instance of conscientious judgement it is effected, or, on the other hand, the claim may be read as conscience has a specific feeling that is associated with it. It is unlikely that Kant maintains the latter as such a claim would compromise the notion of

---

account above and Vujosevic's claim that 'Kantian conscience should not be constructed as a feeling' because, as she states, 'conscience is a kind of self-appraisal that *causes feelings* (emphasis mine)' ('The Judge in the Mirror', 453). Similarly Vujosevic states that 'conscience […] is meant to trigger certain emotional responses' (ibid. 460) i.e. reference to self-appraisal can be seen as alluding to intellectual conscience and the subsequent moral feelings that occur.

65   With respect to the view which maintains that Kantian conscience is both practical reason and feeling, it becomes clear that these views fail to recognise that conscience is fundamentally practical reason. For example when Wood states that conscience as a feeling 'is the *outcome* of the process of moral reflection' (emphasis mine, *Kantian Ethics*, 184–5), he fails to make clear the fact that the 'process of moral reflection' is conscience (as related to intellectual conscience) and that the feelings associated with this moral reflection are the feelings that result as a consequence of this process rather than conscience itself. Indeed, phrases by Wood, that discuss conscience as a 'morally motivating feeling', require unpacking (ibid., 183). Similarly when Hill distinguishes between the judgement of conscience and the thing that an agent 'hears' (*Human Welfare*, 301), there is frustratingly little by way of analysis of this claim (which may be read as a claim that the verdict of the judgement is experienced as a voice from the same capacity).

66   The account of conscience that Paton defends, which takes conscience to involve a feeling and an intellectual aspect, functions by building upon a claim that practical reason 'may contain volitional and even emotional elements within itself' ('Conscience and Kant', 241). What Patron is doing here is drawing attention to the same interpretive problems that are found when attempting to explain how the moral feeling of respect can motivate an agent, the question is simply broadened to moral feelings generally i.e. how can any moral feeling (considered as feelings of reason) motivate an agent by enacting an effect upon the (sensible) self of an agent. This is a legitimate concern, however as stated earlier it does not concern the present discussion. Rather, what is of concern is the fact that once again Paton's position is that there is a judgement of practical reason i.e. intellectual conscience and that this in some way *results* in a morally motivational force. (Quote also cited by Vujosevic, 'The Judge in the Mirror', 452).

conscience as practical reason. Indeed, such a reading would mean that there
are straightforwardly identifiable feelings that one could denote as conscience
and thereby conscience would appear to be similar to a moral sense. Although
this is the case, the claim can nonetheless be maintained that the determination of conscience effects moral feeling and that such feeling is specifically
associated with conscience. To defend this, it is not necessary to postulate a
unique nature to the phenomenological consequence of conscientious determination, rather one simply can point out that because the feeling *proceeds*
the determination of conscience it is to be an instance of moral feeling associated with conscience. It would be puzzling to present a counter claim that
an agent may pass a judgement of conscience, then experience a feeling, and
then question whether that feeling is as a result of such judgement. Indeed, an
agent would naturally conjoin the two (even if the moral feeling is the effect
of the determination of conscience rather than conscience itself). In other
words, the moral feeling is experienced, and thereby understood, within a context of an agent being conscious of the activity of conscience.

In the following sections I will expand upon intellectual conscience by providing a definition of the judgement of conscience and explicating that it is a
higher-order form of moral imputation.

2.4   Conscience as Judgement

In this section I will show that intellectual conscience is a higher-order judgement as to whether an agent has diligently examined their actions.[67] Following
this I will argue that the process of conscience is structured disjunctively.[68]

---

67   Here first-order judgement is a judgement about an object (for example, X is the right
      thing to do), a second-order judgement is a judgement about the first-order judgement
      (not an object: for example, judging whether the first judgement was made correctly) and
      a higher-order judgement is any judgement that is passed upon a judgement.

68   Interestingly within Kant's discussion of conscience in *Vigilantius* he discusses at length
      the metaphor of the court and conscience as syllogistic. For example Kant states that, 'legal
      imputation (*imputatio legis*) involves a syllogism that is the subsumption of the fact (fac-
      tum) under the law' (27:572). In this chapter, because I see no difference in the respective
      treatments of conscience as a syllogism, I will not be exploring at length Kant's treatment
      of conscience as a syllogism in *Vigilantius* but will instead explicate the relevant passages
      from *Religion* and *Metaphysics of Morals*. For a discussion that touches, albeit briefly, on
      Kant's symbolic representation of conscience see H. Bielefeldt, *Symbolic Representation
      in Kant's Practical Philosophy*, Cambridge University Press (2003), 54–5. It is also interest-
      ing to note that the conceiving of conscience in such a syllogistic manner was typical of

2.4.1 *Examination of Cases*

Earlier I highlighted that Kant's talk of conscience as an 'inner court', an 'inner judge' and as 'condemning and acquitting' (*Metaphysis of Morals* 6:438) suggests that the capacity of conscience involves a judgement. In the *Metaphysics of Morals* the thought process of conscience, which constitutes the proceedings of the internal court, is explained when Kant describes how the various representations of the faculties contribute and are involved in the internal court. He states that

> The internal *imputation* of a *deed*, as a case falling under a law [. . .] belongs to the *faculty of judgement* [. . . which] judges with rightful force whether the action as a deed (an action coming under a law) has occurred or not. Upon it follows the conclusion of **reason** (the verdict), that is, the connecting of the rightful result with the action (condemnation or acquittal). All this takes place before a *tribunal* (bold mine, 6:438).[69]

In this passage two distinct moments are being described. The *first moment* is the imputation of a deed. This falls within the faculty of judgement. What is taking place here is *moral judgement*: an agent generates a proposed action and this action is judged as to whether or not it abides by the moral law. The *second moment* relates to the verdict of reason. The verdict concerns whether or not an act was the right thing to do. This second moment follows from the first moment as a *higher-order judgement* about moral judgements. Indeed, this also clarifies what Kant means when he states in *Religion* that

> Conscience could also be defined as *the moral faculty of judgment, passing judgment upon itself* except that this definition would be much in need of prior clarification of the concepts contained in it (6:186).

The reason that defining conscience as the moral faculty of judgement may cause confusion is that the phrase correlates rather too closely to the notion of moral judgement as it relates to the determination of duties themselves. Three levels can be thought of. The first level being what the law actually is (this relates to the faculty of understanding). Here conscience is not in play,

---

Protestant writing at the time of Kant, suggesting that his conceptualisation is a continuation of this tradition. For a discussion of Protestant writings on conscience as a tribunal and syllogistic see Mayes, *Counsel and Conscience*, 44–5 and Kittsteiner, 'Casuistry and Character', 198–202.

69   See also Esser, 'Inner Court', 277fn6.

rather understanding is providing the basic *principle* that may be applied i.e. the moral law. An agent must first generate a rule, or be in possession of a moral principle, from which a moral judgement in the particular instance can occur upon. The second level relates to the moral judgement regarding what action an agent should undertake (this relates to the faculty of judgement). Here an agent may be presented with a practical decision that they must make a determination upon. As such, the faculty of judgement generates judgements that an agent can follow; it discerns the permissibility of actions that an agent is to undertake. Finally, the third level relates to the judgement of conscience, which tells an agent something about how they have come to their moral judgements ('passing of judgement upon itself') i.e. a judgement upon the second level. Indeed, Kant briefly clarifies what he means by stating that 'conscience does not pass judgement upon actions as cases that stand under the law, for this is what reason does so far as it is subjectively practical' (*Religion* 6:186). Which is to say, conscience does not determine duty in terms of moral judgement and is not involved in the first moment (as referred to above). Rather, the judgement of conscience tells an agent something about how the agent came to determine that the particular moral judgement is a case that stands under the law.[70]

The question remains as to what exactly is meant by the claim that the judgement of conscience judges whether or not an act was the right thing to do. In other words, what exactly is it that the judgement of conscience reveals to an agent regarding their moral judgements. A double meaning can be revealed here. Firstly, in noticing in the passage cited above from the *Metaphysics of Morals* (6:438) that Kant talks of 'a case', a straightforward reading of conscience as judging a particular moral judgement can be inferred. By 'case' I read a practical judgement in a particular instance (hence Kant's talk of 'connecting the rightful *result* with the *action* (emphasis mine)'. For example, in the case of a shopkeeper who is presented with a situation where there is a claimant in their shop who is producing evidence (in the form of a receipt) that they have been overcharged, the shopkeeper in this scenario may actually be committed to a number of duties. Along with say, the moral judgement 'when customers are overcharged, the overcharged money should be refunded', there may also be the moral judgement of a duty to one's self not to be conned, a duty to one's family to not be reckless with money, or a duty that when someone is lying the lie should not be rewarded. Due to the possibilities presented by these sets of duties, depending on the particular circumstance agents will have to evaluate

---

70   As Kant tells us it is 'understanding, not conscience, which judges whether an action is *in general* right or wrong' (6:186, emphasis mine).

the situation and come to a decision about which duty they are obligated to actualise (in other words, which case is appropriate to the situation). When an agent decides upon a particular course of action, if the agent chooses to consult their conscience then it will pass a judgement regarding the *rightfulness qua the action*. Here the first dimension of what is meant by the judgement of conscience is to be read as a concern for the veracity of a moral-practical judgement.

A second dimension regarding what exactly the judgement of conscience reveals to an agent can be drawn from Kant's discussions in *Religion*. Here Kant makes it clear that the judgement of conscience is a judgement as to whether or not the agent has been 'diligent' in the examination of their actions. He states

> Here reason judges itself, whether it has actually undertaken, with all diligence, that examination of actions (whether they are right or wrong), and it calls the human being to himself to witness for or against himself whether this has taken place or not (6:186).

In the above passage Kant is referring to two things. The first concerns the examination of 'actions' and the second involves the consciousness that follows from the examination of actions i.e. consciousness as to whether actions have been diligently examined. Here I read Kant's use of the term 'actions' i.e. the plural form, as instructive and in contrast to the specificity of 'cases' that was discussed above. The plural form suggests a broader notion of reflection, which I read as indicative of the role that conscience may play in bringing to the awareness of an agent the bindingness of morality to *oneself*. By calling 'the human being to *himself* to witness for or against *himself* (emphasis mine)' Kant is emphasising the role of conscience in the reflection of moral duty itself.[71] Indeed, within the same context of stating that 'reason judges itself [...whether an agent has] actually undertaken, with diligence' the 'examination of actions', he goes on to emphasises action in terms of that which '*I* want to undertake' (6:186) i.e. the first-personal importance of morality. It is no surprise that Kant highlights this dimension of conscience in *Religion* where his broader concern is with moral evil. An agent may indeed be aware of moral judgements but have no concern for them with respect to their own personal conduct. For example, an agent passing moral judgements where the focus is

---

71   Hoffman's article is particularly pertinent on this point as he takes conscience as a practical analogue of apperception by which an agent comes to regard duty as binding upon themselves ('Gewissen als praktische Apperzeption', 424–43).

on other agents: the judgements that person X is a liar, has been unjust, has stolen etc., may occur without resulting in an agent, via reflection, realising that they themselves are condemnable *qua* the moral judgment for lying, for unjustness, for theft etc. For the moment I will bracket this particular dimension of conscience. In Chapter 5, where the concern is with moral self-improvement, I will discuss how it is that conscientious reflection can cultivate an attitude towards the moral bindingness of duty to oneself within discussions of moral perfection.

Thus, at this stage I will read 'diligence' more specifically in terms of particular actions (cases) and as such it becomes possible to explicate more precisely what the judgement of conscience is:

> Judgement of Conscience: a judgement about the diligence with which an agent examines a case (that has been judged to fall under the law).

Kant's use of legal terminology and more generally the metaphorical talk of conscience as a court of law requires further comment. Indeed, throughout the corpus Kant employs judge/judgement as metaphorical terms (First *Critique* A84/B116, A751/B732, *Metaphysics of Morals* 6:227, 350, *Mrongovius* 29:781–2, *Vigilantius* 27:562–3). The fact that he employs the metaphor of a court with respect to conscience is telling.[72] One reason why Kant may be describing the internal court in such a way is because of the theological connotations that conscience has within the historical context. Thus, rather than conscience being conceived in terms of confession before a priest or God (and subsequent absolving of sin thereby), conscience is to be thought of in terms of a secular court of law. This would fit into a reading of Kant's contribution to the Enlightenment (read here in terms of secularisation). However, this suggestion is problematic. As I will show in Chapter 5, Kant does speak of conscience in religious terms (going so far as to refer to the inner court as a 'divine court'). An alternative reason why he speaks of conscience as a legal metaphor is because he envisions conscience as both an impartial judgement and as a mechanism of imputation to one's self. Two aspects of the process

---

72 For a selection of articles on this point see, I. Proops, 'Kant's Legal Metaphor and the Nature of Deduction', *Journal of the History of Philosophy*, 4, 2, (2003), 209–29, D. Henrich, 'The Proof Stricture of Kant's Transcendental Deduction', *The Review of Metaphysics*, 22. 4, (1969), 640–659, and 'Kant's Notion of a Deduction and the Methodological Background to the First *Critique*', in *Kant's Transcendental Deductions: The Three "Critiques" and the "Opus Postumum"*, ed. E. Forster, Stanford University Press, (1989), 29–46.

of conscience can be thought of, the first involving verification of the facts (diligence), and the second involving the imputation of the verdict to the agent themselves (acquittal or condemnation). Indeed, as Proops correctly points out, *quid facti* and *quid juris* are not the same, *a fortiori imputatio facti* and *imputatio legis* are to be distinguished (see also *Metaphysics of Morals* 6:227).[73] To know something is not the same as conceiving that something in terms of reprehensibility or in the more general terms of moral responsibility. As Reath points out, imputation for Kant is 'a question for practical reason, rather than a straightforward factual, causal or metaphysical issue'.[74] The courtroom metaphor satisfies the double movement of firstly envisioning a deliberative/ evaluative act that occurs upon facts and secondly that this process of deliberation is one that occurs under the remit of practical action (moral responsibility). Conscience conceived of as a courtroom ensures that the facts about the matter are of concern *because of* the moral imputation that the inner judge symbolises. There is more to say on this matter, in particular how it is through the notion that agents are free (self-conscious of their freedom and hence morally responsible) that the facts attributed to agents can then be (morally) imputed upon the agent. As Kant explains in *Collins*, 'we can attribute a thing to someone, yet not impute it to him; the actions, for example, of a madman or drunkard can be attributed, though not imputed to them. In imputation the action must spring from freedom' (27:288).[75] In Chapter 5, I read Kant's notions of an 'inner court'/'divine court' and 'inner judge'/'God' as metaphors that serve a specific function in the rational representation through which conscience is cultivated. Importantly I read these in terms of an agent's

---

73   Proops, 'Kant's Legal Metaphor and the Nature of Deduction', 213. It should be noted that Proops analysis is conduced within a discussion of Kant's Transcendental Deduction.

74   See A. Reath, 'Agency and the Imputation of Consequences in Kant's Ethics', *Annual Review of Law and Ethics*, 2, (1994), 251. See also J. Timmermann's commentary on this paper, 'Agency and Imputation: Comments on Reath', *Philosophical Books*, 49, 2, (2008), 114–124. Here I used imputation in terms of an agent being self-conscious of how the facts of the matter relate to or command a particular conscientious judgement. This is in contrast to the broader notion of imputation taken in terms of the imputation of the consequences of a particular action upon the agent themselves. On this latter point Reath's analysis is particularly germane. See also M. Timmons, 'Evil and Imputation in Kant's Ethics', *Jahrbuch fur Recht und Ethik*, 2, (1994), 113–141.

75   See also, A. Marques, 'Imputation Judgement in Kant's Practical Philosophy', in *Kant und die Philosophie in Weltbürgerlicher Absicht. Akten des XI. Internationalen Kant-Kongress, Bacin, Ferrarin*, Walter De Gruyter, (2013), 385–93.

self-consciousness of their freedom and hence moral responsibility. As such I will return to a discussion of this point in Chapter 5.[76]

In the following subsection I will expand upon the definition of the judgement of conscience provided above by outlining the nature of this judgement further. I will detail what the constituent 'matter' is and how the judgement of conscience is structured.

2.4.2   The Judgement of Conscience

In order to understand the nature of the judgement of conscience it is necessary to explore Kant's view of judgement generally and then apply this view to the judgement of conscience.[77] Kant defines judgement in the *Lectures on Logic* as 'the representation of the unity of the consciousness of various representations, or the representation of their relation insofar as they constitute a concept' (9:101). He then differentiates between the 'matter and forms' of all judgements (9:101), of which he provides the following definition

> The matter of the judgement consists in the given representations that are combined in the unity of consciousness in the judgement, the form in the determination of the ways that the various representations belong, as such, to one consciousness (9:101).

When applying the above to conscience the questions that arise are 'what given representations are involved?' and 'in what way does conscience determine i.e. unify in the consciousness of an agent, the various representations?'

With respect to the matter of conscience, it is relatively straightforward to point out what representations are present. As noted earlier, in the *Metaphysics of Morals* Kant explains that the 'verdict of conscience' (6:440) is presented as

---

76   Sticker discusses the metaphor of the internal court of conscience in a critical manner by reconstructing the metaphor such that it is construed in a manner that puts forth the notion that the judgement of practical reason is the object that seeks to provide 'justifications' for apparent faults (read here as lack of diligent examination, 'When the Reflective Watch-Dog Barks'). As it is my contention that Sticker misunderstands the role of the metaphor with respect to the nature of the judgement of conscience, I will not address this here but will do so in Chapter 4.

77   The account of Kant's view of judgement that I will provide will only be an outline as detailing precisely what Kant understands judgement in general to be is a matter of intense debate by scholars and such detail is not required for the present purpose. For extended discussions on Kant's notion of Judgement see B. Longuenesse, *Kant and the Capacity to Judge*, Princeton University Press (1998), part 2, and Allison, *Kant's Transcendental Idealism*, section 2.

a cooperative achievement of the faculties of judgement and reason (6:438).[78] These two faculties can be thought of in terms of producing the following representations:

a. Consciousness of the moral judgement i.e. seeing that a case falls under the law (Faculty of Judgement).
b. Consciousness of the verdict of consulting conscience (Faculty of Reason).

These two representations can be thought of as the constituent matter of the judgement of conscience.[79]

Although the matter of conscience involves these distinct representations, the judgement of *conscience results in a consciousness of a unity*, which is a unification of the individual representations. In the First *Critique* Kant takes judgement to be the relating of given cognitions (B141) i.e. representations, and then expands on the nature of those relations with respect to syllogistic forms.[80] The exact nature of *how* these cognitions are brought together in the consciousness of an agent i.e. the relating of the faculties of understanding and imagination etc., is beyond the remit of this study as it will require excursions into Kant's theory of imagination and self-consciousness.[81] What is of relevance to the internal court of conscience is that it is a judgement that takes place which brings together immediate representations (that are the matter of conscience) within the mind of an agent.

---

78   See also Esser, 'Inner Court', 271.
79   Esser does refer to the fact that the judgement of conscience is 'syllogistic' in form, however he does not elaborate. Indeed, to the best of my knowledge this is the first attempt at such an explication ('Inner Court', 274).
80   Kant explains that 'All judgements are functions of unity among our representations; instead of an immediate representation, a *higher* representation, which comprises the immediate representation and various others, is used in cognizing the object, and thereby many possible cognitions are collected into one' (A68–9/B93–4). This passage points out that disparate cognitions i.e. each constitutive immediate representation, is pulled into a unity of some sort.
81   For a succinct discussion of Kant's attempt to relate appearances to the concepts of understanding see D. Bell, 'The Art of Judgment', *Mind*, 96, 382, (1987), 221–44. For an expanded discussion of how these faculties can be related in judgements see Allison, *Kant's Transcendental Idealism* and Longuenesse, *Kant and the Capacity to Judge*.

Kant explains in the First *Critique* that the relating, that is to say the unifying of the cognitions, takes place in syllogistic forms (A68–9/B93).[82] In the *Lectures on Logic* he explicates that there are three forms that a syllogism (which he also terms an 'inference of reason') can take and that on this 'is grounded the division of all inferences of reason into *categorical, hypothetical* and *disjunctive*' (24:121–2).[83] The basic structure of a syllogism is a major premise (the rule) which is related to a minor premise through a middle term from which a judgement is deduced as a conclusion (A304/B361, A330/B386).[84] As such the form that a syllogism can take differs with respect to how the major premise relates to the minor premise. The major premises of the syllogistic forms differ in their condition i.e. the categorical syllogism invokes a categorical clause,[85] the hypothetical syllogism involves the 'If/Then' clause, and the disjunctive syllogism invokes the 'Either/Or' clause. It is with respect to the condition that is present in the major premise that the minor premise is related to and hence why the three syllogistic forms differ. As Kant explains in the *Lectures on Logic*, the differing relations of such syllogistic forms is also expressed in the conclusion, 'the conclusion may be universal or a particular proposition, for nothing depends on the conclusion; rather, it depends on the ways in which the consequential of one judgement is drawn from another' (24:94). The nature of the conclusion i.e. if it is universal or particular, depends on the form of the syllogism (24:94). Kant is stating that the nature of the major premise, how the subject and predicate are related, dictates the particular form that a syllogism will take, with each being 'a wholly different way of reasoning' (24:95).

The question remains as to what the activity of conscience is structured according to. In order to answer this question it is first necessary to note that in Kant's account of the judgement of conscience there are only two possible verdicts, 'acquittal' or 'condemnation' (*Metaphysics of Morals* 6:400). The possible conclusions that can be stated as following from the major premise are: an agent's act either falls under the law (acquittal), or an agent's act does not fall under the law (condemnation). Thus it becomes clear from this that the major premise is an either/or clause. This makes the form of the structure that the judgement of conscience takes disjunctive. In cases of condemnation this would be:

---

82   I have taken the example that Longuenesse uses to show the relation between judgement and syllogism (*Kant and the Capacity to Judge*, 90–3).

83   See also First *Critique* A304/B361.

84   See also *Lectures on Logic* 9:93, First *Critique* A322/B378, A307/B364.

85   This may take numerous forms such as 'all', 'some', 'a particular'.

- Major premise: either the case falls under the law, or this is not a case that falls under the law.
- Minor premise: the case did not fall under the law.
- Conclusion: the agent is condemned.

Where 'under the law' is the middle term.[86]

Turning from an explication of the judgement of conscience to the motivation of conscience, in the following section I explore what is meant by the consulting of conscience.

2.5   The Motivation of Conscience

In the previous section I outlined what the judgement of conscience is. Indeed, this was done in a manner that took conscience as a higher-order judgement. In this, and the following section, I will say more on the claim that in comparison to the first-order moral motivation of respect, conscience is to be considered a higher-order judgement and thereby a higher-order motivation.

Kant's account of moral feeling is an account of moral imputation. As such, both respect and the feelings that result as a consequence of the determination of conscience (it is in this manner that I speak of the 'motivation of conscience' in this, and the following, subsection) can in some sense morally motivate an agent. In the opening of this chapter, it was shown that the capacities of moral feeling are constitutive capacities that relate duty to an agent and thereby can motivate an agent. It was also noted that in moral deliberation it is the feeling of respect that is the moral motivation that occurs with moral judgement. What occurs in this case is that an agent voluntarily applies the Categorical Imperative to determine their will. Stating this in an alternative idiom, an agent can be said to experience the moral motivation of respect only after they have consulted (i.e. applied) the Categorical Imperative to their will. In a similar fashion, the motivational efficacy of conscience—in the form of the effect on moral feeling—is experienced by an agent only after they have

---

86   Note that Kant does something very similar with respect to the treatment of the three authorities that exist within a state: namely, the sovereign authority in the person of the legislator, the executive authority in the person of the ruler, and the judicial authority in the person of the judge (*Metaphysics of Morals* 6:313). Kant tells us that this can be read as the three propositions of a *practical syllogism* (6:313).

voluntarily consulted their conscience.[87] As such, both respect and conscience can be characterised as motivating only after voluntary moral judgement.[88]

Given that both respect and conscience can motivate an agent, the question arises regarding the respective contexts of each motivation. In the case of respect the motivation concerns first-order moral judgements (I will flesh this out further in the next section). As was shown above, the judgment of conscience is a judgement about the diligence with which an agent examines a case (that has been judged to fall under the law). As such the motivation that is of concern with respect to conscience is one that is related to the diligence with which an agent examines an act. The implication and important point here is that the motivations of respect and conscience differ.

Nonetheless, irrespective of the fact that the motivations of respect and conscience differ it may be the case that the motivation of conscience is similar to respect insofar as it is first-order. Indeed, there are passages that can be pointed to which are ambiguous with respect to where the motivation of conscience is located i.e. first-order or higher-order. For example, in *Religion* Kant states

> [T]he question here is not, how conscience is to be guided (for conscience does not need any guide; to have a conscience suffices), but how conscience itself can serve as guiding thread in the most perplexing moral decisions [?] (6:185).

---

87   'Voluntarism' is a term that is employed within epistemology with regard to beliefs. Discussions centre upon the voluntariness of belief acquisition and assent, they typically involving discussion of the role of the will and the nature of a particular belief proposition. Here I employ the term with respect to the role of the will in an agent choosing or not choosing to *consult their capacity of conscience*. On the concept of voluntarism with regard to belief see A. A. Buckareff, 'Acceptance and Deciding to Believe', *Journal of Philosophical Research*, 29, (2004), 173–90 and 'Doxastic Decisions and Controlling Belief', *Acta Analytica*, 21, (2006), 102–14, J. Cohen, 'Belief and Acceptance', *Mind*, 98, (1989), 367–89, *An Essay on Belief and Acceptance*, Oxford University Press (1992), R. Feldman, 'Voluntary Belief and Epistemic Evaluation', in *Knowledge, Truth, and Duty*, ed. M. Steup, Oxford University Press (2001), 77–92 and B. C. Van Fraassen, 'Belief and the Will', *The Journal of Philosophy*, 81, (1984), 235–56.

88   In this sense of the term Smith is also a voluntarist. Smith states that an agent's conscience functions when they have 'submitted themselves to [its] reproach and to the punishment' and that 'only by consulting this judge within' the impartial judgement can occur (A. Smith, *The Theory of Moral Sentiments*, Penguin Books (2009), 143, see also 158).

The relevant question is 'how conscience itself can serve as a guiding thread in the most perplexing moral decisions', which I read as, *given* the capacity of conscience present in moral agents *how* is this capacity to be utilised. On the one hand the suggestion is that conscience is not related to first-order moral judgement because if Kant did conceive of conscience in such a manner it would then be puzzling to find him asking the question of how conscience is to guide an agent in moral decisions. Indeed, his talk of 'perplexing moral decisions' suggests a higher-order form of moral inquiry. However, on the other hand, the passage can be read as maintaining that conscience is a guide in complex first-order moral situations.

Indeed, when Kant asserts that 'conscience *speaks* involuntarily and unavoidably' (emphasis mine, *Metaphysics of Morals* 6:401), he may be read as referring to a first-order character of the response of conscience. Nevertheless, this assertion may still be read in terms of a higher-order account. Recall that in section 2.3 above intellectual conscience was characterised as the determination of practical reason, and that the effect that this determination has on the capacity of moral feeling was identified as the experienced feelings that are produced following the judgement of conscience. This two-part analysis allows Kant's assertion that conscience speaks involuntarily to be read as, firstly, the consulting of intellectual conscience is voluntary and, secondly, the type of feeling that this brings about is involuntary once conscience has been consulted.

Evidence for an account of conscience that is higher-order can be found in *Religion* where Kant states

> There are tendencies in the souls of many to make no rigorous judgment of themselves—an urge to dispense with conscience. [...] We find in such people that they are averse to any close examination of their actions, and shy away from it [...] (6:616–7).

In Kant's condemnation of agents who seek to dispense with conscience a reference is being made to the choice of not undertaking the 'rigorous judgment of themselves'. Importantly he is not condemning the agent for not paying heed to the judgement of conscience rather he is condemning the agent for failing to *consult* their conscience. This fits naturally with the idea that conscience is a higher-order judgement concerning the diligence [read: rigour] with which an agent has examined their act. It suggests something distinct from first-order moral motivation. Indeed, the suggestion is that an act— based on a first-order judgement—has occurred and that conscience is part of a mechanism whereby an agent engages in 'close[r] examination of their

actions'. Furthermore, there is ample textual evidence that Kant takes conscience as occurring upon, which I read as *after*, first-order moral judgement.
For example, the passage cited earlier from the *Metaphysics of Morals* 6:438,
where Kant differentiates the judgement of conscience from moral judgements, offers strong support for this reading.[89] The thought here is one of an
asymmetry: every instance of the consulting of conscience requires a relating
to duty; however every instance of moral judgement i.e. duty, does not relate to
the consulting of conscience.[90]

A question that may be raised from this account of conscience is 'what
motivation does an agent have to consult their conscience?' In order to answer
this question it is possible to read Kant's generic discussion of moral feeling
as a set of feelings that are interconnected in a hierarchy. In this account, the
moral feeling of respect forms the first-order moral motivation upon which
the higher-order moral motivation of consulting one's conscience can follow.
Such a model is presented by Guyer who states that Kant is explicating a 'mul-
tistage model of the role of feeling in the performance of morally requisite
and worthy action'.[91] Guyer argues that 'the feeling of respect [...] is the first
stage in making the moral law effective in the phenomenal etiology of action'.[92]
Upon this first stage subsequent stages may occur. This can be explained by
stating that the moral imputation of respect can impute upon the agent a
motivation to submit their moral judgements to the judgement of conscience
as a mechanism that *evaluates the moral judgement itself*.[93] The motivation to
consult one's conscience could be read as an attempt by an agent, following the
experience of respect with moral judgement, to examine the manner in which
they have come to justify a particular act. As such, the motivation of respect
must be seen as correlated to the motivation to consult one's conscience. As
pointed out by Esser

> Kant assigns to conscience a role that is subordinate to moral reflection.
> Conscience does not directly contribute to moral orientation, but merely

---

89   See also *Miscarriage* 8:268, *Vigilantius* 27:614–5 and *Collins* 27:354, where Kant also dif-
     ferentiates moral judgement from the judgement of conscience.
90   See also Timmermann, 'Kant on Conscience', 296.
91   Guyer, 'Moral Feeling', 138.
92   Ibid.
93   As Guyer claims, '[the] moral feeling [of respect], which itself needs to be cultivated and
     strengthened in the normal course of human life, works by in turn motivating the cul-
     tivation and strengthening of the further aesthetic preconditions' that Kant mentions,
     namely conscience, understood as the empirical disposition to hearken to the voice of the
     moral law when presented with particular situations' ('Moral Feeling', 142).

exhorts us to always subject our actions to moral reflection and criticism, and to appeal to the 'inner court of justice'.[94]

Esser is pointing out that the capacity of conscience addresses the problem of 'correct moral self-description and correct moral self-criticism'.[95] The judgement of conscience is not moral judgement, it neither produces its own moral judgement nor does it generate a more diligent moral judgement. Rather, conscience is a judgement about the nature of an agent's moral judgements. The claim here is that the judgement of conscience directs the attention of an agent towards their responsibility to investigate how the moral judgements that occur in an agent have taken place.[96] I will say more about this in Chapter 3.[97]

In the next section I rebut an alternative reading of Kant's conception of conscience. This reading, articulated and defended by Moyar, claims that

---

94   Esser, 'Internal Court', 272.

95   Ibid., 272.

96   Similarly Hill points out that 'the point [...] is to distinguish conscience [...] from the general activities of moral deliberation, reasoning and judgment. Conscience presupposes and makes use of these activities' (*Human Welfare*, 301). However Hill then asserts that the judgement of conscience brings to the awareness of an agent whether their action, or intended action is at odds with their own judgement (*Human Welfare* 301–2), which he then explicates as conscience asking the question 'What sorts of acts, in what circumstances, are morally permissible, and what sorts are morally forbidden?' (*Human Welfare*, 302). In doing so Hill is alluding to the fact that the judgement of conscience can lead to the answering of these questions by the fact that the awareness of whether or not an action has been diligently examined leads to an agent being acquitted or condemned, which itself is a motivation to either act upon the particular moral judgement or reconsider it, respectively.

97   Sticker briefly notes that the motivation of conscience can be viewed in comparison to respect by suggesting that respect provides a 'positive certain[ty] that an action is obligatory or forbidden, whereas [...] conscience [involves] realis[ing] that [an agent is] not certain that their action would be morally right' ('When the Reflective Watch-Dog Barks, section 2.1). Firstly, this account does not take into account cases when an agent may reflect conscientiously and realise that their action is indeed conscientious (see Chapter 3), as such it would be peculiar to describe these cases as realising a 'negative' motivation. Secondly, if by 'negative' something akin to the claim that conscience can tell an agent that they should refrain from an action is understood, then a similar 'negative' motivation can be ascribed as an analogue to respect i.e. in cases when an agent realises that the action is not permissible a negative motivation is experienced (c.f. humiliation). As such, the hierarchical picture that I have provided above is a more natural reading of the relationship between respect and conscience *qua* motivation.

Kant's conception of conscience is *the* mechanism of moral imputation i.e. that conscience is the first-order form of moral imputation.

2.6   Moyar: Conscience as Constitutive of Moral Judgement

Moyar provides an account of the activity of the capacity of conscience as constitutive of all moral judgements i.e. the first-order form of moral imputation. Below I will outline his account and show that it is incorrect.

Moyar argues that in contrast to the 'narrow capacity' of respect conscience is a wider capacity, which 'is a general enough notion to accommodate all the dimensions of moral feeling, rather than simply the [...] feeling of respect'.[98] Moyar asserts that Kant's various claims about conscience are to be read as aspects of 'the more basic idea of a capacity for self-imputation through which duty is represented in a motivationally efficacious manner'.[99] Moyar develops the view that conscience *is the basic act* of moral self-consciousness. He states that

> [Conscience is] the self-consciousness that makes possible judgments imputing an action to the subject. [...] Kant's [...] claim is best understood as restricted to the claim that there is a basic act of self-consciousness that is constitutive of a judgment of duty.[100]

And elsewhere

> Conscience as self-consciousness is constitutive of moral judgment [...]. As moral self-consciousness, conscience is how the agent becomes conscious of his duty, which I read as making imputation of a duty possible.[101]

According to Moyar, Kant is claiming that 'the subjective judgment of conscience is necessary for there to be moral judgment at all', which is to say that an agent's conscience is the first-order mechanism by which duty is imputed

---

98   As Moyar states, 'we should take Kant's doctrine of conscience, rather than the narrow doctrine of respect, as the key to Kant's theory of 'moral sensibility'' ('Unstable Autonomy', 357).

99   Ibid.

100   Ibid., 349.

101   Ibid., 353.

in practical situations.[102] The point that Moyar is making is this: when an agent makes a moral judgement they are still faced with deliberating about practical situations in which they may or may not choose to take into account their moral judgments. Judging that 'X is what ought to be done', is not the same as determining 'X is what I ought to be motivated to do'. The motivating factor, that 'I should do X in this situation', according to Moyar, is the work of conscience.[103] On Moyar's account conscience is necessary to 'even conceive of' a duty, which he takes to mean that 'one could not even have a moral will without the self-consciousness through which deeds become imputable'.[104] It becomes clear that Moyar ascribes to conscience the role that a (failed) notion of respect had played in the *Groundwork*'s and the Second *Critique*'s account of moral motivation. Moyar presents the view that Kant's notion of conscience represents his mature views on moral imputation. Moyar claims that the reason Kant brings conscience to the fore in his 1790's writing is because of the problem of complex moral judgements.[105]

It is clear that the central difference between Moyar's account and the account I am defending lies in the claim that conscience is constitutive of moral judgements. Moyar understands constitutive to mean *constitutive of all moral judgements* in contrast to the account of constitutive that I articulated, namely that conscience is only a constitutive capacity that all agents possess by virtue of being a moral agent and that the feelings of conscience occur subject to the capacity being voluntarily engaged, resulting in higher-order

---

102 Ibid., 348–9. Moyar defines this as the 'Self-Consciousness in Deliberation View' stating, 'One role that Kant ascribes to conscience is self-consciousness of the will. As such a capacity, conscience can be seen as enabling a subjective unity of the diverse aspects of a case of action, and thus as enabling the deed to be imputed to a unitary subject' (ibid., 343).

103 Concerns with rationalistic accounts of morality were raised by the predecessors of Kant. The issue rested upon how rationalistic moral judgements are able to move an agent to act i.e. moral motivation. As Hume famously states 'Reason is perfectly inert' see D. Hume, *A Treatise of Human Nature (Second Edition)*, Oxford University Press (1978), Chapter 3, section 1.1.

104 Moyar, 'Unstable Autonomy', 348.

105 Ibid., 330–1, 335. Indeed Kant only mentions conscience in the *Groundwork* twice (4:404, 422) and in the Second *Critique* once (5:98), and in both texts he does not explicate the concept. The issue is particularly potent with respect to the Second *Critique* given the fact that the purpose of Chapter III of the Second *Critique* is precisely to address the motivational issue of the practicality of reason (Second *Critique* 5:42, 114). For an in-depth discussion of the origin and aim of the Second *Critique* see H. F. Klemme, 'The Origin and Aim of Kant's Critique of Practical Reason' in *Kant's Critique of Practical Reason*, ed. A. Reath and J. Timmermann, *Cambridge University Press* (2010), 11–30.

moral motivation. Indeed, the higher-order account of conscience that I am defending does not encroach upon the first-order account of respect in moral motivation. By arguing that conscience somehow subsumes and surpasses the account of respect that Kant had articulated in the pre-1790's Critical texts, Moyar is making an incredibly strong claim. Such an account would place a central burden upon Kant's conception of conscience, formulating it as the first-order form of moral imputation.

The first problem with the Moyar account is that, as explicated in the previous section, Kant states clearly in *Religion* (a text from the 1790s) that some agents choose not to engage their capacity of conscience (6:616–7). Thus, to assert that conscience accompanies all moral judgements would involve explaining this passage accordingly. A second contention is that a strong argument can be made that Kant maintains the position that respect is the first-order form of moral motivation throughout his post-Critical texts (the 'consistency thesis'). Below I will expand upon this second contention by arguing for the consistency thesis and establishing a negative result, namely, that because of the consistency thesis Kant cannot be ascribing to conscience the role of first-order moral imputation.[106]

2.6.1   *The Consistency Thesis*

Via an inspection of Kant's texts it becomes clear that a strong argument can be made to the effect that his account of respect as the first-order form of moral motivation is a position that he held throughout his post-Critical corpus. Beginning with the shift from the *Groundwork* to the Second *Critique*, within the secondary literature there are proponents of the view that Kant's notion of a 'Fact of Reason' (5:31, 47) can fulfil the role of moral imputation and that this Fact of Reason (that describes the consciousness of the moral law within an agent (5:31)) is a result of the feeling of respect.[107] Such scholars move from Kant's assertion that

---

106   More specifically, it is *highly implausible* to maintain the position that Kant claims that conscience is the first-order form of moral imputation. Importantly it should be noted that the consistency thesis that I will defend does not entail the claim that Kant's notion of respect remains the *same* throughout his post-Critical corpus. An argument that asserts that Kant's view of respect developed, was modified and even that it had radically differed from the notion of respect that is presented in the *Groundwork* is entirely compatible with the consistency thesis. The only claim here is that Kant maintains respect as the first-order form of moral motivation.

107   For a discussion of the 'Fact of Reason' thesis see P. Kleingeld, 'Moral consciousness and the "fact of reason"', in *Kant's Critique of Practical Reason: A Critical Guide*, 73–89. On the fact of reason and imputation see Proops, 'Kant's Legal Metaphor', 209–29 and

> Consciousness of [the] fundamental law may be called a fact of reason [...] it must be noted carefully that it is not an empirical fact but the sole fact of pure reason which, by it, announces itself as originally lawgiving (5:31)

to a claim that respect can be read as falling within the remit of bringing to the awareness of an agent the consciousness of the moral law.[108] For example, Schonecker presents a three step account of this relation:

i. The factum theory explains our insights into the binding character of the moral law; it is a theory of justification.
ii. In our consciousness of the [Categorical Imperative], the moral law is immediately given in its unconditional and binding validity.
iii. The unconditional validity of the [Categorical Imperative] is given in the feeling of respect.[109]

Another example of an account that broadly follows this line is that of Zinkin.[110] Zinkin defends the view that respect can motivate an agent by asserting that the 'account of respect as feeling is not separate from the use of reason, but intrinsic to willing'.[111] Similarly to the account provided above, she explicates her account by developing upon Kant's work in the Second *Critique*.[112] It is important to note that issues of interpretation and analysis concerning the Fact of Reason thesis are highly contentious, and as such the point that I make here is to be read only as the modest claim that Kant maintains the notion of respect as first-order moral motivation in the Second *Critique*. Indeed, Moyar himself acknowledges that this is the case, and it is from this point forward (post Second *Critique*) that Moyar argues that the shift from respect to conscience occurs.

Moyar's account of the moral feeling of conscience may indeed fall into an expanded and/or modified account of the Fact of Reason, the move being from the Fact of Reason to moral motivation (however, in this case respect

---

D. Schonecker, 'Kant's Moral Intuitionism: The Fact of Reason and Moral Dispositions', *Kant Studies Online* (2013), 1–38. See also Sargentis, 'Moral Motivation in Kant', 93–121.

108 For example see O. Ware, 'Kant, Skepticism, and Moral Sensibility' (PhD diss. University of Toronto 2010).
109 Schonecker, 'Kant's Moral Intuitionism', 3.
110 Zinkin, 'Respect for the Law', 31.
111 Ibid.
112 Ibid., 39–45.

is replaced by conscience). Indeed Moyar makes precisely this hermeneutic move. He states that that the feelings of conscience represent a

> [C]oncept of conscience that could do most of the work of the original [Fact of Reason] while avoiding the main pitfalls of the original account.[113]

The issue here is that even if it was granted that Kant's Fact of Reason thesis has many pitfalls, it does not follow that he abandons this thesis.[114] Indeed, even if it is argued that he did, it does not follow that this led Kant to posit an entirely new concept of first-order moral imputation i.e. conscience, rather than provide a modified account of respect. Moyar fails to provide any textual evidence to substantiate such a fundamental shift in Kant's thoughts.[115]

Indeed there is textual evidence to the contrary. For example in *Religion*, where Kant also discusses conscience, there is evidence that he takes respect as the basic, first-order form of moral motivation. He states

> This capacity for simple **respect** for the moral law within us would thus be moral feeling, which in and through itself does not constitute an end of the natural predispositions except so far as it is the motivating force [*Triebfeder*] for the will. Since this is possible only when the free will incorporates such moral feeling into its maxim, the property of such a will is a good character (bold mine, 6:27–8).[116]

---

113 Moyar, 'Unstable Autonomy', 331.

114 For a discussion that attempts to address some of the criticism directed at the Fact of Reason thesis see P. W. Franks, *All or Nothing: Systematicity, Transcendental Arguments, and Skepticism in German Idealism*, Harvard University Press (2005), 260–336.

115 At the end of the section where Moyar address the apparent failure of the Fact of Reason thesis, Moyar simply moves from highlighting the failures of the Fact of Reason's attempt to explain moral imputation to the fact that Kant introduces conscience in the later works (post-1790's), and claims from this the tenuous link between the failures of the Fact of Reason and the introduction of conscience ('Unstable Autonomy', 335).

116 Here a note on translation is necessary. In the above *Triebfeder* has been translated as 'motivating force', however the word can also be translated as 'incentive'. This translational discrepancy is exhibited in this study where in Chapter 5, sections 5.2 and 5.5 I discuss the notion of 'incentive' with respect to moral improvements *qua* rational representation. Although this should be noted, the differing translations of the term do not impact the analysis that I provide.

This passage is germane to the defence of the consistency thesis as it treats respect as '*the* motivating force for the will' (emphasis mine).[117] It can also be pointed out that Kant uses the same term *Triebfeder* (translated as 'motivating force') in the passage from *Religion* (6:27–8) and in the Second *Critique*, where he states that it is 'the subjective determining ground of the will of a being whose reason is not already in virtue of its nature necessarily in accordance with the objective law' (5:72).[118] Moreover, in *Mrongovius* Kant uses a similar phrase of 'moving force' in a discussion of moral feelings after referring directly to respect (27:1428). This thread suggests that his view on respect as the 'moving/motivating force' of moral imputation remained consistent from his early-Critical *Lectures on Ethics* (*Mrongovius* 1785), to the latter Second *Critique* (1788), until, at the very least, the post-1790's text *Religion* (1793).[119] As such, Moyar's claim that Kant's views on moral imputation changed in his later works would have to explain why he was still clearly talking about respect as the 'motivating force' whilst simultaneously introducing the concept of conscience that is supposed to supersede it.

Moyar may argue that by 'mature view', what is being referenced is specifically the *Metaphysics of Morals* (1797).[120] However, even if this was granted, he would still have to explain why Kant, in an almost identical fashion to how he spoke about respect in the *Groundwork* (4:401fn), states in the *Metaphysics of Morals* that 'respect for the law, which in its subjective aspect is called moral feeling is identical with consciousness of one's duty' (6:464). Furthermore, when Kant states

> Every determination of choice proceeds from the representation of the possible action, through the feeling of pleasure or displeasure in taking

---

117   For an exegesis of this passage that follows the line of argument that I am presenting see Morrison, *Kant and the Role of Pleasure in Moral Action*, 152–3.

118   For a discussion of Kant's use of the term *Tribfeder* in the Second *Critique* see S. Engstrom, 'The *Triebfeder* of pure practical reason', in *Kant's Critique of Practical Reason: A Critical Guide*, 90–118. For an additional discussion of Kant's use of the term *Tribfeder* in the Second *Critique* see Reath, *Agency and Autonomy*, 10.

119   It should be noted however, as pointed out by Esser, Lehmann has argued that between the years of 1775 and 1791 Kant presented the same material in his lectures even after publishing his critical works ('Inner Court', 276). However, irrespective of this claim the argument still stands with respect to the continuity between the Second *Critique* and *Religion*.

120   For an account that defends the view that the *Metaphysics of Morals* is the final and therefore mature view of Kant's practical philosophy see A. W. Wood, 'The Final Form of Kant's Practical Philosophy', in *Kant's Metaphysics of Morals: Interpretive Essays*, ed. M. Timmons, Cambridge University Press (2004), 1–21.

an interest in the action or in its effect, to the deed; and here the sensitive condition (the affection of the internal sense) is either a pathological or a moral feeling. The former is that feeling which precedes the representation of the law; the latter is that which can only follow the representation of the law (6:399)

he is outlining the picture of every determination of choice, be it moral or immoral. Kant is stating that actions result as a consequence of a presented choice between pathological and moral feeling. What is important to note here is that Kant is presenting a model of moral motivation that includes all the specific moral feelings i.e. love of one's neighbour, conscience and respect, which may result as a consequence of the representation of the law. Moyar may argue that in the introduction to the section 'Moral Feeling', Kant uses the similar phrase of 'the moral vital force' (6:400)—which I have argued remained constantly as a reference to respect in his previous works—however this time in a fundamentally distinct manner. The first issue with this is that Moyar would also have to explain what role the moral feeling of love of one's neighbour (discussed under the same section) plays. Moreover, bracketing the issue of where to place the moral feeling of love of one's neighbour, if Kant's view had changed in terms of the role of respect (which would have been a major shift in his account of moral motivation), why, in the *Metaphysics of Morals* (6:399–403) passages that Moyar relies so heavily upon, did Kant expend such a short treatment (a few paragraphs)? And why, given the gravity of this shift, did he not make this claim explicitly clear? In light of these problems and the strong evidence supporting the consistency thesis, Moyar's claim that Kant had replaced respect with conscience as the first-order form of moral imputation must be rejected.

2.7   Conclusion

In this chapter I argued that Kant takes conscience to be a particular manifestation of practical reason, which results in a feeling that is produced as a result of its determination. I also argued that should an agent choose to consult their conscience, it will pass a disjunctively structured higher-order judgement with respect to whether or not an agent has been diligent in the examination of their actions. This chapter constitutes the first stage in the defence of the Unity Thesis by outlining the fundamental nature and function of conscience *qua* the judgement of conscience. However, at various points I have bracketed certain issues that have been raised. Most importantly, I have not fully explored the function that conscientious reflection plays in revealing a bindingness of duty to *oneself*. In order to fully explicate this point, it is necessary to delve deeper into the nature of the judgement of conscience. In the following chapter I will explore Kant's insistent denial of an erring conscience. Not only will this shed light on a central element of Kant's notion of conscience, it will also bring to the fore concepts such as subjective certainty and conscientiousness. As will become clear, these concepts are vital to understanding how conscience functions, and building upon these, the role of conscience in Kant's ethics will be elaborated.

CHAPTER 3

The Errors and Failures of Conscience

3.1   Introduction

Kant's theory of conscience belongs to a historical tradition of discussing the errors and failures associated with conscience.[1] Hobbes, Locke, Wolff, Grotius, Crusius and Baumgarten argue that the judgement of conscience can err.[2] Shaftesbury, Hutcheson and Rousseau discuss the relationship between conscience and error in terms of false notions of conscience, where 'false conscience' is a form of reflection which, despite appearing to be the reflection that is conscience, is not in fact conscientious reflection.[3] The former can be

---

1 Kant discusses the notions of an 'erring conscience' (*Metaphysics of Morals* 6:401, *Miscarriage* 8:268, *Vigilantius* 27:614–5), an 'erroneous conscience' (*Religion* 6:185–7) and an 'errant conscience' (*Collins* 27:354).

2 Both Hobbes and Locke make the claim that, because the judgement of conscience is erroneous, agents are never to base their civic action upon this (I will say more about this below). Wolff argues that errors in the judgement of conscience (which he refers to as an 'erring conscience') result from the incompetence of some agents in rational demonstration (*Vernüfftige Gedancken*, 399). Grotius talks of conscience erring because it has not been fully developed (*On the Law of War and Peace*, 94). This position is similarly articulated by Crusius (*A Guide to Rational Living*, 580). Crusius explains that 'because the conscience, like other basic drives, can err, we must transform its feelings, as far as possible, into clear conclusions or at least beware lest self-love or other corrupt inclinations make us partial' (ibid., 584). Baumgarten, whose notion of conscience is situated within his perfectionist philosophy, attributes the liability of conscience to err to the fact that human agents are finite beings. Agents should seek, but cannot attain perfection, and as such an agent cannot make the unerring judgements that would be characteristic of perfection (Osawa, 'Perfection and Morality', 131). Smith refers to the ambiguous notion that conscience is 'unerring in its rectitude' (*The Theory of Moral Sentiments*, 154). It is unclear whether he is referring to conscience being active in every moral event, or whether he is referring to the judgement of conscience (or some other alternative possibility). As such it is not possible to categorise Smith's view within one of the broadly outlined positions above.

3 Shaftesbury describes the notion of 'false consciences' that provide agents with unclear 'sentiment' (*Characteristics of Men, Manners, Opinions, Times*, 209). Hutcheson discusses 'erroneous conscience' occurring because of 'false notions of religion [...] informed by superstition and wrong education' (*A System of Moral Philosophy*, 159). Despite this, and in direct contradiction to Hobbes and Locke, Hutcheson asserts that the 'liberty of conscience is [...]

thought of as errors associated with the judgement of conscience. The latter can be thought of as errors associated with the consulting of false conscience. In addition to these categories there are other errors and failures: these being the failure of an agent to consult their conscience, the failure to act upon the judgement of conscience (when conscience has been consulted), and finally the consulting of conscience upon a false principle of morality (Kant refers to this as an 'errant conscience' (*Collins* 27:354, see also *Brauer* 132). Throughout Kant's various discussions of conscience there is an insistent denial of the possibility of an erring conscience, which in the *Metaphysics of Morals* he calls 'an absurdity' (6:401).[4] Herein this shall be referred to as the 'Absurdity Thesis'.

Given the centrality of the Absurdity Thesis to Kant's overall notion of conscience this chapter concerns the explication of this notion. This will involve exploring what exactly Kant takes the Absurdity Thesis to mean, how he argues for it and to what and to whom he is responding. As is clear from the secondary literature, there is a considerable lack of clarity and scholarly consensus

---

an unalienable branch [of right]' (F. Hutcheson, *A System of Moral Philosophy*, R. and A. Foulis (1755), 257, see also 258, 260). Indeed, in *A Short Introduction to Moral Philosophy* Hutcheson asserts that 'conscience [...] should be the governing power in man' (F. Hutcheson, *A Short Introduction to Moral Philosophy*, The University of Glasgow (1787), 41, see also 256). Although Rousseau characterises conscience as constitutive, he does acknowledge that many agents behave in manners that seem to suggest otherwise. Despite this he tells us that even such morally reprehensible agents still possess some morality in their 'heart'. He opposes the claim that conscience is simply the expression of moral notions that have been conditioned within an agent by customs that come from society and/or by an authority such as a priest, or as expressions of 'errors of childhood, prejudices of education' (*Emile*, 289), by first acknowledging that there are various phenomena that agents often conceive of as conscience and then differentiating what he takes to be genuine conscience from such falsely identified phenomena. Rousseau refers to the illegitimate forms of conscience as 'acquired ideas' that are introduced by experience (ibid., see also 258, 286–7fn, 293). Although Pufendorf explains that natural law 'can be investigated and learned as a whole, by the light of man's inborn reason and a consideration of human nature' (*The Duty of Man and Citizen*, 161), he does not believe the claim that 'the law is known by nature' entails that the law was 'inherent in men's minds at the hour of their birth' (ibid., 164). Instead, introducing conscience, he argues that '[O]nce [natural law] find[s] assent, and grow[s] up in our minds, [it] can never again be destroyed, no matter how [...] impious [the] man, [...] we think of this knowledge exactly as if we had had it already at birth' (ibid., see also 180). This seems to commit Pufendorf to the view that conscience is 'acquired' and yet still morally authoritative.

4   For examples see *Metaphysics of Morals* 6:401, *Miscarriage* 8:268 and *Vigilantius* 27:614–5.

on these matters.[5] My central claim in this chapter is that Kant is found to have two expressions of the Absurdity Thesis. In *Miscarriage* and *Vigilantius* he expresses the following:

> Absurdity Thesis$_1$: it is impossible for an agent to have a mistaken belief about their belief regarding the rightfulness of an action.

In a passage from *Metaphysics of Morals* Kant contrastingly expresses an alternative version:

> Absurdity Thesis$_2$: it is impossible for an agent to be mistaken in their belief as to whether or not they have consulted conscience.

Through textual exegesis I will outline these expressions.[6] I will argue that whereas Absurdity Thesis$_1$ is philosophically coherent, Absurdity Thesis$_2$ is problematic and implausible. I will then discuss the relationship between the two expressions. I will point out that although Kant is being inconsistent both expressions nonetheless share the notion of a higher-order judgement that concerns subjective belief. I will also argue that the two expressions are a result of Kant responding to two different questions in the historical context: where Absurdity Thesis$_1$ is a response to the Hobbes-Locke conception of conscience and Absurdity Thesis$_2$ is a response to Bayle's and Wolff's conception of conscience. Following this I will discuss the notion of 'subjective certainty', which concerns the propositional subjective *beliefs* that an agent assents to. I will show that Kant does indeed have a coherent theory of subjective certainty. Following this I will explicate Kant's notion of conscientiousness by showing that a conscientious agent is one that takes a sceptical stance towards their beliefs and evaluative procedures, and thereby is always in an active state of re-evaluation. Finally, I will discuss further the categories of error and failure (explicated in the introduction above), which are associated with conscience and highlight in particular their relation to moral judgement. Here I explicate Kant's warning against a 'certain conscience' (*Vigilantius* 27:619), the cases

---

5   See Wood, *Kantian Ethics*, 191, Hill, *Human Welfare*, 303fn50, Moyar, 'Unstable Autonomy', 348, Despland, 'Can Conscience Be Hypocritical?', 368–9, Timmermann, 'Kant on Conscience', 303 and Howard, 'Kant and Moral Imputation', 616.

6   It is necessary to point out that Kant does address the Absurdity Thesis in *Religion* (6:185–7) by discussing the case of an Inquisitor condemning a heretic to death. I will explore the case of the Inquisitor in *Religion* only after I have explicated the more fundamental issues regarding the Absurdity Thesis.

of the 'analogues of conscience' i.e. false conscience, cases of failing to act upon the verdict of conscience, and Kant's discussion of an Inquisitor condemning a supposed heretic to death (*Religion* 6:183). The latter will involve explication of the notion of an errant conscience (*Collins* 27:354), i.e. a conscience that judges according to a false principle of morality. I then offer a brief conclusion that ties the results of this chapter to the Unity Thesis.

3.2 The Absurdity Thesis

3.2.1 Miscarriage *and* Vigilantius: *Absurdity Thesis₁*

In this section I explicate Kant's expression of the Absurdity Thesis as found in *Miscarriage* and *Vigilantius*. I will also argue that this expression is philosophically plausible.

In *Miscarriage* and *Vigilantius* Kant asserts that through the judgement of conscience an agent can be 'certain they have acted rightly' (*Miscarriage* 8:268) and this certainty comes about because conscience judges whether the agent was 'completely certain' of the action (*Vigilantius* 27:614–5). For example, in *Vigilantius* Kant states

> The judgement of conscience is addressed to a *factum* [i.e. a case], the judgement of understanding to a general proposition [i.e. the law]. [...] Now [an] assurance, up to **complete certainty**, that in order to accept a thing we have previously examined everything, and that the *factum* can accordingly be no otherwise, is the object of conscience (bold mine, 27:614–5).

There are two steps to this passage. Firstly, that the judgement of conscience is addressed to a *particular* proposition i.e. a case. Secondly, that the judgement of understanding is addressed to a *general* proposition i.e. a moral law. Here Kant is differentiating moral judgement from the judgement of conscience, where the latter is directed to a particular proposition. For example, a shopkeeper may have a general proposition that they ought to refund overcharged customers, and a particular proposition regarding a case of a particular customer. Kant makes it clear that the 'complete certainty' that an agent has 'examined everything' is in relation to the particular proposition and that this therefore is the domain of the judgement of conscience.

In *Miscarriage* Kant again begins by first differentiating the judgement of conscience from moral judgements in terms of the possibility of erring. He states

I can indeed err in the judgment in which I believe to be right, for this belongs to the understanding which alone judges objectively (rightly or wrongly) (8:268).

Following this he then goes on to say that

If there were such a thing [as an erring conscience], then we could never be **certain** we have acted rightly, since even the judge in the last instance can still be in error (bold mine, 8:268).

Here Kant is contrasting the fact than an agent can err with respect to moral judgements, but that such errors do not carry themselves into the judgement of conscience.

In order to understand what Kant means by 'acted rightly' it is necessary to point out that he is referring to the fact that the judgement of conscience is a higher-order judgement as to whether an agent has 'diligently examined' their actions (*Religion* 6:186).[7] To clarify, the assertion is not that an agent has *done the right thing* i.e. 'I acted rightly'. Rather what Kant is actually claiming here is that acting rightly is akin to the assertion 'I diligently examined my action'. That he is making this claim is evidenced by the following assertion in the *Metaphysics of Morals*

If someone is aware that he has acted in accordance with his conscience, then as far as guilt or innocence is concerned nothing more can be required of him (6:401).

Here Kant links acting in accordance with conscience (conscientiously) with acting rightly, where acting rightly is taken to be synonymous with the action that is 'required' of an agent. Crucially, the manner in which Kant develops this claim is by highlighting that the judgement regarding what an agent *believes about their own beliefs* is certain. He states

[B]ut in the judgment whether I in fact **believe** to be right (or merely pretend it) I absolutely cannot be mistaken, for this judgment—or rather this proposition—merely says that I judge the object in such-and-such a way (bold mine, *Miscarriage* 8:268).

Central to this passage is the fact that Kant is talking about first-person declarations ('I believe that p') i.e. the subjective belief that an agent holds with

---

7   As shown in Chapter 2.

respect to a particular proposition. Kant is neither talking about the objective truth of the proposition, nor is he making a claim about the proposition from a third-person standpoint. With respect to the objective truth of the proposition, agents can certainly be mistaken in their judgement: all that would be taking place here is the claim that an agent believes that p but it is in fact the case that not p. With respect to third-person standpoints a claim can be made 'it is the case that p, but the agent believes that not p'. Here all that is occurring is the *observation* that an agent believes a proposition that does not correspond to the matter of fact. The kind of claims that Kant is denying here are of the form of an agent asserting 'I believe that p and it is not the case that p'. Cases such as these were pointed out by G. E. Moore and have come to be known as 'Moore's paradox'.[8] Regarding these types of statements, Moore distinguishes between what he refers to as the paradoxical and the absurd. In short, the paradoxical issue here is that such statements strike one as contradictory but are in fact logically coherent.[9] There is nothing logically contradictory in stating 'I believe that p but it is not in the case that p'. The absurdity that is being referred to is in the *assertion* of these kinds of statements. This follows from the fact that 'I believe that p' follows neither from p nor from 'I assert that p'. Nonetheless, in 'assertively uttering' an indicative statement an agent *implies* that they believe it (where imply is understood in a non-logical common usage sense). As such, when an agent asserts 'it is not the case that p', this implies that they do not believe that p, and from this the assertion *presents* itself as an agent stating that 'I believe that p and that not p'. Relating this to Kant's claim that 'I absolutely cannot be mistaken' with respect to what 'I in fact believe to be right', a claim is being asserted that it is *psychologically contradictory* to pretend to oneself that one believes something other than what one believes.[10] The key step being 'the judgment whether *I in fact* believe to be right' (emphasis mine), which reveals the higher-order reflection that leads to certainty in terms of an agent's *subjective belief*. To reject Kant's position here would be to commit oneself to the claim that assertions such as 'I believe that p (but I am merely pretending to believe p)', are plausible and psychologically coherent.

8   G. E. Moore, 'A Reply to My Critics', in *The Philosophy of G. E. Moore*, ed. P. A. Schlipp, Northwestern University Press (1942), 543.

9   Here I follow the introduction to Moore's Paradox provided by Green and Williams in *Moore's Paradox: New Essays on Belief, Rationality, and the First Person*, ed. M. S. Green, J. N. Williams, Oxford University Press (2007), 5. This book also presents an excellent series of contemporary discussions on Moore's paradox.

10   An alternative articulation can be put in terms of an agent's actions: 'I believe that p but act as though it is not the case that p'. In this case an agent is expressing a performative contradiction i.e. acting contradictorily to a belief that they hold.

In order to fully explicate Kant's position it is necessary to make clear what exactly he means by 'certainty' in this context. As noted above, Kant is referring to first-person subjective beliefs regarding the rightfulness of an action. Hence when he claims that an agent's conscience cannot err he is claiming that an agent can be *subjectively certain* of their conscientious judgement. In a discussion of the Absurdity Thesis he states

> The consciousness of its truth [i.e. a factum] calls for examination of the truth of the circumstances, and is founded, therefore, on **subjective certainty** after suitably conducted tests (bold mine, *Vigilantius* 27:614).

He then explicates this by explaining that what is relevant is only that which is 'known to us' (27:614). In other words he is excluding a duty to examine objects that are not known to the agent i.e. objective standards of evaluation (I will say more about this in the subsequent sections). It is following the above that Kant goes on to talk about conscientiousness and being 'totally certain that a thing could not have occurred otherwise (27:615).[11]

The unambiguous connecting of the notion of subjective certainty (of the judgement of conscience) with the Absurdity Thesis allows for the following expression to be made:

> Absurdity Thesis$_1$: it is impossible for an agent to have a mistaken belief about their belief regarding the rightfulness of an action.

Given that Kant couples the judgement of conscience with the propositional subjective *beliefs* that an agent assents to, I believe that it can be asserted that Absurdity Thesis$_1$ is plausible and coherent.[12] This is the kind of case where

---

11   Kant then completes the section by asserting, 'It also follows very clearly from this, that the judgement founded on examination of the *factum* does not, by itself, constitute conscience, and that indeed this judgement may be an error, whereas conscience can never be that, whence the division *inter conscientiam erroneam et rectam* [between a right and erring conscience] is totally false and unthinkable' (my translation, 27:615).

12   Interestingly, Kant speaks about the certainty of conscience with almost exactly the same terminology in *Notes on Moral Philosophy* (1783–4) when he states 'Conscience is 1. the capacity to become conscious of the rightfulness or wrongfulness of all of one's own actions. 2. The inner standing of this capacity for judging, *a* as a judge, *b* to give an account of the authorization of our actions. The supreme principle of conscience is that nothing is permitted to be done about which the agent is not entirely certain that it is allowed for him to do it (in general). We cannot undertake anything at the risk of acting wrongly' (18:579). Nonetheless, in this note Kant does not mention the vital caveat that is

an agent is simply stating 'I believe that p because p is the case', where 'case' is in reference to that which an agent is subjectively certain about. Given Kant's notion of subjective certainty, to deny Absurdity Thesis$_1$ is to claim that an agent can coherently assert 'I believe that p and it is not the case that p', which is what Kant rightly points out as absurd because of the very nature of assertion. Importantly, it should be noted that the plausibility of Absurdity Thesis$_1$ has nothing to do with the subject matter at hand, namely the moral concern of conscience. Rather, the plausibility here rests on a claim about the nature of belief and assertion itself, which is applied in the context of conscience.

Kant expresses an alternative version of the Absurdity Thesis in the *Metaphysics of Morals*. I will explicate this version below and explain why it is philosophically implausible.

3.2.2 Metaphysics of Morals: *Absurdity Thesis$_2$*

In the *Metaphysics of Morals* Kant introduces the notion of an erring conscience and explains why it is an absurdity. He states

> An erring conscience is an absurdity. For while I can indeed be mistaken in my subjective judgement as to whether something is a duty or not, I cannot be mistaken in my subjective judgement as to whether I have submitted it to my practical reason (here in its role as judge) for such a judgement; for if I could be mistaken in that, I would have made no practical judgement at all, and in that case there would be neither truth nor error. *Unconscientiousness* is not a lack of conscience but rather the propensity to pay no heed to its judgement (6:401).

In stating that an agent can 'indeed be mistaken in [their] subjective judgement as to whether something is a duty or not', similarly to Kant's other treatments of the non-erring claim regarding conscience, the assertion is that the denial of an erring conscience does not relate to moral judgement. Therefore the key sentence in the passage above is

---

observed in his other writings, namely that this certainty is *subjective certainty*. However there is an allusion to this notion when he completes the note by stating 'The guideline for conscience in the case of a morally good intention is not to pretend to more conviction than we are capable of having in order to be certain of doing nothing wrong by means of this cognition'.

I cannot be mistaken in my subjective judgement whether I have submitted it to my practical reason (here in its role as judge) for such a
judgement.

Here Kant's assertion appears to refer to the submitting of the moral judgement to the capacity of conscience i.e. practical reason, which itself will pass
the judgement of conscience. Formulated in this way it appears as though
there are two steps: the first being the consulting of the capacity of conscience,
and the second being the passing of the judgement itself. However Kant completes the sentence (proceeding the semicolon) with 'for if I could be mistaken
in that, I would have made no practical judgement at all' and in doing so couples consulting conscience with practical judgement itself. As such, the above
expresses the following reading of the Absurdity Thesis:

> Absurdity Thesis$_2$: it is impossible for an agent to be mistaken in their
> belief as to whether or not they have consulted conscience.

I will argue that this articulation of the Absurdity Thesis commits Kant to an
implausible position. In order to forward this claim it is necessary to explicate
what exactly Kant is alluding to in Absurdity Thesis$_2$. I shall turn to this task
now.
    Consider the following:

- First-order: 'I ought not to X' i.e. the moral judgement. This is the rule.
  As has been shown above, Kant categorically denies that this is what
  conscience judges.
- Second-order: 'is 1. True?' Here the agent is passing a judgement regarding the rightfulness of an action in the particular case. The second-
  order judgement is merely an attempt, that is to say any judgement
  that is passed upon the first-order judgement. At this level an agent
  may believe they have consulted their conscience and this belief may
  indeed be false (as is the case with false conscience).
- Third-order: 'have I answered the second-order question correctly?'
  Here the agent is passing a third-order judgement. The agent is genuinely trying to ascertain whether they have passed judgement according to conscience itself. The agent cannot err in this because this *just is
  consulting conscience and passing the judgement of conscience.* In this
  third-order question the issue of whether or not this is really a judgement of conscience does not arise because the very third-order questioning is conscience proper. Simply asking the third-order question is
  conscientiousness, i.e. doing the real thing.

From the above, Kant's articulation of Absurdity Thesis$_2$ is a claim that, when an agent asks the third-order question then the agent cannot have a false belief about whether or not the agent has submitted the question to their conscience.

The first point to note is that the schematic that I have provided above seems to suggest that second-order judgements are not occasions of consulting one's conscience. This is problematic because the higher-order judgement of conscience appears precisely to be the asking of this second-order question. However this issue is resolved when it is considered that the second-order judgements regarding particular cases are in fact first-order judgements regarding the case and not the rule. The question of 'is 1. True?' could be either 'is the rule correct?', or 'is this a case that falls under the rule?' In other words the judgement is first-order with respect to a case. This judgement is a judgement that may indeed err and thereby be mistaken. The judgement regarding the case may have occurred without regard to whether the agent has consulted conscience. This leads to the third point which is that it is specifically with respect to the examination of actions that the higher-order (termed above as third-order) question is addressed. Kant is stating that it is this that cannot be mistaken because to ask this question is precisely to pass the judgement of conscience.

An alternative manner in which to explicate Kant's position is to point out that 'the consulting of conscience' is being taken as a 'success' or 'achievement' verb. The notion of an achievement verb is discussed by Ryle in *The Concept of Mind*.[13] Using the examples of 'seeing' and 'hearing', Ryle argues that there are many verbs that are used to signify achievements rather than tasks or processes.[14] Ryle explains that achievement verbs are used to report the termination of a process: words such as 'win', 'find' and 'solve' express 'not merely that some performance has been gone through, but also that something has been brought off by the agent going through it. They are verbs of success'.[15] In order to clarify his position Ryle contrasts task verbs with achievement verbs 'play/win, treat/heal, travel/arrive' (where the first words signify a process and the second words signify the result of the process).[16] All that Ryle is pointing out here is a conceptual difference that clarifies the appropriate use of various words. An agent can certainly look (a task) without seeing (an achievement) and can certainly listen without hearing. However, when the words are used appropriately, an agent cannot see (an achievement) without having seen and

---

13   Originally published in 1949. For a more recent edition see G. Ryle, *The Concept of Mind*, Routledge (2009), 131–38.

14   Ryle, *Mind*, 149–53, 222–3.

15   Ibid., 130.

16   Ibid., 149.

cannot hear without having heard. Importantly to Kant's claim regarding the consulting of conscience Ryle clarifies that in achieving something one is not doing two things but 'one thing with a certain upshot'.[17] This is applied to Kant's account of Absurdity Thesis$_2$ in the fact that the consulting of conscience and the passing of its judgement are not two things, rather the consulting of conscience is akin to an achievement insofar as to do so is to pass the judgement of conscience. In other words, to consult conscience is to pass the judgement of conscience.[18] A contrast can be made between an agent's mathematical capacity and their capacity of conscience. With respect to the former an agent can certainly consult their mathematical capacity and pass a false judgement i.e. be mistaken with respect to the correct mathematical result. With respect to the latter Kant is claiming that to consult the capacity of conscience is to successfully pass a judgement ('one thing with a certain upshot') and as such the notion of the consulting of conscience is an achievement notion.[19]

---

17   Ibid., 150. Ryle's claims are situated within his theory of perception and as such further explication of his particular work is beyond the scope of this chapter. For further discussions of Ryle's notion of 'achievements' see C. C. Pfisterer, 'Ryle on Perception' in *Ryle on Mind and Language*, ed. D. Dolby, Palgrave Macmillan (2015), 146–64, A. Quinton, 'Ryle on Perception', in *Ryle*, ed. O. P. Wood and G. Pitcher, Palgrave Macmillan (1971), 107 and R. J. Hirst, *Problems of Perception*, Routledge (2013), 126.

18   Wood provides a reconstruction of the Absurdity Thesis passage in the *Metaphysics of Morals* (6:401) which appears to conform to the account that I have presented above. Wood claims that the Absurdity Thesis is an assertion that when an agent does successfully consult their conscience the agent 'cannot fail to be aware of this' (*Kantian Ethics*, 191). According to Wood, Kant is asserting that when in fact an agent genuinely submits their moral judgements to conscience it is impossible for the agent to be mistaken in their belief that they have successfully consulted their conscience. According to this reading an agent will *know* that they have successfully consulted their conscience. I take Wood's assertion that Kant is denying the possibility of being mistaken that the 'inner judicial process has taken place' to be a denial in cases when 'we do in fact genuinely submit ourselves to the judgment of conscience' (ibid.) the judgement may or may not have taken place. The assertion being that to genuinely consult conscience is just what it is to pass its judgement. As such, although Wood's account is presented in a frustratingly undeveloped manner, I take his claim to be akin to the account that I have presented above.

19   Hill reads the passage from the *Metaphysics of Morals* (6:401) as a claim that the representations of the act and the moral standard must be presupposed (all 'internal') in order for the capacity of conscience to be consulted (*Human Welfare*, 303fn50). As such, if these representations are not present then Hill tells us 'we did not make any prior moral judgment on the particular act, and so our conscience [...] never operate[s] and so cannot have yielded a false verdict' (ibid.). The problem with this argument is that it maintains a hidden premise, namely that the 'act of scrutinising' is the act of conscience. Hill's account fails to address the question as to whether or not the judgement of conscience

Kant's claim centres upon a technical point. His assertions are in regard to the proposition 'it is the case that it is false that conscience has passed a judgement', rather than the proposition 'it is not the case that conscience has passed a false judgement'. This form of reasoning would suggest that the only type of judgement an agent can make about a matter is a true judgement. This is a technical point akin to the claim that if an agent makes a false judgement about a moral matter then one could say that no moral judgement has occurred at all because the person did not really judge about morality. This would mean that an agent can only successfully consult their conscience because anything else would simply have to be rejected as a judgement of conscience.[20] It follows that there can be no such thing as an erring judgement of conscience because an erring judgement would not be a judgement of conscience at all.[21]

Although Kant's claim is technically correct his position is problematic and implausible because it avoids the problem of an erring conscience by appealing to a technicality rather than addressing the intuitive sense in which an agent would view such an error. The first point that must be made is that the belief that an agent has consulted their conscience is, similarly to Absurdity Thesis$_1$, a matter of subjective certainty. Kant is not denying that an agent can be subjectively certain that they have consulted their conscience when in fact they have not. This is problematic because it generates cases where an agent may be subjectively certain that they have consulted conscience but passed an erring judgement and therefore despite being subjectively certain that they have consulted conscience, technically it must be said that they have not passed the judgement of conscience at all. From the perspective of the agent, the agent would have done all that is required of conscientiousness (in being subjectively certain) and would be acting according to what they believe is the judgement of conscience. However when the judgement errs the agent cannot be said to be acting upon the judgement of conscience irrespective of the fact that an agent is unaware of the fact that what they believe is the judgement of conscience is in fact not a judgement of conscience at all. Considering the

---

can err even in cases where the 'background facts' are in place and have been submitted to the capacity of conscience. As such the background fact of having successfully consulted conscience, referred to by Hill, cannot be what Kant is denying in the Absurdity Thesis.

20 Picking up on this point Wood states 'In the self-deceptive belief that I have acted conscientiously when I have not, there has been no genuine judgment of conscience at all, so there cannot have been an erroneous one either (*Kantian Ethics*, 192).

21 Although Sticker does identify the Absurdity Thesis as concerning second-order judgements, his analysis is nonetheless brief (one page) and fails to explore the fact that Kant's assertions on this point are *prima facia* in contradiction ('When the Reflective Watch-Dog Barks', section 2.1).

perspective of the agent, for all intents and purposes the agent is acting according to an erring judgement of conscience. However, Kant is simply blocking this claim by appealing to a technicality. It would be more plausible to claim that an agent is doing the wrong thing for the right reasons, rather than simply deny that conscience is operating in these scenarios on a technical point. Thus Kant's Absurdity Thesis$_2$ is implausible.[22]

3.2.3   The Absurdity Theses

The questions that arise from the two accounts of the Absurdity Thesis are what relationship the two articulations have with one another and why does Kant offer two expressions at all? As a point of departure, it is necessary to note that both expressions have in common the notion of a higher-order judgment that concerns subjective belief. Below I will argue that the reason why Kant offers two expressions is because he is responding to two different issues within his historical context. I will claim that Absurdity Thesis$_1$ is a response to the Hobbes-Locke conception of conscience as unreliable and that Absurdity Thesis$_2$ is a response to Bayle's and Wolff's conceptions of an erring conscience in terms of false judgements.

As noted in the introduction, within the historical context the notion of an erring conscience was widespread and debated. Hobbes, Locke, Wolff, Grotius and Crusius argue that the judgement of conscience can err. In the context of the discussion above, both Hobbes's and Locke's views are germane. In *Leviathan* Hobbes rejects the idea that conscience can be a source of law or action in a commonwealth.[23] Indeed he refers to this as 'repugnant'.[24] The reason for this is because in following their own conscience an agent makes

---

22   Moyar also provides a formulation of the Absurdity Thesis. He states that 'Kant's no-erring-conscience claim is best understood as restricted to the claim that there is a basic act of self-consciousness that is constitutive of a judgment of duty' ('Unstable Autonomy', 349). As explicated in Chapter 2, according to Moyar conscience is the first-order form of moral motivation that accompanies all moral judgements. As such Moyar reads the Absurdity Thesis as a claim that confirms his view, namely that conscience is always consulted with moral judgement. In Chapter 2 I have addressed Moyar's account by showing that conscience is a higher-order judgement that results via the voluntary consulting of conscience. As such Moyar's version of the Absurdity Thesis also follows as false.

23   T. Hobbes, *Leviathan*, Cambridge University Press (2012), 233 (when quoting I use the modern forms of the relevant word, for example 'evil' instead of 'Evill'). On Hobbes's social and political theory see J. Hampton, *Hobbes and the Social Contract Tradition*, Cambridge University Press (1986). See also Schneewind, *The Invention of Autonomy*, 91–4.

24   Hobbes, *Leviathan*, 233.

'himself judge of good and evil'.[25] Hobbes grounds this rejection upon the fact that an agent's conscience and an agent's judgement 'is the same thing, and as the judgment, so also the conscience may be erroneous'.[26] What must be noted is that Hobbes makes this point with respect to agents living in a commonwealth. Indeed, he distinguishes between 'private' and 'public' consciences: where the former would be a sin to go against when an agent 'has no other rule to follow' and the latter is a conscience that is subordinate to the sovereign power.[27] Hobbes's position is not simply that private conscience is inferior to public conscience: rather that it is diametrically opposed to it. This seems to follow from the fact that adopting private conscience as a legitimate source by which to decide action would entail that all agents will act according to action that they themselves ascribe to, thereby contradicting public authority. This assumption appears to rest on the notion that following private conscience will lead to divisions in the civil society, the destruction of the civil society will follow from this and therefore agents should follow the public 'civic' conscience of the sovereign that is embodied by the civil law.[28]

Given Locke's famous defence of toleration it is surprising to notice the similarity of his position with that of Hobbes.[29] In the *Second Tract on Government* Locke argues that if all agents were to follow their own conscience then this would lead to an unstable situation.[30] This seems to rest upon the notion that the justification of action based upon what an agent's conscience is apparently telling them will lead to a chaotic situation that will compromise the civic state. In accordance with his empiricist views, as expressed in *An Essay*

---

25 Ibid.

26 Ibid. Hobbes discusses how the metaphorical talk of conscience has resulted in a false notion of conscience that can be exposed via an etymological analysis (ibid. 48). I shall not discuss this further here. For a discussion of Hobbes's analysis of metaphorical conscience and its etymological root see K. S. Feldman, 'Conscience and the Concealment of Metaphor in Hobbes's Leviathan', *Philosophy and Rhetoric*, 34, 1, (2001), 21–37, and Ojakangas, *The Voice of Conscience*, 110–17.

27 Hobbes, *Leviathan*, 233.

28 Ibid. See also K. C. Pepperell, 'Religious Conscience and Civic Conscience in Thomas Hobbes's Civic Philosophy', *Educational Theory*, 39, 1, (1989), 18, and G. Edward, 'Hobbes on Conscience within the Law and Without', *Canadian Journal of Political Science*, 32, 2, (1999), 203–25.

29 J. Locke, *A Letter Concerning Toleration*, Hackett (1983). See also Schneewind, *The Invention of Autonomy*, 141. For a discussion of Locke's ethical thought see J. Marshall, *'John Locke'*, Cambridge University Press (1994), and Darwall *British Moralists*, 23–6, 33.

30 Indeed this mention of conscience is in the chapter titled 'Tyranny'. Found in *Locke: Political Essays*, ed. M. Goldie, Cambridge University Press (2002), 54–78 (see in particular 67).

Concerning Human Understanding, Locke rejects the notion that conscience is an innate moral idea.[31] Instead he argues that the voice of conscience is reducible to custom and education and that particular perspectives, which are 'errors' and 'absurdities', are legitimised as 'divine' through the claim that they are conscientious.[32] Indeed, he argues that it is not an agent's conscience, but rather their fear of God and the punishment of the hereafter that provides the true foundation and motivation of moral action.[33]

Both Hobbes's and Locke's discussions of conscience highlight an important distinction between conscience *qua* belief and conscience *qua* action. Hobbes expressly states that inner beliefs are not a legitimate domain that the (otherwise absolute) sovereign can legislate.[34] Hobbes's negative views of conscience are as such grounded on the relation of conscience to action. Similarly (the otherwise tolerate) Locke is arguing against conscience with respect to actions taken in a civil state.[35] In the cases of both Hobbes and Locke the inference is made from, *because the judgement of conscience is erroneous* (here taken in the sense of unreliable), to, agents *are therefore never to base their civic action upon the judgement of conscience*. This may be referred to as the sceptical argument. Put in these terms the idea can be expressed as: because the judgement of conscience is erroneous it is impossible to know that one acts rightly through the

---

31   Locke states that 'all ideas come from sensation...', (*An Essay Concerning Human Understanding*, ed. A. S. Pringle-Pattison, Oxford University Press (1947), 42, see also 20), hence his view concerning the nature of conscience neatly corresponds with his more general epistemological framework of empiricism. See also Schneewind, *The Invention of Autonomy*, 144.

32   Locke, *An Essay Concerning Human Understanding*, 20, 25. For a discussion of conscience in *Essays on the Law of Nature*, where Locke extends his attack on conscience by pointing out that there are agents who have committed numerous crimes and yet experience no pang of conscience, and that there is considerable evidence that conscience is not present in all individuals, see Ojakangas, *The Voice of Conscience*, 114. See also Darwall's discussion of *Essay*, where he argues that this work is Locke's final and considered views on autonomy and obligation (*British Moralists*, 149–75).

33   Locke, *An Essay Concerning Human Understanding*, 147–8. See also Schneewind, *The Invention of Autonomy*, 146–9. For a further discussion of Locke's notion of conscience see M. Ayers, *Locke*, Routledge (1996), 132, 266n, 271, 325n87.

34   Hobbes, *Levitation*, 323.

35   Sorabji explicates Locke's position by highlighting that Locke distinguishes between 'restriction' in terms of the permissibility of an action, and 'imposing' with respect to the beliefs that an agent holds. The principle point being that to restrict an action is not to impose a belief upon an agent and thereby Locke can be tolerate with respect to conscientious belief whilst maintaining a relative intolerance with respect to apparent conscientious actions. See Sorabji, *Moral Conscience Through the Ages*, 145–7.

judgement of conscience. As such Absurdity Thesis$_1$ is to be read as a response to this position. Kant's response comprises of a notion of conscience that is grounded upon subjective certainty and as such the claim that it is absurd that an agent can be mistaken with respect to their subjective belief regarding the rightfulness of their actions. In other words, Kant is asserting that agents can be subjectively certain of their judgements of conscience and thereby resist the Hobbes-Locke conception.

An alternative character in the historical context that Kant is likely to have been responding to is Bayle. Bayle's discussion of errors and conscience is one where an agent can be right in an action even if this is based upon a belief that is false.[36] Giving the example of a wife who sleeps with an imposter posing as her husband, Bayle claims that on the part of the woman nothing immoral has occurred. In other words, those who mistakenly believe that they have a duty do in fact have a duty. For Bayle, an agent has a duty to follow what he refers to as an 'erroneous conscience'.[37] Although Bayle's conception of conscience is such that an agent is still obligated to follow its dictate, the notion nonetheless is presented in such a way as to depict a scenario of doing what is in fact the wrong thing. It is likely that Absurdity Thesis$_2$ is a response to this characterisation by Bayle. Firstly, in a notion shared by both expressions of the Absurdity Thesis, Kant can be read as countering the claim that an erring conscience is when an agent does the objectively wrong thing but for the right (conscientious) reasons. Kant is able to maintain this position by stating that the judgement of conscience does not concern the objectively correct moral judgement but rather concerns the subjective judgement concerning an agent's efforts in ascertaining to the best of their ability ('diligent examination') what the right thing to do is. Secondly, although I have argued above that Absurdity Thesis$_2$ is implausible there is good reason to see why Kant would have maintained such a position in the context of Bayle's views. The reason for this is because Kant may argue that although it seems as though a technical point is being made, what is really taking place is the emphasis that agents should not view conscience as unreliable (cf. Rousseau).[38] Hence, although it may seem as

---

36   Here I follow Kilcullen ('Bayle on the Rights of Conscience', 60–1).

37   Ibid., 69.

38   Here it is perhaps the case that Rousseau's influence on Kant is exhibited. Rousseau's positive characterisation of conscience is indefatigable ('Conscience, Conscience! Divine instinct, immortal and celestial voice, certain guide of a being that is ignorant and limited but intelligent and free; infallible judge of good and bad which makes man like unto God; it is you who makes the excellence of his nature and the morality of his actions' *Emile*, 290).

though an agent is following an erring conscience, by making what seems
as though a mere technical point what is really being highlighted is the fact
that when conscience does seem unreliable it is perhaps because in truth the
agent has not really consulted conscience.

An additional explanation as to why Kant would have maintained Absurdity
Thesis$_2$ is by reading it as a response to the notion of an erring conscience in
the rationalism of Wolff. In the cases of both Wolff and Crusius the notion of
an erring conscience is a claim that refers to the variant ratiocinative abilities
of agents. Wolff argues that the manner in which conscience judges whether
actions are good or bad is through 'insight into the connection of truths'.[39] Here
Wolff is referring to the process of rational deduction: by claiming that truths
are made manifest 'because reason consists of insight into the connection of
truths, it follows that conscience comes from reason. Man has a conscience
because he has reason'.[40] He follows this by stating that in order to be certain
that judgements of conscience '[a]gree with other truths, nothing more will
be needed than our putting the proof into rational form and earnestly investigating whether the matter and the form are correct. [...] So demonstration
is the means to decide whether or not conscience is right'. Wolff explains that
disputes concerning what the correct judgement of conscience is derive from
the fact that there are agents who 'cannot understand demonstrations [and
therefore] will not be convinced by them'. So long as agents cannot 'attain
facility in demonstration' in 'matters of conscience', Wolff asserts that the
phenomena of an 'erring conscience' will occur.[41] The basic assertion being
that errors of conscience are errors in the reasoning of an agent, hence the
phenomena of an erring conscience is 'wide spread' because so few people
know 'the art of demonstration'.[42] Wolff's assertion can be stated in terms of
the consulting of conscience. According to Wolff an agent may have successfully consulted their conscience but the judgement that follows from this successful consultation may err because of variant ratiocinative ability. Absurdity
Thesis$_2$ is to be read as a response to this claim. Although Kant would certainly
agree that the rational ability of agents vary and as such accept the account of
error that Wolff's notion of conscience presents, as has been shown, Kant
asserts that to call this ratiocinative error an erring conscience is absurd
because a false judgement of conscience is not to be considered a judgement
of conscience at all.

---

39   *Vernüfftige Gedancken*, 338, see also 399.
40   Ibid.
41   Ibid.
42   Ibid., 340.

In this section I have explored two expressions of the Absurdity Thesis. I have argued that whereas Absurdity Thesis$_1$ is plausible, Absurdity Thesis$_2$ is implausible. I have discussed the relationship between the two expressions as one of Kant addressing different conceptions of conscience in the historical context. As I have argued that Absurdity Thesis$_1$ is a plausible claim, for the remainder of this chapter the discussion will be conducted in terms of Absurdity Thesis$_1$. What is clear is that the notion of subjective certainty is central to Kant's denial of an erring conscience and as such in the following section I shall expand upon the notion of subjective certainty and discuss it under the broader notion that conscience requires conviction.[43]

3.3 Subjective Certainty

To understand the notion of subjective certainty it is necessary to explore Kant's notions of belief and knowledge, and how these concepts relate to his notion of conscientiousness. In order to achieve this I will firstly expand upon Kant's theory of assent (attitudes that an agent may hold towards a particular proposition). Secondly, I will show that this is related to conscience by pointing out that a conscientious action is one where an agent holds a proposition with conviction (which, when understood in terms of practical believing, involves subjective certainty). Thirdly, I will explicate the role of choice in the notion of 'voluntary conviction' that subjective certainty is related to.[44] As the analysis proceeds, it will become clear that the *minimum* condition for conscientiousness is subjective certainty, which relates to subjective standards of evaluation and concerns practical belief. However conscience may also provide conviction *qua* objective certainty, which relates to objective standards of evaluation i.e. knowledge.[45]

---

43 An example of an account of the Absurdity Thesis that correlates with the account of subjective certainty that I am defending can be found in the work of Howard ('Kant and Moral Imputation', 616). Similarly Despland's and Timmermann's accounts of the Absurdity Thesis contrast the objective fallibility of moral judgement with the subjective certainty of conscience ('Can Conscience Be Hypocritical?', 359, 'Kant on Conscience', 303).

44 For a discussion of the relation between justification and awareness see P. J. Markie, 'Justification and Awareness', *Philosophical Studies: An International Journal for Philosophy in the Analytic Tradition*, 146, 3, (2009), 361–77.

45 Although Ware does discuss conscience *qua* conviction his account is both brief and lacks the nuance that I present here ('The Duty of Self-Knowledge', 694–5).

3.3.1   *Justification and Assent*

In order to explicate what Kant is referring to by subjective certainty, it is necessary to explore his notion of assent (*furwahrhalten*).[46] Assent is a genus under which a spectrum of attitudes may fall under: for example, assent may involve postulating an axiom as a prop for mathematical theoretical speculation, or opining about the quality of the craftsmanship of a particular ornament, or holding a logical proposition with absolute certainty.[47] As such, assent is a broad category. Moreover, the context within which the proposition is being considered affects the manner in which the particular type of assent is viewed. Thus, in the building of a ship the assent that a builder holds with respect to a particular material becomes crucial: by a high standard of safety (that holds that the material used to build a ship should be 'known' to be strong), the notion of postulating, or opining with respect to the strength of a particular material would be viewed as inappropriate (as the safety of passengers on the ship will be placed at risk). Put more generically, a particular claim can be thought of as justified or not according to a context sensitive criterion of justification.[48]

Important to note is that there is a difference between assent, which is a psychological concept, and a strict definition of judgement (*Urteil*), which is a logical concept.[49] By logical concept what is meant is a subject-predicate structure of a particular proposition. This can be taken in two ways, judgement *qua* an object (or possible object) of an act of judging, that is a proposition (First *Critique* A6–9/B10–13), and judgement *qua* a mental act of judging, in which an agent judges a proposition (which means judging something to be true—not merely postulating it) (A69/B94, A130/B169).[50] As such, judgement is to be differentiated from assent, where assent is a wider concept that

---

46   Here I have offered a straightforward translation of *furwahrhalten* as assent. I do so in order to express a general concept that I will flesh out below. For a more nuanced discussion on the translation of this word see L. Stevenson, 'Opinion, Belief or Faith, and Knowledge', *Kantian Review*, 7, (2003), 73.

47   As A. Chignell points out, it is in this sense that Early Modern philosophers such as Locke and Leibniz used the term ('Kant's Concepts of Justification', *Nous*, 41, 1, (2007), 34). See J. Locke, *Essay Concerning Human Understanding*, ed. P. H. Nidditch, Clarendon (1979), IV.20.16, and Leibniz, *New Essays on Human Understanding*, 520.

48   For a discussion on this point see A. Plantinga, 'Epistemic Justification', *Nous*, 20, 1, (1986), 3–18.

49   See Chignell, 'Kant's Concepts of Justification', 35.

50   A third way of taking judgement is simply as the faculty of judging considered as an ability. The above characterisation of judgement are taken from Stevenson, 'Opinion, Belief or Faith, and Knowledge', 74.

does not necessarily hold the type of subject-predicate structure of judgement 'strictly speaking' (here taken to be in reference to the logical object of an attitude that always has a subject-predicate structure).[51] Indeed Kant often talks imprecisely when using terms such as 'forming' or 'making' judgements when in fact what is being referred to is 'forming' or 'making' assents that are of a subject-predicate structure.[52] Although judgement strictly speaking and assent can be differentiated in this way, judgement strictly speaking is also a form of assent. The reason is that if an agent makes a judgement that is of a subject-predicate form, the agent can still be said to have a propositional attitude towards it: it is simply that this attitude is justified via the rules of logic.

Kant believes that an agent can have a host of attitudes and that these attitudes hold different epistemic statuses. For example he maintains that agents can adopt particular beliefs (*Glaube*) towards certain propositions such as freedom, the immortality of the soul and the existence of God.[53] Crucially, within this context he states that assent is still a **voluntary** (*freiwillig*) determination of our judgment' for which agents are nonetheless fully responsible (bold mine, Second *Critique* 5:146).[54] Thus an additional dimension of assent concerns the notions of assent that are involuntary and voluntary. Assent that is involuntary is of a kind that if the proposition at hand is 'fully' justified an agent cannot help but hold-it-to-be-true. Assent that is voluntary relates to propositions that an agent may hold but the agent is not compelled to hold-to-be-true.[55] Kant refers to propositions that an agent involuntarily assents to as 'convictions' (*Uberzeugungen*)' (*Lectures on Logic* 24:733).[56] I shall say more about the notions of voluntary and involuntary convictions below.

In the *Lectures on Logic* Kant makes explicit the different categories of assent. Below I summarise this spectrum:

i.   Knowing: involuntary conviction. This can be either conviction *qua* judgement (i.e. true and structured in a subject-predicate form), or conviction *qua* overwhelming evidence in support of a proposition.

---

51   Chignell, 'Kant's Concepts of Justification', 35fn3.

52   See First *Critique* A6–9/B10–13 and *Lectures on Logic* 24:273–4, 9:101fn. For an extended treatment of Kant theory of judgement see Longuenesse, *Kant and the Capacity to Judge*.

53   In fact Kant claims that such assent is demanded of all rational agents. See Chignell, 'Kant's Concepts of Justification', 35–6.

54   See also *Lectures on Logic* 9:67–70.

55   For a discussion of voluntary and involuntary assent see F. A. Siegler, 'Voluntary and Involuntary', *The Monist*, 52, 2, (1968), 268–87.

56   See Chignell, 'Kant's Concepts of Justification', 36.

Here the distinction between the two types of conviction can be made clear through examples. The proposition, 'the part is smaller than the whole' (derived from the definitions of 'part', 'smaller' and 'whole') falls under the remit of conviction *qua* judgement. The proposition, 'the University will be closed on Christmas day' (based on the evidence that the University has always closed on Christmas day and it has been announced that it will close on the approaching Christmas day), falls under the remit of conviction *qua* overwhelming evidence.[57] Due to the fact that knowing is a form of assent that is of the involuntary type of conviction, Kant refers to this as 'certainty' (24:148). The difference between these two types of conviction can be stated more explicitly by noting that Kant differentiates between the *objects of certainty*, where the first kind of conviction *qua* judgement he calls apodictic (giving the example of mathematical intuitions) and where the second kind of conviction *qua* overwhelming evidence he refers to via the example of historical claims (24:733).[58]

ii.   Opinion: can be either voluntary or involuntary.

Kant states '*Opining* is not yet conviction, for otherwise it would have to be at least subjectively sufficient, for me in the condition of mind in which I find myself. With opining, our judgement is problematic, i.e., I settle nothing; rather, I only have a degree of holding-to-be-true, although this degree is not sufficient' (24:850). Kant explicates that this is to judge something 'incompletely' (24:148), or that opinions result from 'imperfect cognitions' (24:218). He states that 'in these *opinions*, however, the grounds, and thereby also the degrees of holding-to-be-true, can grow and increase; but it is to be noted that in the case of *opining* one always remains undecided' (24:148). The key element here is that opinions vary: hence why it is possible to talk of either voluntary or involuntary opinions, as the degree to which they are assented to changes (24:218–37, 227–9). Kant tells us that opinions can be held when the grounds for the particular opinion are greater than the grounds for the opposite (24:148, 227, 850–7).

---

57   For a discussion of conviction see D. J. Anderson, 'Knowledge and Conviction', *Synthese*, 187, 2 (2012), 377–92.

58   See also C. A. Kirwan, 'Truth and Universal Assent', *Canadian Journal of Philosophy*, 11, 3, (1981), 377–94 and H. W. Johnstone, 'The Logical Powerfulness of Philosophical Arguments', *Mind*, 64, 256, (1955), 539–41. For discussions of knowing see P. A. Carmichael, 'Knowing', *The Journal of Philosophy*, 56, 8, (1959), 341–51, T. Wilhelmus, 'Knowing', *The Hudson Review*, 41, 3, (1988), 548–56 and W. H. F. Barnes, 'Knowing', *The Philosophical Review*, 72, 1, (1963), 3–16.

iii. Belief: voluntary.[59]

Kant introduces this notion after the explication of opinions by stating that 'to opine something practically [...] involves believing'. To believe and to opine are differentiated with respect to believing's relation to practical concerns. Where believing is to hold something to be true to such a degree that it is sufficient for deciding to act i.e. of practical concern (24:227–8), and 'opining has nothing harmful about it, as long as I am conscious of the insufficiency of my holding-to-be-true' (24:850), i.e. opining is neutral with respect to practical concerns. Kant then explains that 'to accept something without a subjective necessity according to logical concepts is *to believe*' (24:148). What he means by this is that an agent may hold-to-be true a proposition that they are not involuntarily/immediately convicted to believe in (i.e. voluntarily holding-to-be-true). He tells us that in believing an agent can even hold-to-be-true with certainty a particular proposition when the belief at hand is of the status of *practically* holding-to-be-true, *provided* that the belief is not 'irrefutable according to the laws of logic' (he provides two examples of this: that 'there is a God' and 'there is another world' (24:149–50)).[60]

The definitions that I have offered above are cursory and should be read with caution. That these epistemological categories are far more complex is evidenced from the numerous, and somewhat inconsistent, treatments that Kant provides throughout his corpus.[61] A distinction that is necessary to point out is the ambiguity in what I have referred to generally as 'belief' above. Two notions of 'practical belief' can be observed: belief in relation to theoretical reason (alluded to above in terms of God and another world) and belief in relation to practical actions. The former can be thought to relate to the postulates of practical reason that are a product of Kant's Transcendental Idealism (products of theoretical judgements). The latter concerns propositional claims that can be incorporated into a maxim of action (practical judgements based on empirical propositions). As the concern of this study is with conscience

---

59   Kant also talks of 'acceptance', which I read as analogous with belief (*Lectures on Logic* 24:735–7). I will not explore the extent to which the two notions are analogues as such an exploration is immaterial to this study.

60   For an in-depth discussion of Kant's theory of belief see A. Chignell, 'Belief in Kant', *The Philosophical Review*, 116, 3, (2007), 323–60.

61   A good example that demonstrates this complexity is Stevenson's analysis of opinion, 'Opinion, Belief or Faith, and Knowledge', 75–82.

and therefore practical actions, unless stated otherwise my references to belief should be taken in terms of the latter notion of belief.[62]

In the following subsection I will discuss these forms of assent by explicating how these relate to the notion that subjective certainty is the *minimum criterion* of assent that must be satisfied for an agent to be conscientious.

3.3.2   *Conscience Requires Conviction*

The notions of assent outlined above provide the possible candidates that the judgement of conscience is in reference to. In *Religion* Kant makes it clear that the type of assent that relates to an acquittal by the judgement of conscience is an assent that is held with *conviction*. He states

> It is not absolutely necessary to know, of all possible actions, whether they are right or wrong. With respect to the action *I* want to undertake, however, I must not only judge, and be of the opinion, that it is right; I must also be certain that it is. And this is a requirement of conscience to which is opposed probabilism i.e., the principle that the mere opinion that an action may well be right is itself sufficient for undertaking it (6:186).

Here Kant begins by bracketing out that conscience does not *necessarily* relate to *absolute* knowing i.e. according to *objective standards of evaluation*. Rather, by emphasising that the judgement of conscience relates to the 'I', Kant is stating that the concern is with the conviction that the agent has towards a particular proposition ('*I* must also be *certain* [read: have conviction] that it is)'.

The notion of conviction can be fleshed out by noting Kant's elaboration on the difference between belief and knowing in the *Lectures on Logic*. He states that 'believing is a subjectively sufficient but objectively insufficient holding-to-be-true. [...] Knowing is an objective holding-to-be-true' (24:852). In order to understand what Kant means here it is necessary to explicate what is meant by subjective and objective sufficiency in the above. One manner in which to explicate Kant's position is by pointing to his assertion in the First *Critique* (A820/B848), where subjective sufficiency appears to refer to judgements that are 'only in the particular constitution of the subject', which can be read as a reference to the individual subject and as having only 'private validity' (A820/B848).[63] This may be coupled with a notion of 'objective' that is taken as a

---

62   Here Stevenson's analysis is particularly strong as he identifies five ways in which belief is discussed by Kant. For a summary of his analysis see ibid., 96–7.

63   See Stevenson, 'Opinion, Belief or Faith, and Knowledge', 84.

publically accessible standard of justification.[64] However such an approach is problematic as it fails to acknowledge the centrally important notion of how the agent self-consciously views the particular proposition (whether subjectively or objectively certain). As Stevenson points out, it is necessary to recognise that by subjectively sufficient in Kant's notion of *glauben* what is meant is that 'the subject can have a ground or reason which she acknowledges not to amount to objective justification, but which she takes to be *good enough in its own distinctive way* to justify her in holding the proposition to be true'.[65] As such, when distinguishing between subjective and objective sufficiency what is of concern is not the relation between the subject's own view of their justification and a publicly evaluable fact, rather the concern is with the standard of justification the agent applies to themselves.

The question then becomes: what are the standards that Kant is referring to? In a few paragraphs after he offers a definition of belief in the First *Critique* he asserts that 'only in a practical relation [...] can something that is theoretically insufficient to be true be called believing' (A823/B851). As such the two standards are objective-theoretical and subjective-practical, where knowing refers to the former, and believing refers to the latter. In an analysis by Wood of knowing and believing, it is pointed out that Kant holds that both epistemological notions are based on universally valid grounds.[66] By 'universally valid' what is being referred to are reasons that appeal to the judgement of any rational (human) agent. In contrast to opining, both notions involve *conviction*, however the nature of the respective convictions differs (as noted above, knowing is via logical judgement or overwhelming evidence, and believing is via practical commitments).[67] As such, objectively sufficient holding-to-be-true is a reference to the type of assent that falls under the remit of objective standards, which is termed knowing (considered knowledge), and subjectively sufficient holding-to-be-true is a reference to the type of assent that falls under the remit of subjective standards, which is termed (practical) believing. As such, the first result of the exegesis of this passage is that what Kant means

---

64 Such a reading may appeal to Kant's assertion in the Third *Critique* regarding aesthetic judgements, which he takes as having universal (for all agents) and yet subjective validity (5:215, see also 467, 472). For a discussion on this point see ibid.

65 Ibid.

66 A. W. Wood, *Kant's Moral Religion*, Cornell University Press (1970), 14–16.

67 The crucial distinction here is that although the grounds for believing are universal, they are still subjective insofar as they do not solely concern the object that is the subject of the judgement but rather also the nature in which an agent is said to view a particular proposition.

by 'it is not absolutely necessary to know' is that *knowing is a sufficient but not necessary condition for conscientiousness.*

The central point here is that conscience provides conviction. As was stated in the previous subsection, Kant asserts that in both knowing and believing an agent can hold a proposition to the point of *conviction.*[68] Conviction itself is divided into involuntary conviction i.e. knowing, and voluntary (practical) conviction i.e. believing.[69] Kant expands on the notion of practical conviction by stating that

> [T]his practical conviction, or this *moral belief of reason,* is often firmer than all knowledge. With knowledge one still listens to opposed grounds, but not with belief, because here it does not depend on objective grounds but on the moral interest of the subject (*Lectures on Logic* 24:72).

In this passage Kant is stating that the context within which a particular proposition is being considered changes the nature of how the particular proposition is viewed. With many knowledge claims, such as scientific or historical propositions that fall within the remit of knowing conviction, an agent 'still listens to opposed grounds'. This is because the knowledge is of a proposition that

---

68   See *Lectures on Logic* 24:227–8.

69   This division is further warranted by noting that Kant states in the First *Critique* that 'Subjective sufficiency is called **conviction** (for myself), [and] objective sufficiency [is called] **certainty** (for everyone)' (A822/B850). However, frustratingly Kant does not see the need to explicate these conceptions of conviction. Kant's underdeveloped terminology presents two confusions: the first is that he talks of subjective sufficiency as something that is agent specific ('for myself') whereas objective sufficiency is spoken about as something that is not agent specific ('for everyone'). The second is that he then talks of certainty with respect to something that is non-agent specific, thus suggesting that certainty relates to objective standards of evaluation. These two points clearly contradict the reading of conviction and certainty with respect to conscience because, as I have argued, Kant can be seen to be referring to subjective and objective sufficiency with respect to believing and knowing respectively, which are concepts that accord to different standards of evaluation, and certainty/conviction as something that an *agent* must possess in cases of conscience i.e. not 'for everyone' but 'for myself'. The discrepancies between the notions of objective and subjective sufficiency in the *Lectures on Logic* and the First *Critique,* and the notion of certainty (with respect to conscience) in *Religion* and the First *Critique,* can be explained by the fact that Kant's use of these terms are not treated precisely in the First *Critique* where he passes them over by stating 'I will not pause for the exposition of such readily grasped concepts' (A822/B850). See also *Lectures on Logic* 24:72. On this point see also Stevenson, 'Opinion, Belief or Faith, and Knowledge', 77.

is value neutral, whereas in the case of beliefs they can be 'often firmer than all knowledge' because they relate to the *practical concerns* of an agent. Kant mentions specifically that the conviction of beliefs depends not on 'objective grounds but on the moral interest of the subject'. The reason for this is because in a situation where an agent must act they must make a definitive judgement (a 'biting of the bullet', so to speak).

When Kant states that an agent 'must not only judge, and be of the opinion' that their action is right, but also that the agent must be '*certain* that it is', he is stating the *necessary* conditions for an action to be considered a conscientious action. Kant rejects the idea that opinions are a sufficient condition for actions to be based upon in cases deemed conscientious. This is because opinion is based on 'probabilism', which, within his discussion of opinions (as explicated above), is merely grounds for a particular proposition being greater than the grounds for the opposite.[70] Moreover, if the primary concern was opining with regard to moral matters then conscience would be judging morally neutral propositions. This is precisely not what Kant conceives conscience as doing.[71] Believing conviction is, as he states, the '*practical* conviction (*I am certain*)' (24:72) and as such practical believing conviction is a necessary and sufficient condition for conscientiousness. This is termed *subjective certainty*.[72]

To reiterate, *subjective certainty* is in reference to practical believing *voluntary* conviction. However, as has been argued, there are of course cases where an agent may possess a higher standard of certainty i.e. *objective sufficiency*: knowing *involuntary* conviction (objective certainty). All that is meant by this distinction is that propositions are evaluated according to their differing natures. In the following subsection I will explain how it is that Kant can talk of practical voluntary conviction with respect to when an agent is subjectively certain about a particular position and why it is that an agent cannot voluntarily assent to any proposition.[73]

---

70   See *Lectures on Logic* 24:148, 227, 850–7.

71   For an extended discussion on the various nuances of Kant's notion of opining see Stevenson, 'Opinion, Belief or Faith, and Knowledge'.

72   For a succinct summary by Kant of the notion of conviction see *Lectures on Logic* 24:735, 9:70.

73   Due to the fact that the concern of this chapter is with moral practical concerns and subjective standards of evaluating a proposition, the concept of justification as it relates to apriority will be bracketed here and will not be the primary subject of the analysis below. Such concerns fall within the remit of Kant's Transcendental Idealism. For a discussion that touches upon this domain of Kant's work see D. Pereboom, 'Kant on Justification in Transcendental Philosophy', *Synthese*, 85, (1990), 25–54.

3.3.3   *Voluntary Convictions and the Role of the Will*

In the *Lectures on Logic* Kant discusses the differences between voluntary and involuntary conviction. He explicates his point by giving an example of a businessman inspecting their accounts (24:157–8).[74] What he alludes to in this example is the case of an involuntary conviction: the facts about the arithmetic directly demand that the businessman acknowledges what is the case. As such the businessman can be said to be objectively certain with respect to propositions that relate to his accounts. Kant tells us the evidence is 'too much' and that the businessman is 'too evidently convinced' (24:158). In cases of propositions that an agent holds with objective certainty, the highest level that a propositional attitude may hold is at play.[75]

However objective certainty is not a necessary condition for the acquittal of an agent by the judgement of conscience. Rather, the *minimal* condition that is to be met, as explicated above, is subjective certainty i.e. believing voluntary conviction. As such, the notion of voluntary conviction requires further elaboration. For example, Kant claims that there are activities that an agent can engage in that have the consequence of resulting in convictions about said propositions

> Insofar as the will either impels the understanding toward inquiry into a truth or holds it back therefrom, however, one must grant it an influence on the *use of the understanding*, and hence indirectly on conviction itself,

---

74   Kant states, 'a businessman, e.g., who sees from his bills that he owes much, more than he possesses or can hope to possess, will of course not be able to withdraw his approval and consent (*Beifall und Consens*) from this cognition, which is so evident, however much he might like to [...] since he is too much and too evidently convinced (*uberzeugt*) of the correctness of the arithmetic in this matter, [...] The free *arbitrium* in regard to approval [...] disappears entirely in the presence of certain degrees of the grounds, and it is always very hard, if not utterly impossible, to withhold approval' (24:157–8). This example and the following two quotes from the *Lectures on Logic* are also quoted in Chignell, 'Kant's Concepts of Justification', 36, 37.

75   Stevenson's discussion on this point is framed in terms of consciousness, where the condition upon which a valid belief or knowledge proposition is held depends upon an agent's awareness of the nature of the proposition. The idea here is that an agent may hold a proposition as a belief whilst lacking an awareness (conscious reflection) of the properties of the relevant proposition (in terms of epistemological justification, 'Opinion, Belief or Faith, and Knowledge', 75–8). However, Stevenson's discussion primarily concerns opinion and as such the analysis I present below will not utilise his terminology. Instead it will concentrate on beliefs rather than opinions, and will be framed in terms of conscience.

since this depends so much upon the use of the understanding (*Lectures on Logic* 9:74).

Here he is referring to the fact that cases of voluntary conviction are when an agent may make inquiries that relate to propositions that cannot be evaluated to the point of objective certainty but rather can *only* be evaluated to the point of subjective certainty.[76]

In the *Lectures on Logic* Kant explains that presented with a situation where an agent cannot determine a proposition through simple logical judgement (which would result in involuntary convictions) the agent can make further inquiries as to the nature of the proposition

> If approval does not arise immediately through the nature of the human understanding and of human reason, then it still requires closer direction of choice, will, wish, or in general of our free will, toward the grounds of proof (24:158).

What Kant is referring to by approvals that arise 'immediately' are cases where objective certainty can be met without an effort on the part of the agent. When immediate approval does not occur what is required is that an agent makes a choice to conduct other forms of inquiries. When an agent conducts all of the choices that they are aware of with respect to 'the grounds of a proof' of a proposition, then depending on the result and nature of these inquires an agent can become objectively certain *qua* overwhelming evidence, or perhaps subjectively certain i.e. when there is a lack of overwhelming evidence.

In cases of subjective certainty, because the evaluated proposition cannot be substantiated in a manner that may result in objective certainty (i.e. involuntary conviction), such certainty is said to relate to voluntary conviction. This is because of the role of the will in choosing to assent i.e. hold-to-be-true, the non-objectively ascertainable proposition.[77] Importantly, Kant is clear that an agent cannot, by a pure act of the will, claim to hold any proposition.[78] He states

---

76 For contemporary theories that closely correlate to this picture of conviction see R. Stalnaker's notion of 'acceptance' in *Inquiry*, MIT University Press (1984), chapter 5. See also J. Cohen, *An Essay on Belief and Acceptance*, Oxford University Press (1992), and M. Bratman, 'Practical Reasoning and Acceptance in a Context', *Mind*, 101, 401, (1992), 1–15.

77 Interestingly Kant talks of the desire of an agent's understanding to expand and 'enrich itself with cognitions by judging' (9:74) and of 'reason's drive for cognition' (8:139fn). These assertions suggest a kind of inbuilt propensity towards engaging in such activity.

78 For a discussion that touches upon this theme see J. Barnes, 'Belief is up to Us', *Proceedings of the Aristotelian Society*, 106, (2006), 189–206.

The question arises, accordingly, *whether willing has an influence on our judgments.* The will does not have any influence immediately on holding-to-be true; this would be quite absurd. When it is said that *we gladly believe what we wish,* this means only our benign wishes, e.g., those of a father for his children. If the will had an immediate influence on our conviction concerning what we wish, we would constantly form for ourselves chimeras of a happy condition, and always hold them to be true, too. But the will cannot struggle *against* convincing proofs of truths that are contrary to its wishes and inclinations (9:73–4).[79]

The above passage can be broken into a number of steps. The first step relates to the fact that the will cannot have any influence on immediately holding-to-be true. What Kant means by this is that an agent possesses immediate representations that relate to particular propositions and that the agent has no choice with respect to how they view these propositions.[80]

The second step has Kant referring to 'benign wishes' in cases where agents 'gladly believe what [they] wish [to believe]'. Here he makes reference to the wishes of a father relating to the behaviour and ability of their child. What he is referring to here are propositional claims that are not related to any form of inquiry and do not result in practical action. For example, a father may wish that their child is well behaved and thus gladly believe that their child is well behaved. This is a *benign* belief because the father, in such cases, is neither evaluating any evidence (say, report cards from the child's teachers etc.), nor basing any moral action upon this benign belief. The case of this father is voluntary belief, but not *practical* believing voluntary conviction.

Hence in the third step, when Kant denies that it is possible for the will to have 'an immediate influence on our *conviction* concerning what we wish' (emphasis mine), what he is stating is that (in cases of convictions that are held-to-be-true) an agent has undergone a certain amount of evaluation. Thus it is impossible for the agent in light of these evaluations, by the pure act of their will i.e. wishing, to hold-to-be-true with conviction that for which there is 'convincing proofs of truths that are contrary to [an agent's] wishes'. Although the father may possess a desperate wish to believe in the proposition 'my child

---

79   See also *Lectures on Logic* 9:94–95 and *Collins* 27:354, where Kant states 'the accusation of conscience cannot be dismissed, and neither should it be, [...] *it is not a matter of willpower*'.

80   For a discussion of this see G. Soldati, 'Direct Realism and Immediate Justification', *Proceedings of the Aristotelian Society*, 112, (2012), 29–44 and P. Gilbert, 'Immediate Experience', *Proceedings of the Aristotelian Society*, 92, (1992), 233–50.

is well behaved at school', he cannot simply will such that he holds this proposition to-be-true in the face of overwhelming evidence that substantiates the contrary.[81]

Thus, through an exegesis of the above passage it has become clear that although cases of voluntary conviction involve an agent choosing to assent to a particular proposition this voluntary conviction is not arbitrary but conditioned.[82] As Chignell points out within this context, '[f]or Kant, only broadly-speaking practical reasons can provide adequate motivation for adopting a positive attitude towards a proposition (rather than suspending judgment) in the absence of sufficient epistemic grounds'.[83] This falls within the remit of believing voluntary conviction. Indeed with respect to the moral practical concerns of conscience, it has been shown that an agent must be subjectively certain for the voluntary belief to be held with conviction. This is a condition that is satisfied if and only if an agent undergoes all of the evaluative actions the agent can conduct that an agent is aware of at a particular time.

It is important to note here that the reading that I have provided suggests that in the context of conscience, assent to practical claims is generally non-epistemic i.e. not based on objective standards of evaluation and unable to achieve the status of knowledge.[84] Indeed, given that Kant's theory of conscience relates to subjective certainty, his account of conscience is to be read as fallibilist (defined broadly as the principle that a proposition can be accepted even though the proposition cannot be proved to the point of objective certainty). The reason for this is because cases that would satisfy a non-fallibilist theory of justification would be extremely limited. Indeed, as Kant himself asserts, in common life most of an agent's judgements do not meet the standard of 'knowledge' (*Lectures on Logic* 24:38). Of course, practical concerns are far more acute than the everyday judgements of common life and as such

---

81   See R. Robinson, 'Necessary Propositions', *Mind*, 67, 267, (1958), 289–304.

82   The above analysis falls into Kant's account of 'reflection' presented in the *Lectures on Logic* (24:163). Kant explains that agents have 'provisional judgements' that can become 'decisive judgements' with reflection. Kant holds that, in cases of provisional judgements (related to practical matters), a 'suspension of judgement' would be 'useful and very necessary'. This is because 'in many cases it keeps us from many wrong turns and errors in cognitions' (24:163). Indeed he expands upon this by stating, '*Reflection is, however, an important* [,] *very great and certain path, if not for extinguishing the affects, nevertheless for quieting them, for hindering their dangerous consequences, and thus for avoiding errors*' (24:163). See also B. Stroud, 'Epistemological Reflection on Knowledge of the External World', *Philosophy and Phenomenological Research*, 56, 2, (1996), 345–58.

83   See Chignell, 'Kant's Concepts of Justification', 33–63.

84   A view congruent with Chignell's analysis (ibid.).

I acknowledge that the point is contentious and requires further investigation.[85] A full exploration of this point will bring the discussion beyond the purview of this chapter.[86] Below I turn to discussing conscientiousness, which I believe is a notion that informs this debate. As will become clear, Kant certainty envisions a robust process of justified conscientious assent.

3.4   Conscientiousness

In this section I will expand on the notion of subjective certainty with respect to Kant's notion of 'conscientiousness'. I will explicate that an agent's conscientiousness depends on the nature of the proposition, the circumstances within which evaluation occurs and the readiness of always being open to new possibilities of re-evaluation.[87]

3.4.1   *Material and Formal Conscientiousness*
In *Miscarriage* Kant introduces a distinction between 'material conscientiousness' and 'formal conscientiousness'. This distinction is expressed in the following passage

> "material conscientiousness" consists in the caution of not venturing anything on the danger that it might be wrong, whereas "formal" conscientiousness consists in the consciousness of having applied this caution in a given case (8:268).

Here material conscientiousness is a state or attitude that an agent ought to be in or take, to be considered conscientious. This relates to the general norm of holding the following principle: 'I cannot will an action unless I am in a state of conscientiousness' i.e. subjectively certain. Formal conscientiousness

---

85   See Stevenson, 'Opinion, Belief or Faith, and Knowledge'.

86   It should be noted that 'fallibilism' usually attaches to theories of knowledge. That is, one can have a fallibilist theory of knowledge if one thinks it suffices to know that p if one's claim that p does not entail infallible certainty that p. Within this context it might be thought to be slightly incorrect to call Kant a fallibilist or an infallibilist regarding practical belief, since he does not think that it counts as knowledge in any sense (as such Kant cannot hold an infallibilist theory of knowledge here).

87   This can also be discussed in terms of 'subjective justification'. For discussion in the secondary literature of subjective justification see G. De Pierris, 'Subjective Justification', *Canadian Journal of Philosophy*, 19, 3, (1989), 363–82 and J. L. Kvanvig, 'Subjective Justification', *Mind*, 93, 369, (1984), 71–84.

relates to particular circumstances i.e. 'with respect to this particular moral action, I cannot will this action unless I am in a state of conscientiousness' i.e. subjectively certain of the particular proposition.[88] Thus material and formal conscientiousness are distinguished only by the fact that material conscientiousness is a broader state that an agent can be in, whereas formal conscientiousness relates to a particular situation.

An additional term that Kant employs with respect to actions being evaluated conscientiously is 'sincerity'. In *Vigilantius*, within the context of discussing conscience, Kant states

> Consciousness must be accompanied with an attitude of sincerity, i.e., that the subject be aware of having entered upon his examination with an eye to probability; this examination always has to do, of course, with the merely external circumstances in the action; it calls for a customary rigour, in order not to view a *factum* as other than it really is (27:616).

As such, sincerity is conceptually equivalent to conscientiousness. It is to hold a particular attitude (material conscientiousness) and evaluate particular cases (formal conscientiousness) in a manner that grounds an action upon suitable evaluation of propositions.[89] This last point is important as it qualifies other terms that Kant uses in this passage such as 'probability', 'external circumstance in the action', 'customary rigor' and 'factum'. Indeed the passage above can be reconstructed to read as a statement of two parts: the first part (ending with the first semicolon) represents the broader material conscientiousness, and the second part represents the narrower formal conscientiousness, i.e. actions that qualify a particular proposition as having been evaluated according to its own properties and external circumstances. In this second part Kant is using the term 'factum' which is equivalent to my use of the term

---

88   As Despland succinctly puts it 'formal conscience can always function as a double check on the attention which the self, by itself, has paid to the dictates of its own material conscience at any given stage of its life or development' ('Can Conscience Be Hypocritical?', 368–9). See also Howard's similar treatment of material and formal conscientiousness ('Kant and Moral Imputation', 616).

89   As Despand puts it 'Sincerity is the quality that results from conscientiously going through this second stage of moral self-scrutiny, or from passing judgment on the first stage, which formulated the moral judgment. The sincere man cannot claim to speak the truth: he is fallible, and his moral judgments may err. But he can claim that what he says is truthful [i.e. conscientious] and is an exact statement of his state of mind, as honestly reflected upon' ('Can Conscience Be Hypocritical?', 359). See also *Religion* 6:178 and A. D. M. Walker, 'The Ideal of Sincerity', *Mind*, 87, 348, (1978), 481–97.

proposition. The properties of the factum dictate what type of 'customary rigour' is to be employed and the context constitutes the external circumstances that the factum is related to. Due to the fact that individual factum have different properties and are situated in different contexts, the customary rigour will of course differ according to the particular factum. Sincerity with respect to a particular proposition is simply formal conscientiousness.[90]

Within the discussion above, a term that I have left unexplored is 'probability'. In the following section I will explain how Kant employs this term as well as other notions such as 'plausibility' and in doing so I will further flesh out his notion of conscientiousness.

3.4.2   Suitable Evaluation: Subjective Probability and Plausibility

It should be noted that although Protestantism advocated a greater directness of the individual to God, an interesting development following the Reformation is the proliferation of 'casuistry', the study of individual cases of conscience by counsels.[91] One reason for this was the competing claims to various truths (be they points of beliefs or right actions) coming from the split Church (Catholic and Protestant), as well as the further division into the denominations of Protestant sects. Another reason had to do with specific cases of moral dilemmas. One of the consequences of this development was the introduction of nuances regarding moral decisions centring upon the notion of 'probabilism'.[92] The central idea pivoted upon the notion that in cases where clear and definitive evidence is not available, the most probable solution should be taken.[93] Indeed, in the historical context the issue of probability with respect to conscience is raised by Pufendorf, Hutcheson, and Wolff.[94] Pufendorf discusses the notion of a 'correct conscience' as cases where an action is 'absolutely to be done or omitted' because the action is 'in agreement with certain and indubitable divine

---

90   Notice that Leibniz seems to allude to this type of phenomena, 'But in the great [and fearful day of judgment], wherein the secrets of all hearts shall be laid open, [we are entitled] to think, that no-one shall be made to answer for what he knows nothing of; but shall receive his doom, his conscience accusing or excusing him' (*New Essays on Human Understanding*, 243).

91   See Sorabji, *Moral Conscience Through the Ages*, 117–25.

92   For an in-depth discussion on this point see Mayes, *Counsel and Conscience*, 21–38.

93   Sorabji, *Moral Conscience Through the Ages*, 117–25.

94   *The Political Writings of Samuel Pufendorf*, 76. Similarly Crusius also asserts 'there is indeed an erring and doubtful conscience (*A Guide to Rational Living*, 580), however he does not explicate the notion and thus in the above I will only explore Pufendorf's and Hutcheson's claims on the matter (Hutcheson, *A System of Moral Philosophy*, 236). See also, Wolff, *Vernüfftige Gedancken*, 340.

and human law'.[95] This is to be contrasted with 'a probable conscience [...] based on an opinion constructed out of reasons that are not thought to be evidently infallible but only probable, so that it is not deemed impossible that the opposite side can be true'.[96] This picture corresponds to Kant insofar as correct conscience can be thought to be a case of knowing and probable conscience to a case of believing, where Kant takes the former to be a sufficient condition and the latter to be a necessary and sufficient condition of certainty. Pufendorf also describes a 'doubtful conscience', where the 'conscience hangs [...] in equilibrium', as cases where there are comparable probabilities between two alternatives.[97] In this situation an agent's action 'ought to be suspended' until further evidence comes to light.[98] Hutcheson also talks of a 'doubtful conscience' which is a scenario where there are only different probabilities (rather than definitive evidence) regarding the rightfulness of an action.[99] Like Pufendorf, Hutcheson asserts that in such situations the action must be 'deferred till further inquiry be made'. However unlike Pufendorf, Hutcheson stipulates that when there is 'no time for delays' an agent should act upon the action with the higher probability of rightfulness.[100] In other words: the need to be practical triumphs. The prioritising of the practical concern is also present in Wolff who asserts that 'occasionally probability will have to be enough'.[101]

In contrast to Pufendorf, Hutcheson and Wolff, Kant does not employ the phrases of 'probable conscience' and 'doubtful conscience'. In fact Kant's use of the term probable/probability is idiosyncratic. Hence, although he asserts that for an agent to be sincere they must have been 'aware of having entered upon his examination with an eye to probability' (*Vigilantius* 27:616), it is neither necessarily the case that probability will be something that is involved in the evaluative actions that constitute the customary rigour by which a proposition is going to be evaluated, nor may it be possible (given the context) for an agent to determine a probability with respect to a particular circumstance.[102] Rather,

---

95   *The Political Writings of Samuel Pufendorf*, 76.

96   Ibid.

97   Ibid., 110–1.

98   Ibid.

99   Hutcheson, *A system of Moral Philosophy*, 236.

100   Ibid.

101   Wolff then states that for this reason 'we can see how important it is to peace of conscience that the rational art of probability be brought into good condition' (*Vernüfftige Gedancken*, 340).

102   Where probability is defined in a mathematical sense as 'the extent to which an event is likely to occur, measured by the ratio of the favourable cases to the whole number of cases possible', see D. R. Cousin, 'Probability', *The Philosophical Quarterly*, 4, 14, (1954), 82–4.

probability is being used by Kant in a broader sense to mean that agents are conscientious when it is the case that there are no more evaluative actions that an agent is conscious of at a particular time (which the agent can do to substantiate a proposition).

Hence, although there are a host of propositions that may not be viewed 'with an eye to [mathematical] probability', these propositions can nonetheless be evaluated conscientiously. For example, in the *Lectures on Logic* Kant describes the phenomena of *plausibility*. He defines plausibility as resting 'merely on the subject' and contrasts this with probability that 'rests on the object' (24:194). In order to explicate this he provides the example of attempting to ascertain the size of the Moon (24:196–7). In this context, he asserts that the concern of probability is from the perspective of objective standards of evaluation because the reference is to the Moon in-itself i.e. the object, which is as it is in itself independent of an agent's beliefs about it.[103] There is a truth that is true in all circumstances, which may provide an objective criterion (the barometer i.e. the 100%) by which the percentage is gauged.[104] When there is no such 'certain grounds for the truth of the thing, and [...] no one who is in a position to teach us more grounds against the truth of the thing than for it', a particular cognition, Kant tells us, is 'nothing more than plausible' (24:196).[105]

The notion of plausibility is premised precisely on this lack of a clear criterion by which a probability would be gauged. Indeed, because of this inherent lack of a clear criterion, notions of plausibility are riddled with the possibility of great errors.[106] As Kant states

> With *plausibility* an error can actually be met with [...], since one is not conscious of the insufficient grounds. The first rule is thus: with all cognitions, even true ones, seek first of all to become conscious of the uncertainty that arises and ever could arise from insufficient grounds [;] one should place himself, as it were, in the position of the opponent, of the doubter, who believe themselves to have sufficient grounds for maintaining the opposite of this cognition; for otherwise one will almost always, in most cases, err and deceive oneself (24:194–5).

---

103   This notion of probability is discussed as objective probability in E. Eells, 'Objective Probability Theory', *Synthese*, 57, 3, (1983), 387–442.

104   See also *Lectures on Logic* 24:194–7, 742–4, 879–84, 9:81–4 .

105   For a discussion of the concept of certainty in epistemological theories see P. Keith, *Certainty*, University of Minnesota Press (1981).

106   Kant discusses general cases of error in the *Lectures on Logic* see 24:77–8, 87–8, 101–3, 160, 824–6, 719–20, 832–4, 9:52–5.

Here Kant is telling us that an agent should always be cognisant of the fact that they may not, or do not, have sufficient grounds to substantiate the *objective plausibility* of the plausibility of a particular proposition.[107] Indeed, Kant makes clear that there are many cases where an agent may find themselves as having determined that a particular proposition is plausible when in fact it is not (9:53–4).[108] Due to this, an agent must hold a stance towards their beliefs that is akin to the position of a sceptical doubter (here defined broadly as one that is suspicious of their held beliefs and who actively seeks additional information and evidence that relates to the plausibility of the proposition held).[109]

Although Kant talks of probability relating to the object (rather than the representation of the object in the mind of the agent), it is nonetheless not always the case (or even typically the case), that an agent is aware of the value of the objective criterion. Indeed, *even in the case of probability* an agent 'can never know whether one cognizes more grounds for than against the thing' (*Lectures on Logic* 24:194). In such cases Kant can be seen to be talking about *subjective probability*.[110] Thus he tells us

> [W]ith *all cognitions* one must seek first of all to acquaint oneself with the sufficient ground, or to know and to cognize how many grounds are properly required for full certainty of a thing, so that one can distinguish suitably whether something is plausible or probable in the first place (emphasis mine, 24:194–5).

107　Consider the difference between judging whether someone is lying (plausible) and judging the size of the moon (probability). For a discussion of this problem see D. Henige, 'The Implausibility of Plausibility/The Plausibility of Implausibility', *Historical Reflections*, 30, 2, (2004), 311–35.

108　In such cases Kant talks of the notion of 'persuasion'. Persuasion relates to plausibility in an analogous fashion of percentage to probability. The higher the percentage the greater the probability, and likewise with persuasion, the greater the level of persuasion the more plausible a proposition becomes to an agent (9:81). See also *Lectures on Logic* 24:143–7, 218, 226–7, 848–51, 854–5, 732–4, 747, 889–91.

109　Within this context doubt is termed by Kant as 'scruples': Scruples must be treated positively because they invite an agent to engage in 'expanding', 'extending' and 'elucidating', that which substantiate a particular proposition (24:83–6, 743–7). For Kant's extended views on the different types of doubt in the *Lectures on Logic* see his distinction between doubt *qua* dogmatic/sceptical (24:205–18, 884–6), *qua* objective/subjective (24:201–2, 881–3) and *qua* sceptical Pyrrhonic/academic (24:208–9, 745).

110　For a discussion of subjective probability see R. Jeffrey, *Subjective Probability*, Cambridge University Press (2004).

By an agent acquainting themselves with respect to a particular proposition, first of all with the knowledge of whether or not it is possible to gain sufficient ground i.e. objective probability, an agent can know whether their judgement relates to a subjectively probable or a plausible proposition (*Lectures on Logic* 24:81–2).[111] Although in the passage about the Moon Kant talks of probability with respect to the object in-itself i.e. objective standards of evaluation, in the case of conscience, because all conscience can judge according to is the representations of the object within the mind of an agent—as he states '[conscience] is not directed to an object but merely to the subject' (*Metaphysics of Morals* 6:400)—the agent must evaluate what standard of evaluative action is appropriate according to the properties of a particular proposition. This also involves an evaluation of the circumstances that the proposition is being evaluated within. This is all there is to conscientiousness. As Kant states, 'a man, in the utmost exertion of his dutifulness, can only get so far as to be conscientious', which he asserts is based upon 'subjective certainty after suitably conducted tests' (*Vigilantius* 27:617).[112]

The conscientious agent will readily concede that they may have failed in their evaluation and failed in *knowing* what evaluation was appropriate, but the agent will not concede that they have failed to act in accordance with what evaluative procedures they were aware of at a particular time *and that they did their best to determine if those evaluative procedures were appropriate with respect to the particular proposition.* Indeed this sentiment is alluded to by Kant. With respect to conscientiousness he states

> In order to attain to this, a repeated awakening of conscience is needed, i.e., the frequent evocation of the consciousness of his deeds (27:617).

What Kant is stating here is that for an agent to be considered a conscientious agent, the propositions that are being held as subjectively certain must be continually reassessed. What is required of an agent is the maintenance of their awareness with respect to the extent to which an agent is being 'honest with

---

111   See also *Lectures on Logic* 24:143–6, 742, 882–4. For a contemporary discussion of the relation of beliefs to probability see J. Pollock, 'Epistemology and Probability', *Synthese*, 55, 2, (1983), 231–52.

112   In *Vigilantius* Kant states 'nobody can take a thing to be right or wrong, even when probability is present, so long as he cannot dismiss the possibility of the opposite [...] nobody can take a chance on this danger, without acting in a conscienceless way' (27:614–5).

themselves' (27:616).[113] For example, at a particular point an agent may have acted conscientiously upon a proposition but then, after a period of time, continue to hold (and thereby act according to) the proposition despite not having re-evaluated the proposition according to re-evaluated and updated circumstances. Such an agent would thereby be acting unconscientiously.[114]

Importantly this last point defeats the philosophical concern that is raised with respect to subjective standards of evaluation being too low a criterion for conscientiousness. The intuitive concern is that if there were evaluations that an agent should have been aware of, but was not for a seemingly frivolous reason (such as laziness) then it does not seem that the agent should be exonerated as having followed their conscience. This concern is dispelled by the stipulation above that the agent cannot be deemed conscientious if they are not in a state such that they are always open to new evaluative possibilities and in the active pursuit of these. An alternative way of putting it is to think of conscientiousness as a state that is a duty in itself, or as Kant states elsewhere 'now a conscience consists in the ability to impute one's own factum to oneself, through the law itself, and the **readiness to do this is conscientiousness**' (bold min, 27:576). Indeed this also defeats the concern that it seems as though so long as an agent fails to consult their conscience then they can never be found to be unconscientious, because simply failing to take the first step of evaluating action *is* unconscientiousness (a failure to maintain a 'readiness to do this').

In this section I have outlined Kant's notion of conscientiousness. I explicated that an agent's conscientiousness depends on the nature of the proposition and the circumstances within which evaluation occurs. I argued that for an agent to be conscientious they must have engaged in suitable evaluation to

---

113   See also *Metaphysics of Morals* 6:341, where Kant talks of the 'general duty of so disposing [oneself] to being capable of observing all moral duties', and Wood, *Kantian Ethics*, 187.

114   Indeed, the manner in which an agent views a particular proposition is typically rooted in a bevy of psychological states, such as recollections of memories, tiredness, bias and prejudices (Kant talks extensively about various sources of prejudice, such as custom, inclination, imitation, antiquity, mistrust, modernity, pride, meekness, taste, etc. see *Lectures on Logic* 24:165–6, 737, 9:75–81). An agent may in fact be prejudiced but be unaware of this prejudice and therefore believe that they are acting rightly. Importantly, if it is assumed that at a particular time an agent was unaware of the possible distortion of their evaluations then such an agent *can* be said to be conscientious. As Despland rightly points out, 'the genuinely sincere self remains aware of the frailty of its perceptions and of the shakiness of its convictions. In time it will discover its own contradictions. This means the self remains open to education. Whether such education will be available is another issue [...]' ('Can Conscience Be Hypocritical?', 370).

the best of their ability and that an agent should always bear in mind that their certainty of a particular proposition (in all but analytical-demonstrative, and cases of overwhelming evidence) is only subjective. They must take a sceptical stance towards their beliefs and evaluative procedures, and thus they must always be open to new possibilities of re-evaluation. Building upon the above, in the following section I will categorise the failures and errors of conscience primarily in terms of moral judgement.

3.5   Conscience: Moral Failures and Errors

The various errors and failures that can be associated with conscience can be summarised as:

  i.   The moral failure of choosing not to consult one's conscience.
  ii.   Moral failure of taking the subjective certainty of the judgement of conscience to be an objective moral judgement i.e. a certain conscience.
  iii.   The errors of the analogues of conscience i.e. a false conscience.
  iv.   The moral failure of choosing not to pay attention to the verdict of conscience i.e. unconscientious action.
  v.   The error of passing a judgement of conscience upon a false principle of morality i.e. an errant conscience.

I will not explicate i. as these are simply the cases of the moral failure of agents choosing not to consult their conscience. As such I will address points ii–v in turn below.

3.5.1   *Certain Conscience*
As noted numerous times above, Kant's notion of conscience is one of a higher-order judgement upon the moral judgement that an agent makes. The central point is that conscience is not moral judgement and as such the subjectively certain judgement of conscience is not to be taken by the agent as certainty regarding whether an action is right or wrong. Indeed Kant's explication of this point is neatly summarised by his student *Vigilantius*

> Professor Kant finds fault with *conscientia certa* [certain conscience] insofar as this is taken to mean the objective certainty of the rectitude of the action. It is the business of the understanding to examine whether an action be right or wrong; conscience presupposes this, and is subject only

to the duty of providing an awareness of having undertaken the examination with great thoroughness (27:619).

All Kant is cautioning against here is the taking of the judgement of conscience in terms of the objective certainty of the rectitude of an action i.e. conscience is not moral judgement but rather concerns whether the examination of the rectitude of the action is done 'with great thoroughness'.

3.5.2   Analogues of Conscience: False Conscience

Kant does much to distinguish his notion of conscience from various intuitively held notions which can be mistaken for conscience.[115] He asserts that the 'pangs of conscience' are not to be mistaken for the type of feelings that occur from what he terms an 'acquired conscience' that has been inculcated in an agent through custom, prudential reasons, or through being cultivated in an agent by art and education. He deems that these are not conscience but rather 'analogues of conscience' (*Collins* 27:353), i.e. false conscience.[116]

In as early as the *Herder* notes, Kant is careful to distinguish between what he terms 'acquired conscience' and 'natural conscience' (which is the real concern of his philosophical attention). By 'natural' Kant can be read as referring to the status of conscience as a constitutive capacity of moral agents. He asserts that distinguishing between the two is 'often difficult [because] much that is acquired is taken to be natural' (*Herder* 27:43).[117] An example of an acquired conscience may be of a sense within an agent to obey their parents' wishes with respect to who the agent should marry (27:43). Assuming that the agent is a fully rational adult and is not breaking any laws etc., the disapproval of the agent's parents may lead to a 'pang of conscience' that is generated through a sense of loyalty and respect that the culture within which this is taking place has inculcated within the agent. Obeying of parents in such circumstances is not a

---

115   For a discussion in the German literature that explores the relationship between good conscience and false conscience, see Funke, 'Gutes Gewissen, falsches Bewußtsein, richtende Vernunft', 226–51.

116   Similarly, Hutcheson argues that there are erroneous forms of conscience that occur from 'false notions of religion [...] informed by superstition and wrong education' (*A System of Moral Philosophy*, 159), and that this 'false conscience' can be exposed through reflection (ibid., 160).

117   Although Kant acknowledges that 'to what degree our conscientious feelings are acquired, in particular cases, is hard to say' (*Herder* 27:43), he does not deny that there are conscientious feelings that are solely due to constitutive natural conscience. Kant ascribes the view that conscience is reducible solely to custom and education to Voltaire (27:43). For a discussion on Voltaire's views on conscience see Ojakangas, *The Voice of Conscience*, 121–4.

duty in Kantian terms but rather a notion of 'duty' that has 'been acquired only through custom' (27:43).[118] Elsewhere in later *Lectures on Ethics* Kant makes further distinctions within this vein. In this circumstance he refers to *conscientia artificialis* (artificial conscience) (*Collins* 27:355–6), which can be taken as analogous to an acquired conscience. He states two things about artificial conscience. The first point he makes is that the artificial conscience is a product of 'art and education'.[119] The second point is that irrespective of whether artificial conscience has been cultivated in the agent, the agent still has a conscience nonetheless (the aforementioned constitutive 'natural conscience').[120]

In addition to the false feelings of the 'pangs of conscience' with respect to acquired/artificial conscience, Kant also distinguishes between the feelings of

---

118   Notice that Kant is employing a concept that Rousseau articulates as 'acquired ideas', which are 'ideas that come to us from outside [i.e.] experience' (*Emile*, 289). See also Kant's description of other ways in which conscience can be 'corrupted, errant, depraved, or crooked/distorted/perverse/wicked' (*Herder* 27:43). See also *Religion* 6:124, 168, 172, 177–8.

119   See also *Brauer* 133.

120   As pointed out to me by Prof. Timmermann, in *Collins* (27:352) Kant asserts that 'many people [only] have an analogue of conscience', where 'only' is parenthetical as the word is omitted in Heath's translation (see also *Brauer* 130–1). Here I do not read this claim as an assertion to the effect that some agents do not have a capacity of conscience i.e. that conscience is not constitutive. Instead I read this as a claim that many agents do not utilise, consult, engage with, etc. their natural-constitutive conscience. This reading is justified because the assertion is followed by Kant describing why the analogues of conscience are to be avoided and denounced as non-conscientious, which would only be a coherent critique of such agents if they possessed a real conscience. The idea is that an agent cannot be condemned unless they have at the very least a potential for genuine conscientiousness. Furthermore, textual evidence can be pointed to. The view of conscience detailed in Chapter 2 also clarifies the sense in which within the same context *Kant denies that conscience can be cultivated* (a theme that I will detail in Chapter 5). Kant is making the claim that conscience cannot be cultivated in the context of differentiating 'natural conscience' i.e. the constitutive capacity ('intellectual conscience') that is an activity of practical reason, with 'artificial conscience' which is an analogue of conscience. Kant states, 'The *conscientia naturalis* [natural conscience] might be contrasted to the *conscientia artificialis* [artificial conscience]. Many have contended that conscience is a product of art and education, and that it judges and speaks in a merely habitual fashion. **But if this were so, the person having no such training and education of his conscience could escape the pangs of it, which is not in fact the case.** Art and instruction must admittedly bring to fruition that to which nature has already **predisposed** us; so we must also have prior knowledge of good and evil, if conscience is to judge; but though our understanding may be cultivated, conscience does not need to be. It is therefore nothing but a natural conscience (bold mine, 27:355–6)'.

being content or discontent with oneself. This distinction comes from an agent feeling such feelings either pragmatically or ethically (27:251). What occurs is that an agent 'often thinks he has pangs of conscience, although he is only afraid of a tribunal of Prudence' (27:251).[121] For example, Kant explains that the pangs of conscience that are generated by worrying about the consequences of offending someone, are a result of worrying about the possible enmity of the person offended (27:251). This comes about due to the 'tribunal of prudence' because it may occur to the agent that they are going to have to face the person they have offended at some later point and this may lead to an uncomfortable experience at best or a conflict at worse. This is not a moral concern but rather a reproach that arises because of the possibility of harm that the agent anticipates.[122]

It is important to note that in the cases of the analogues of conscience the judgements that they generate can never be moral. For example, a case may occur when an agent consults an analogue of conscience and a verdict is passed such that it directs the agent to what is the morally correct thing to do. Although such chance cases may occur, the reason why such a case would still be deemed immoral is because, as Kant points out in the *Groundwork*, moral action is action done for the *sake* of the moral law not action that merely *conforms* to the moral law.

3.5.3 The Moral Failure of not Paying Attention to the Verdict of Conscience i.e. Unconscientious Action

A moral failure that can be ascribed to conscience is the case of an agent consulting their conscience and then failing to act according to the verdict that it generates.[123] As Kant states '*Unconscientiousness* is not a lack of conscience but rather the propensity to pay no heed to its judgement' (*Metaphysics of Morals* 6:401). This point touches upon a wider issue of moral motivation. In the case of respect two pictures can be drawn. One account of respect is that

---

121 Shaftesbury also talks of prudential interest causing 'disturbances from conscience' (*Characteristics of Men, Manners, Opinions, Times*, 211).

122 Smith also rejects the remorse of the 'bed of death' (*Theory of Moral Sentiments*, 155, see also 160). Although Crusius does not refer to the 'conscience of prudence' he does take 'prudence' as that which an agent does to achieve their 'own ends' (*A Guide to Rational Living*, 577). From this comes the 'obligations of prudence' that are derived from an agent's 'nature'. This is contrasted with the obligations that derive from the divine law i.e. from conscience (ibid., 577–8).

123 Timmermann comments on this point, 'Kant could add that one can also be guilty of not enacting the command of practical reason even if one has taken all due care in determining what exactly practical reason wants one to do ('Kant on Conscience', 304).

once an agent passes a moral judgement the agent will straightforwardly be motivated to act in accordance with this judgement. Another account of the motivation of respect can be given such that an agent may consider what to do and think that the best thing to do is to act according to the Categorical Imperative. In addition to this, a competing motive may be present that is grounded in inclination. In this case the agent may still decide that it is best to act morally, despite the presence of the sensibly grounded motivation, and yet, in spite of this decision, the agent may still be akratic and end up acting on the basis of the sensible motivation.[124] On this account, respect is motivating as one motivating element among others.[125] It is important to note that this is a substantive issue. Further investigation into the nature of the choice an agent makes in an action (moral or otherwise) is required and would expand the discussion beyond the remit of the current concern. Regarding conscience, from the *Metaphysics of Morals* passage above something analogous to the second account of the motivation of respect appears to be in play. An agent may choose to consult their conscience and thereby obtain a motivation to act conscientiously, however this does not entail that the agent will necessarily act in accordance with the motivation of conscience.

It is necessary to clarify that although Kant makes the connection between passing the judgement of conscience and not acting upon it in the *Metaphysics of Morals* passage cited above (6:401), this claim is made within what has been explicated as an implausible account of the non-erring claim i.e. Absurdity Thesis$_2$. Although this is true, in *Collins* Kant makes similar claims regarding

---

124   A discussion that touches on this point concerns the idea that a 'real motive' for an action can be identified. Firstly one must consider moral deliberation as an agent possessing two motivations. One motivation that is grounded upon an agent deciding that the best thing to do is to act according to the Categorical Imperative, and another motivation that is grounded in some specific interest. Presented with these two motivations the agent decides between the two. Here the motivational judgement to will according to either the moral judgment or the inclination (immoral) judgement presents itself as a distinct moment that can be described as the voluntary choice between the two (referred to as the 'real motive'). There are two concerns with this picture. The first concerns the incoherence of an agent passing what is a moral judgement (to act out of respect for the moral law) and then deciding voluntarily that it would be moral to act upon the moral judgement. There is in effect a 'doubling up' here of passing a moral judgement upon a judgement that an agent has determined is moral. To determine a judgement as moral is to be morally motivated by that judgement. The second issue, as Wood points out, concerns the lack of textual evidence for such a characterisation (see Wood, *Kantian Ethics*, 25–7). Further discussion of this point is beyond the remit of this study.

125   This account was pointed out to me by Prof. Baiasu.

the consulting of conscience but nonetheless failing to act in accordance with its verdict (27:353).[126] As has been shown above, in conjunction with Absurdity Thesis₁ through an explication of passages found in *Vigilantius* (27:616) and *Miscarriage* (8:268), Kant's theory of conscientiousness and unconscientiousness is a theory that relates to an evaluative disposition that an agent takes towards their actions. As such, Kant appears to have two notions of conscientiousness, one relating to (self) examination and another relating to action. In a passage in *Vigilantius* he seems to suggest that differing notions are indeed present when he explains that there is what 'we might call the examining conscience, in contrast to the judging one', where the examining conscience involves 'consciousness of the fact that the subject has decided on, inaugurated, or is actually engaged in, self-examination', and a judging conscience involves a *post facto* evaluation of an agents action (27:616).[127] Here conscientiousness *qua* examination can be thought to relate to engaging in self-examination and conscientiousness *qua* action can be thought to relate to the enactment of the action. In other words, both notions of conscientiousness are indeed present.[128]

This also introduces an important distinction between conscience before and after an action (a distinction that Kant inherits from Baumgarten). Thus far I have spoken of conscience in terms of a judgement concerning the diligence with which an agent has passed a moral judgement. This characterisation is most natural in terms of the consulting of conscience before an action as the agent is deliberating upon what action they should take. Characterising conscience in terms of the diligence with which an action was examined is less natural in *post facto* circumstances. As the action has already occurred, in these circumstances it appears as though a straightforward first-order moral judgement is occurring i.e. the agent *via* their conscience is simply judging whether the action was good or bad rather than whether the examination of the action

---

126   Kant talks of agents who engage in the 'dismissal of the very accusation, and the prick of conscience' as rebels, and as an act of 'infamy'.

127   See also Esser, 'The Inner Court of Conscience', 278.

128   It should be noted that conscientiousness *qua* acting upon the verdict of conscience is to be more precisely understood as falling under the remit of moral duty generally. As Kant explains, acting in accordance with conscience is all that is required of an agent 'as far as guilt or innocence is concerned' (*Metaphysics of Morals* 6:401). As such, Kant's assertion that 'to act in accordance with conscience cannot itself be a duty; for if it were, there would have to be yet a second conscience in order for one to become aware of the act of the first' (6:401), can be explained by reading him as stating 'acting in accordance with conscience cannot itself *be the duty of conscience....*' i.e. some other moral motivation must operate at the point of examining one's action ('examining conscientiousness'), which I read as a basic choice between either moral or immoral action.

was diligent or not. Although at first instance this reading appears to be what Kant is indeed claiming, *post facto* judgement can still be read in terms of the higher-order judgement that I have characterised above. The reason for this is because a judgement about the diligence with which an agent examines a case (that has been judged to fall under the law) can still occur after the action and *then*, in cases where conscience condemns, the agent can judge the action to be wrong *because* it was not diligently examined. In other words, *post facto* conscientiousness feeds back into moral judgement (I shall say more about this in Chapter 5, section 5.3).

Nonetheless the question still remains: is it coherent to claim that an agent can be conscientious *qua* self-examination and still fail to act upon the verdict of conscience? The short answer is that Kant thought so and that the issue is rooted in broader discussions of moral motivation in Kant. I will not fully explore this problem here as it would take the discussion beyond the scope of this chapter.

3.5.4   *The Inquisitor and the Heretic: An Errant Conscience*
In order to highlight cases of error that are associated with conscience when a verdict is passed according to a false principle of morality, I will explicate the case of an Inquisitor condemning a 'heretic' to death (*Religion* 6:187). Kant raises the example in the following passage

> Take, for instance, an inquisitor who clings fast to the exclusiveness of his statutory faith even to the point, if need be, of martyrdom, and who has to pass judgment upon a so-called heretic (otherwise a good citizen) charged with unbelief. Now I ask: if he condemns him to death, whether we can say that he has passed judgment according to his conscience (though erroneous), or whether we can rather accuse him of plain *lack of conscience*; whether he simply erred or consciously did wrong (6:187).[129]

Here Kant is raising two possibilities: i. that the Inquisitor has failed to consult their conscience and ii. the case of an 'erroneous conscience', that is the consulting of conscience with respect to a false principle of morality (in *Collins*

---

129   Kant's view of moral agency is that all such agents posses the capacity of conscience (it is *constitutive* of moral agency, see Chapter 2). Thus it is relatively trivial to point out the question pivots on the issue of whether or not the Inquisitor's conscience has erred in its judgement or if the Inquisitor has consciously done wrong.

he raises this situation and terms it an 'errant conscience' (27:354)).[130] Below I will show that Kant condemns the Inquisitor because of a failure to consult conscience i.e. the first possibility. Following this I explore the second possible opinion, namely that of an erroneous or errant conscience.

Kant begins by assuming that the Inquisitor is firm in the belief that a 'supernaturally revealed divine will' made this act a duty for him. This is problematic because it appears to be a case of a sincerely held belief. He tells us that the danger of this example is that 'the inquisitor would risk the danger of doing something which would be to the highest degree wrong, and on this score [act] unconscientiously' (6:187).[131] The point here is that the experiential phenomena of the Inquisitor is undeniable. The Inquisitor can in fact be said to involuntarily hold the belief that a divine will has manifested itself to him. However with respect to *conviction* the case is different. Agents can only hold a proposition with conviction in two cases: either involuntarily (in cases of logical judgements or overwhelming evidence), or voluntarily, where a proposition is related to practical concerns. Thus, although Kant can readily grant that the Inquisitor is genuine in their provisional belief, he is not granting that the Inquisitor is *sincere* in the decisive judgement that is conscientiousness. In other words he is denying that the Inquisitor can be subjectively certain of the proposition.

Importantly, when Kant asks if the Inquisitor can be 'really as strongly convinced of such a revealed doctrine, and also of its meaning, as is required for daring to destroy a human being on its basis?' (6:186), at first inspection he does not appear to be posing this question in a determinate manner. It may be *possible* that an agent in a particular circumstance is subjectively certain, for example an Inquisitor that is completely isolated from any other agents and thereby unaware of any of the developments in theology, psychology etc. that would quickly determine (via evaluative actions) the precarious nature of the proposition. Rather the question is posed rhetorically as 'can the inquisitor *really* be as strongly convinced...?' Crucially Kant clarifies that the Inquisitor in question is someone *suitably socially situated* 'since we can always tell him [the

---

130 Germane to the current discussion is Bayle's notion of an errant conscience, cases of conscience judging according to a false principle of morality (see Mori, 'Bayle', 49 and Fulton, 'Bayle', 74). The fact that Bayle also discusses the notion within an example of the judgement of a supposed 'heretic' is further evidence for the claim that Kant is here responding to Bayle (see Mori, 'Bayle', 49).

131 It is interesting to note that Kant's remarks about conscience in the *Notes on Moral Philosophy* (1783–4) are in terms of religion and more specifically false professions of faith (18:602–3).

Inquisitor] outright that in such a situation he could not have been entirely certain that he was not perhaps doing wrong' (6:186). Indeed, the context within which the case of the Inquisitor is being discussed is one where the Inquisitor is aware of the fact that

> God has ever manifested this awful will is a matter of historical documen-
> tation and never apodictically certain. After all, the revelation reached
> the inquisitor only through the intermediary of human beings and their
> interpretation, and even if it were to appear to him to have come from
> God himself (like the command issued to Abraham to slaughter his own
> son like a sheep), yet it is at least possible that on this point error has
> prevailed (6:187).

It is within this context that Kant is placing the Inquisitor and condemning him as unconscientious. Although Kant does not employ the term 'material conscientiousness' in *Religion*, he clearly refers to this notion in the passage preceding his discussion of the Inquisitor by stating 'it is a moral principle [...] that we ought to venture nothing where there is danger that it might be wrong' (6:185). The Inquisitor is aware of a number of things that he can do to evaluate the proposition but he has chosen not to do these actions. As such, of the two options that Kant provides (the Inquisitor erring or consciously doing wrong), the answer must be given that the Inquisitor is consciously doing wrong.

Although I have argued that the case of the Inquisitor is one of unconscientiousness due to the failure to consult conscience, I will now discuss the sec-
ond possibility raised by Kant, namely the case of an 'erroneous conscience'. An erroneous conscience is the possibility that the Inquisitor 'simply erred'. This case would seem to present a situation where the Inquisitor is consulting their conscience and yet coming to take as conscientious what is a flagrantly immoral act. Such cases are problematic because they seem to be the case of a clear error in the moral judgement not being deemed unconscientious. In fact there seems to be evidence that Kant does not view this as problematic. He asserts

> If someone is aware that he has acted in accordance with his conscience,
> then as far as guilt or innocence is concerned nothing more can be
> required of him (*Metaphysics of Morals* 6:401).

Here the evidence suggests that all that matters is acting in accordance with conscience even if (and when) conscience is passed upon a flagrantly false moral judgement. In order to unpack this situation it is necessary to explore

Kant's explanation of the corresponding phenomena that is an 'errant conscience' in *Collins* (27:354).

The phenomena of an errant conscience relates to laws that are not 'natural
obligations'. By natural obligations what Kant is referring to is the universal
moral law, which is the Categorical Imperative. He develops the notion of an
errant conscience by first pointing out that 'the difference between the correct and the errant conscience lies in this, that error of conscience takes two
forms, error *facti* [factual error] *and error legis* [error of fact of law]' (27:354).
In the case of factual errors, he readily acknowledges that conscience may be
errant because by factual here he is referring to matters of fact *qua* objective
standards of evaluation. This is simply cases where it was not possible for an
agent to be aware of some fact that would have altered the particular judgement of conscience. Kant can bracket this and explain that the errant conscience relates to facts of law. He tells us that errors with respect to the law are
of two types; '*errores inculpabiles* [non-culpable error] and *errores culpabiles*
[culpable error]' i.e. legal errors that an agent is not culpable for and legal
errors that an agent can be blamed for (27:355). He then explains that culpable errors relate to 'natural moral laws', whereas non-culpable errors relate
to 'positive law':

> In regard to his natural obligations, nobody can be in error; for the natu-
> ral moral laws cannot be unknown to anyone, in that they lie in reason
> for all; hence nobody is guiltless there in such error, but in regard to a
> positive law there are *errores inculpabiles*, and there one may act in all
> innocence, because of a *conscientia erronea* [errant conscience], whereas
> in regard to the natural law there are no *errores inculpabiles* (27:355).[132]

---

132   Notice here the similarity with Hutcheson's notion of an 'erroneous conscience' (*A Short
      Introduction to Moral Philosophy*, 104)—a phrase which Kant himself employs in the
      passage on the Inquisitor. Hutcheson introduces this notion after a discussion that expli-
      cates the idea of ignorance regarding the law, which he divides into involuntary and vol-
      untary ignorance. The former relates to laws that an agent is unaware of through no fault
      of their own, the latter relates to agents who are blameworthy for their ignorance regard-
      ing the law because 'if they had formerly used the diligence required of good men they
      might have known it' (ibid.). Thus, Hutcheson believes that in cases when an agent has an
      erroneous conscience (i.e. a conscience based upon a false notion of the law) depending
      on whether this is due to voluntary or involuntary error the agent is to be judged as either
      non-culpable or culpable respectively. Hutcheson believes that most agents are culpable
      because 'the laws themselves are more or less easy to be discovered' however, agents have
      'various degrees of natural fagacity', differing opportunities of information and inquiry'
      (ibid) and these need to be considered when evaluating the culpability of a particular

Here Kant is making it clear that unlike positive legal laws, moral laws incumbent upon an agent cannot be 'unknown'. There are two ways in which this claim can be made. The first is that agents are always aware of the moral law. The second is that agents can know the moral law even if they are not aware of it at a particular time. The latter is what Kant seems to be arguing in the *Groundwork* by asserting that it is possible that an agent can come to know the moral law through sufficient moral effort (considered as rational reflection) (4:387–405). Hence the latter must be what he is referring to. Further to this claim, the former possibility (of choosing to act according to another principle of morality while being aware of the moral law), would simply be a moral failure. In the first case agents are guilty because they are aware of the moral law and fail to act upon it and in the second case agents are guilty because they have refused to engage in the rational reflection that would have made them aware of the moral law. Thus, when Kant states that no agent is 'guiltless [...] in such error', he is referring to the rational reflection that is related to becoming aware of the moral law.[133]

Timmermann similarly discusses the case of the Inquisitor. However he does so within the remit of a conflict between actions that are grounded either in revealed religion or in practical reason.[134] Timmermann states, 'Kant does not question the sincerity of the inquisitor's faith, but it can never be certain, as is morally required, that revealed religion justifies the destruction of a human being'.[135] Indeed within this context Kant denies that an action commanded by a positive law grounded on revealed religion (such as making it a law to

---

agent. In an additional interesting historical note, Bayle discusses the non-culpability of agents in terms of 'invincible error' that are errors of conscience based on 'ignorance' that an agent could not have avoided (Mori, 'Bayle', 48).

133   However, what I will postulate is that the agents that Kant is discussing are *typically* agents who do not err in their objective judgement as to what the principle of morality is. Evidence for this comes from the fact that within the discussion of the Inquisitor Kant talks about human beings who have 'made by the slightest beginning in freedom of thought', a move away from their previous state of being 'under a slavish yoke of faith' (6:188). In a footnote Kant refers to this process as 'ripening' (6:188fn), which can only occur if it is assumed that agents are indeed free (see also Second *Critique* 5:73–4).

134   Timmermann states 'There is little evidence [...] in Kant's *oeuvre* that [the principle of moral judgment] should ever be likely to err. The robust nature of moral norms is impressively confirmed by the inquisitor's example. [...] It is perhaps Kant's most fundamental moral conviction, and the starting-point of much of his moral philosophy, that every mature and sane human being has access to moral principles that are essentially objective and correct' ('Kant on Conscience', 306).

135   Ibid., 305.

profess something as an article of faith) can be imposed upon people (*Religion* 6:187). The reason for this is because the

> [G]rounds of proof [are only] historical ones, [... thus] the cleric would be compelling the people to profess as true [...] something which they however do not know with certainty to be such [...] here the people's spiritual authority would himself be acting against his conscience (6:187).

Kant's assertion rests upon the claim that the epistemic status of historical (revealed) religion is fallible and thus *always* liable to the possibility of error.[136] He argues that if an agent engages in rational reflection (read: conscientious reflection) they will never be subjectively certain they have acted rightly in an action that is demanded from revealed religion, even if, as he states, '[there is] perhaps truth in what is believed'.

To summarise the possibility of an erroneous or errant conscience: Kant raises cases where an agent passes a judgement of conscience and yet an apparent conscientiousness which relates to this judgement is clearly an immoral act. He raises such cases in order to show that there can be cases of erroneous or errant conscience, where the judgement of conscience is based upon a false principle of morality. These are cases of moral failure (associated with moral judgement) and not cases of an erring conscience.

3.6   Conclusion

Chapter 3 provided an important step in the defence of the Unity Thesis as it built upon the explication of the judgement of conscience presented in Chapter 2. Indeed, by discussing the non-erring judgment of conscience and the extent and nature of Kant's notion of subjective certainty within this context, the importance of conscience is elevated from merely a higher-order judgement to one where an agent can gain 'certainty' in their actions (an element crucial to Kantian moral practice).

Crucially, by demonstrating the importance of the notion of subjective certainty, and how this relates to conscientiousness, the emphasis of conscience with respect to the first-personal perspective was shown. Conscience concerns actions that 'I must undertake', it involves a fundamental turn to oneself in

---

136   In the *Lectures on Logic* Kant explicates in what sense 'historical belief' can be taken as certain or not certain see 24:74, 293, 225, 893.

light of one's held beliefs regarding propositions (c.f. formal conscientiousness) and actions more generally (c.f. material conscientiousness). This turn
towards the 'I', that is central to the understanding of conscience, is paradoxically facilitated by the notion of an internal court—a court that is premised on
the notion of an 'other' that is represented by the inner judge. In the following
chapter, I will explore in detail how it is that the internal court of conscience
functions. I will do so by specific discussion of Kant's notion of an internal lie, a
notion that itself relies on the concept of subjective certainty *qua* truthfulness
(which I show is understood in terms of conscientiousness).

CHAPTER 4

Conscience and Internal Lies

4.1   Introduction

Within Kant's various discussions of morality the case of lying can be read as a paradigmatic example.[1] Indeed, Kant goes as far as beginning his discussion of lying in the *Metaphysics of Morals* by boldly asserting that lying is the greatest 'violation of a man's duty to himself' when regarded 'merely as a moral being' (6:429). Kant's views on lying are typically characterised by readings of his essay 'On a Proposed Right to Lie from Altruistic Motives'.[2] In this essay he replies to the criticism levelled by Constant, that an absolute duty not to lie would lead to the destruction of society, by affirming that even in cases where an agent is asked by another agent who is intent on murder, the asked agent is still obligated to speak truth to the would-be murderer.[3] Due to this response, the essay lends itself to an apparent *reductio* of Kant's view on lying to a rigorous application of the duty never to lie.[4] As a result some scholars have sought to distance Kant from this essay. For example, Paton argues that the essay does not reflect Kant's more considered view on the possibility of exceptions to practical rules.[5] Other scholars have attempted to reformulate

---

1   I take lying as a category that includes the notions of untruthfulness, dishonesty and insincerity. See *Groundwork* 4:430, Second *Critique* 5:44, *Metaphysics of Morals* 6:429–31, *Religion* 6:159–60, *Miscarriage* 8:268–71.

2   A translation can be found in *Kant's Critique of Practical Reason and Other Works on the Theory of Ethics*, trans. L. W. Beck, The University of Chicago Press (1949).

3   For a discussion of Constant's criticism of Kant see R. J. Benton, 'Political Expediency and Lying: Kant vs Benjamin Constant', *Journal of the History of Ideas*, 43, 1, (1982), 135–44.

4   For typical examples see W. Schwarz, 'Kant Refutation of Charitable Lies', *Ethics*, 81, (1970), 62, 'Truth and Truthfulness: A Rejoinder', *Ethics*, 83, (1972–73), 173–5 and W. I. Matson, 'Kant as Casuist', *Journal of Philosophy*, 51, (1954), 859. Indeed the 'rigorous' characterisation of Kant's view on lying led Bernard Williams to accuse Kant of being 'hysterical' on his treatment of lies, see *Truth and Truthfulness: An Essay in Genealogy*, Princeton University Press (2002), 106.

5   H. J. Paton, 'An alleged Right to Lie, A problem with Kantian Ethics', *Kant-Studien*, 45, (1953), 190. Paton goes as far as to claim that Kant's rigor is a problem begotten by 'bad temper in his old age', (ibid., 201). See also R. Sullivan, *Immanuel Kant's Moral Theory*, Cambridge University Press (1989), 350fn24 and S. Sedgwick, 'On Lying and the Role of Content in Kant's Ethics', *Kant-Studien*, 82, (1991), 61.

more specifically what Kant understands by the duty not to lie.[6] Such scholars point out that there are distinct senses in which lying is discussed in Kant's moral philosophy and thus, by taking these different senses into consideration, a more nuanced approach to his views on lying is observed.[7]

Found within this interpretive vein, Wood challenges the rigorist view by pointing out that Kant's account of lying is far more complex and involves distinguishing between 'declarations' that relate to intentional untruthfulness with respect to legal-right and 'falsifications' which have no such legal-right connotations, notwithstanding that such statements would technically constitute a lie.[8] Wood's treatment of Kant on lying is also particularly instructive as it fleshes out the important distinction between his notion of 'external' and 'internal' lies (*Metaphysics of Morals* 6:430). The former relates to the 'Doctrine of Right' (6:239) and the latter relates to the 'Doctrine of Virtue' (6:429–31). Unlike the notion of lying in the context of the Doctrine of Right, which considers agents lying to other agents (involving social and political considerations), Kant's notion of internal lies has been relatively neglected as a direct subject of analysis.[9] In particular, Kant's specific discussion of the relationship between conscience and internal lies, which he explicitly discusses together (6:430), has been hereunto unexplored.[10]

In this chapter I will provide the first exploration that specifically addresses Kant's notion of an internal lie in relation to his notion of conscience. I will argue that Kantian conscience must be viewed as a capacity that can keep in check self-deception and in a roundabout manner facilitate the fundamental

---

6   For example, H. E. M. Hofmeister argues that truthfulness in Kant involves the moral evaluation of the nature of a statement ('The Ethical Problem of the Lie in Kant', *Kant-Studien*, 63, (1972), 353). See also 'Truth and Truthfulness: A Reply to Dr. Schwars', *Ethics*, 82, (1972), 262–7 and C. M. Korsgaard, 'The Right to lie: Kant on Dealing with Evil', *Philosophy and Public Affairs* 15, 4, (1986), 325–49.

7   For example see both J. E. Atwell, *Ends and Principles in Kant's Moral Thought*, Nijhoff Publishers (1986), 193–4 and J. E. Mahon, 'The Truth about Kant on Lies', in *The Philosophy of Deception*, ed. C. Martin, Oxford University Press (2009), 202.

8   Wood, *Kantian Ethics*, 240–58.

9   As mentioned above, the exception being Wood's analysis. It should be noted that Mahon does discuss the notion of an internal lie however he does so only cursorily (in a single paragraph) ('The Truth about Kant on Lies', 205).

10   Although Sticker does address conscience within the context of self-deception, he does not do so with a specific discussion of the notion of an internal lie ('When the Reflective Watch-Dog Barks'). Indeed, as I will note, Sticker's treatment is flawed because of his failure to consider Kant's notion of subjective certainty as the standard by which conscientious judgement is held to.

duty to oneself, namely to maintain personhood (taken as rational agency).[11] It will also become clear that the analysis presented here supports an interpretation that reads Kant's fundamental value as rational self-governance.[12]

Central to this chapter will be an explication of Kant's treatment of the 'inner judge' as an 'ideal other', as presented in passages from the *Metaphysics of Morals* (6:429–30, 438–9). In order to interpret these passages I will first provide a conceptual analysis of lying. Secondly, I will turn to Kant's discussions of lying in terms of duties. It is only following these treatments that I will be able to fully explicate the above passages. The format of this chapter will be as follows. I begin by providing an analysis of Kant's definition of a lie as an 'intentional untruth' (*Metaphysics of Morals* 6:429–30). I will argue that there are four conditions that a lie should satisfy to be considered a lie, these being: i. intention to deceive, ii. belief, iii. background assumptions of beliefs/context of action, and iv. communicability.[13] In arguing for this I will challenge the

---

11   On Kant's notion of a duty to one's self see L. Denis, 'Kant's Ethics and Duties to Oneself', *Pacific Philosophical Quarterly*, 78, 4, (1997), 321–48 and *Moral Self-Regard. Duties to Oneself in Kant's Moral Theory*, Garland Publishing (2001), S. Engstrom, 'Deriving Duties to Oneself: Comments on Andrews Reath's "Self-Legislation and Duties to Oneself"', *The Southern Journal of Philosophy*, 36, (1997), 125–30, A. E. Hills, 'Duties and Duties to the Self', *American Philosophical Quarterly*, 40, 2, (2003), 131–42, M. Paton, 'A Reconsideration of Kant's Treatment of Duties to Oneself', *Philosophical Quarterly*, 40, 159, (1990), 222–33, A. Reath, 'Self-Legislation and Duties to Oneself', *The Southern Journal of Philosophy*, 36, (1997), 103–24; reprinted in *Kant's Metaphysics of Morals: Interpretive Essays*, ed. M. Timmons, Oxford University Press (2002), 349–70, and J. Timmermann 'Kantian Duties to the Self, Explained and Defended', *Philosophy*, 81, 317, (2006), 505–30.

12   This is of course a strong substantive claim. Discussions of Kant's fundamental value are typically centred upon either the value of the will (read: rationality) or the value of humanity. I will not enter into this debate other than, as noted above, to highlight that Kant's discussion of conscience supports the value of the will interpretation. For discussions that support the rational will interpretation see B. Herman, *The Practice of Moral Judgment*, Harvard University Press (1993), 231, Wood, *Kantian Ethics*, 55 and R. N. Johnson, 'Value and Autonomy in Kantian Ethics', in *Oxford Studies in Metaethics: Volume II*, ed. R. Shafer-Landau, Oxford University Press (2007), 133–47. For an extensive treatment of the value of humanity that explores this value in relation to the value of rational autonomy see R. Dean, *The Value of Humanity in Kant's Moral Theory*, Oxford University Press (2006).

13   This will involve an excursion into the secondary literature on lying. Due to the fact that my approach is conceptual I will only utilise examples of historical approaches to lying as cases that illustrate a particular approach to the notion of a lie. For a selection of contemporary articles that seek to define lying see D. Simpson, 'Lying, Liars and Language', *Philosophy and Phenomenological Research*, 52, 3, (1992), 623–40, C. Bagnoli, 'Self-deception: a Constructivist Account', *HumanaMente* 20, (2012), 93–116, S. Bok,

'semantic' view that language is fundamental to lying by suggesting that the condition of communicability can be fulfilled without the use of language.[14] Following this I will then explicate the distinction between lying as it relates to the duty agents have to others and as it relates to the duty agents have to one-self.[15] I will then build upon this by briefly discussing lying as it relates to the Doctrine of Right (6:239) and the Doctrine of Virtue (6:429–31). This will intro-duce Kant's notions of external and internal lies (6:430), the latter of which I will then expand upon. This involves exploring how internal lies violate the basic duty to oneself to maintain personhood (a duty grounded upon the ratio-nal nature of an agent). Finally, via the employment of the notion of 'multiple consciousness', I provide an account of how internal lies are possible and show how this notion fits with Kant's discussion of the internal court of conscience.

4.2   Lying as Intentional Untruth

In this section I will flesh out the definition of lying as 'intentional untruth' (*Metaphysics of Morals* 6:429, 430).[16] This will primarily involve a conceptual analysis of the notion of lying rather than an exegetical analysis of Kant's texts.

    Lying: Moral Choice in Public and Private Life, Pantheon Books (1978), T. L. Carson, 'The Definition of Lying', *Nous*, 40, 2, (2006), 284–306, *Lying and Deception: Theory and Practice* Oxford University Press (2010), M. L. Knapp, *Lying and Deception in Human Interaction*, Pearson Education/Penguin Academics, (2008), J. E. Mahon, 'Two Definitions of Lying', *International Journal of Applied Philosophy*, 22, (2008), 211–30, 'A Definition of Deceiving', *International Journal of Applied Philosophy*, 21, (2007), 181–94, *Lying and Deception in Everyday Life*, ed. M. Lewis and C. Saarni, The Guilford Press (1993), *Perspectives on Self-Deception*, ed. B. P. McLaughlin and A. O. Rorty, University of California Press (1988) and A. Mele, *Self-Deception Unmasked*, Princeton University Press (2001).

14   As presented by J. Kupfer, 'The Moral Presumption Against Lying', *The Review of Metaphysics*, 36, 1, (1982), 103–26. This 'semantic' view of lying is also held by R. Sorensen, 'Lying with Conditionals', *The Philosophical Quarterly*, 62, 249, (2012), 820–32 and 'What Lies Behind Misspeaking', *American Philosophical Quarterly*, 48, 4, (2011), 399–409, and Carson, 'The definition of Lying', 284–306. See also J. M. Saul, *Lying, Misleading, and What is Said: An Exploration in Philosophy of Language and Ethics*, Oxford University Press (2012).

15   On Kant's notion of a duty to others see K. M. Vogt, 'Duties to Others: Demands and Limits', in *Kant's Ethics of Virtue*, ed. M. Betzler, De Gruyter, (2008), 219–44, J. E. Mahon, 'Kant and the Perfect Duty to Others Not to Lie', *British Journal for the History of Philosophy*, 14, 4, (2006), 653–85 and P. Statton-Lake, *Kant, Duty and Moral Worth*, Routledge (2000).

16   Note also that although undefined in an explicit manner, Kant also discusses lying as untruthfulness in the *Groundwork* 4:402–3, 429–30.

One reason for this is that Kant's assertions on the definition of lying are some-what vague. For example, in the *Metaphysics of Morals* he describes lying in the case of *speakers* 'communication of one's thoughts to someone through words that yet (intentionally) contain the contrary of what the speaker thinks' (6:429) i.e. the specific case of language, whereas in *Vigilantius* he states that an agent lies 'when a person gives *signs* indicative of thoughts that he does not have (emphasis mine)' (27:700), where signs is read as any form of communication (which of course includes, but is not restricted to, words). The texts themselves thereby prove inconclusive with respect to the question as to whether Kant takes lying *qua* words to be lying in general rather than a particular kind of lying, or, whether he takes the *Vigilantius* notion of lying *qua* signs as a broader account. As the subject of this chapter is the relationship between conscience and internal lies, *prima facia* it does not appear as though the notion of 'speak-ers' in the form of an agent communicating to another agent will be in play. Indeed, as will become clear, the notion of an internal lie involves the com-munication an agent has within themselves. As such, by providing a concep-tual analysis of lying as a general class of intentional deception that contains the conceptually equivalent notions of linguistic and non-linguistic lies the necessary conditions that a lie would have to satisfy to be considered a lie will be provided. In light of these conditions the notion of an internal lie will be explored in subsequent sections.

4.2.1 *Intentionality and Untruth*

The notion of intentionality can be understood by stating that the act of lying is an *attempt to deceive*, which is to say that the *end that is sought by the act of lying is a deception*.[17] Deception can be defined widely as an act that occurs which attempts to make an agent believe it is situation A, whereas in fact it is situation B, and this belief or action arises at least in part from the action of some other agent.[18] Put more simply, lying involves intentional deception. The key point here is that lying involves the possibility that an error by an agent has come about, in some part, by the action of another (the deceiver). The error would not be a 'mistake' of some sort: rather it involves a delibera-tion or action by the one deceived that is premised upon information that is harnessed as a result of another agent, which has been presented with the intention to deceive. As such, the act of lying is an attempt at deception by

---

17   The centrality of intentionality to lying in Kant is also explored by Mahon, 'The Truth about Kant on Lies', 205. See also R. M. Chisholm and T. D. Feehan, 'The Intent to Deceive', *Journal of Philosophy*, 74, (1977), 150.

18   I have used a modified version of Simpson's definition ('Lying, Liars and Language', 623).

a deceiver regardless of whether the deception has been successful i.e. it is the intentionality of the liar that matters.[19] Moreover, intentional deception is also insensitive to the objective truth of a particular proposition. An agent may *sincerely believe* that the weather is warm when in fact it is not (in terms of objective truth) and relay this (false) belief to another agent thereby causing the other agent to also hold an objectively false belief. Due to the fact that there is no intentional act of deception taking place, the agent who relayed this (false) belief cannot be considered a liar.[20] Thus, a distinction is to be made between truth and truthfulness, where truth is akin to some matter of fact and truthfulness relates to a statement by an agent which they *believe to be true*. Indeed, in such circumstances Kant considers that such beliefs express 'sincerity', which he himself refers to as 'truthfulness' (*Metaphysics of Morals* 6:429). Thus the two aspects that are involved in lying are intentionality to deceive and belief. In the context of the definition of a lie/untruthfulness, as an intentional untruth a lie would be *the intent to deceive by communicating something that an agent themselves believes to be untrue*.[21]

4.2.2   *Background Beliefs/Context of Action*

The issue of beliefs can be expanded upon to go further than simply the belief that is held by an agent about a particular proposition. A context of action, or, put more simply, a background of beliefs, is crucial to the act of deception.[22] A 'primary deceptive intention' can be thought of as simply making the subject of the deception believe a particular thing that the deceiver believes to be false. A 'secondary deceptive intention' can be thought of as derived from the idea that there is a secondary level to the deception taking place that involves the manipulation of contextual beliefs that the agent being deceived holds. For example, in the case of a waiter providing information about the nature of the food they are serving, the customer's susceptibility to believe that the

---

19   This leads to a further differentiation, between the liar and the lied to, a distinction that Bok expands upon in *Lying*, 17–31.

20   Rather the agent is relaying incorrect information without being aware of the fact that they are wrong about the information that they are relaying. An interesting example of agents relaying incorrect information in this way is that of rumours as explored in G. W. Allport and L. Postman, *Psychology of Rumor*, Henry Hold & Co. (1947).

21   Kant's notions of sincerity and conscientiousness (discussed in Chapter 3), are conceptually identical to his notion of truthfulness. Indeed, he explicitly discusses these two notions within a discussion of conscience in *Miscarriage* and goes as far as to explicate the notions of formal and material truthfulness i.e. equivalents to formal and material conscientiousness (8:268–9).

22   Here I draw upon Simpson, 'Lying, Liars and Language', 625.

information conveyed by the waiter is accurate and true is grounded on a host of assumptions that may be reasonably taken for granted (such as the assumption that the waiter has nothing to gain from lying). Cases of a rival restaurant owner making assertions to the effect of discrediting the restaurant would be different: given the status of the rival as a financial competitor the attempts to deceive may be less convincing. This 'secondary background' is an important aspect by which deception is able to take place. The attempted deception makes use of this secondary background which is part of the act of intentional deception.

An interesting consequence of this can be seen in relation to an example of apparent deceitful sincerity. Take for example Augustine's discussion of a person knowing that there is a bandit on the road that a friend of his is about to travel along.[23] The person knows that his friend does not trust him and therefore he lies by saying that there are no bandits on the road hoping that his friend will not believe him and therefore not travel on that road.[24] The person is said to be sincere but nonetheless deceitful. This is a complicated case because there is an apparent intentional deception whose intentionality is premised on bringing about a belief which is in fact believed to be true. In this case the notion of background beliefs are key. The friend holds various assumptions about the person who is making the assertion that there are no bandits on the road, and it is in the context of these assumptions that the friend will evaluate the assertion. A discussion of whether or not the person has lied will involve considering the status of a lie when considered as a statement standing alone i.e. without consideration of who has made the statement and in what context etc., as well as a deeper analysis of the notion of intentionality to deceive. In the context of the above, it would seem that the person has not lied to their friend when the conditions of belief and the intention to deceive are taken into consideration. Although the statement alone 'there are no bandits on the road' is untrue, it is not being made with the intention to deceive.[25] In other words the person is being sincere i.e. truthful, and they are not being deceitful, if deceitful here is taken to be the intention to deceive an agent *resulting in an end* that is a false belief.

---

23 Augustine's views on lying can be found in *Treatises on Various Subjects*, ed. R. J. Deferrari, Catholic University of America Press (1952), 14, Chapter 14. The specific example of the bandit can be found in Chapters 16 and 18, see also Chapters 1 and 2.

24 Simpson also uses this example ('Lying, Liars and Language', 628).

25 For a detailed discussion of this example see Chisholm and Feehan, 'The Intent to Deceive', 153–4.

The example of the bandit is instructive because it shows that there is more to lying than simply assertions and beliefs that are untrue.[26] Moreover, the above also demonstrates that lying cannot be reduced to linguistic forms alone.[27] I shall show below that lying as 'intentional untruth' encompasses a far greater zone than simply language statements.

4.2.3   Communicability: Not Just Words

Within the secondary literature there are those who claim that lying is a semantic phenomenon.[28] For example, Joseph Kupfer claims that a distinction must be made between, non-linguistic and non-lying linguistic deception on the one hand and lying as a species of linguistic deception on the other.[29] Kupfer's claim is that lying is necessarily related to linguistics. Kupfer is correct in making the distinction between lying and deception: as lying involves intentional deception, but of course an agent can be deceived without being lied to.[30] However, it appears that there are some *prima facia* reasons for rejecting a strict relation between lying and linguistics. For an example that may serve to show how non-linguistic deception may be considered lying (taken as intentional deception rather than merely as being deceived) the case of a military tactic used in antiquity can be given. Consider an approaching or defending army, while camped at night lighting more fires then needed for the number of soldiers in that army to be kept warm and cook their food. Such an act would be done in order to give an impression to the respective opponent that there are far greater numbers than is actually the case. This is clearly an example that would constitute a non-linguistic deception (relating to the number of soldiers in the army).

---

26   This can be trivially demonstrated by examples of statements such as a worker in a company proclaiming, in relation to their employers, 'it's impossible to please them!', or a person who is hungry stating to a friend 'I could eat a horse!' In the former statement, assuming that there is no logical reason precluding the employers from being pleased (which would involve something like the claim that the employers were agents with no 'pleasurable faculty'), the worker is making an exaggerated statement that alludes to a perceived unreasonableness in the expectation of their employers. In the latter statement the hungry person is attempting to convey that they are extremely hungry. It would seem strange, and certainly inappropriate, to declare such people as liars.

27   By this I mean simply the analysis of sentences and the correspondence of claims or assertions that are being made in such sentences with respect to truth as matter of fact.

28   See Introduction to this chapter.

29   Kupfer, 'The Moral Presumption Against Lying', 104.

30   Phenomena such as innocent misunderstandings, mistakes, problems with translations etc. attest to this claim.

Although it is less straightforward to establish the case of a non-lying linguistic deception being considered as lying, it is still possible to provide an example. The example of Augustine's bandit can be modified such that a person tells a friend that there *are* bandits on a road that the friend is about to travel along when the person *knows that their friend does not trust them* and as such believes that the friend will not believe that there really are bandits on the road. The result of this may be that the friend decides to travel along that road because they do not believe the person telling them that there are bandits on the road (precisely the belief that the person was attempting to leave their friend with). In this case the friend believes there are no bandits on the road based on a non-lying statement. If it is assumed that the person claiming that there are no bandits was fully aware that in making this statement it would be taken as a lie and thus the contrary would be taken as the truth, then it seems that an intentional deception has taken place while still involving non-lying linguistics.[31] This would be akin to a non-lying deception. It is unclear how Kupfer's notion of non-lying linguistic deceptions can hold in this case. Moreover, 'non-lying' would have to be considered something like objective truth content of statements irrespective of the context within which such statements are made and the intention behind them. Although Kupfer does in fact take intentionality to be central to an account of lying as linguistic deception, he simply reduces the expressions of intentionality, with respect to lying, to linguistics.[32]

For the reasons expressed above, the idea that lying can be reduced to linguistics is to be rejected based on the notion that linguistic statements that relate to lying are made in contexts that make those statements meaningful (as in the case of the bandit), as well as the counter example of the army fires that seem to suggest non-linguistic lies.[33] To put the point more broadly, lying can be said to be a *communicated intent to deceive. Without specifying the nature of that communication*, let communication be known as any attempt to relate or affect, directed at one agent to another agent.[34] In other words, contra Kupfer's

---

31   Again, by this I mean simply the analysis of sentences and the relation of claims or assertions that may be made by such sentences that relate to the truth claims.

32   Kupfer, 'The Moral Presumption Against Lying', 104.

33   Similarly Simpson alludes to this very same point, 'while it is true that language is present and used in almost all lying, we don't exactly need language each time we lie [...] winks and shoulder shrugs may suffice' ('Lying, Liars and Language', 630).

34   For example, when Bok defines lying as 'any intentionally deceptive message which is *stated*', she does so in full acknowledgment that an agent can deceive another agent 'through gesture, through disguise, by means of action or inaction, *even through silence* (emphasis mine)'. However, although the phenomenon of lying *qua* language is to be

analysis, there are no philosophical reasons for making the claim that lying must be a linguistic phenomenon other than that of convention or definitions.

4.2.4   *The Four Conditions of a Lie*

In the above three subsections the conceptual intricacy of the notion of a lie being an 'intentional untruth' has been fleshed out. In summary: an 'intentional untruth' *qua* communicated intent to deceive, involves the following four elements:

i.   Intention to deceive: regardless of the relative consequences i.e. whether the lied to has been deceived or not.

ii.   Belief: belief about a particular proposition (resting upon the distinction between truth and untruthfulness).

iii.   Background: assumptions, beliefs, and context of action.

iv.   Communicability: very broadly defined to encompass more than linguistic statements.

These elements will be taken as the framework by which I will survey internal lies. However, before I turn to this task I will briefly outline in what sense it is that lying constitutes the violation of an agent's duty to one's self as a moral being. In order to do this it is necessary to explicate the notions of a duty to oneself and a duty to others.

4.3   Lying: A Violation of the Duty to Oneself and to Others

In this section I will outline Kant's account of the duty not to lie by explicating what exactly is being violated in the act of lying. As will be shown, when an agent engages in the act of lying they can be seen to be violating duties that they have to others (duty to others), and also violating the duty that an agent has to their own self (duty to oneself).

Kant begins his discussion of lying in the *Metaphysics of Morals* by asserting that lying is the greatest 'violation of a man's duty to himself' when regarded 'merely as a moral being' (6:429). He qualifies what he means by 'moral being' by stating that it is 'the humanity in his own person' (6:429). In the *Groundwork* he explicates what is meant by 'humanity' by asserting that 'every rational

---

understood within the wider notion of deception, for the purposes of limiting her study she delimits lying as that which is expressed linguistically. As she states, 'deception then, is the larger category, and lying forms part of it' (*Lying*, 13–4).

being exists as an end itself, not merely as a means to be used [by other wills']'
(4:428). He then defines 'rational beings' as 'persons' with the rational nature
of persons being that which is of 'absolute worth'. This absolute worth comes
about because it is the only thing that 'in itself is an end'; all other things
are worthy only conditionally and therefore contingently (4:428). Kant takes
conditionality and contingency to be problematic because if there was nothing of absolute worth then 'no supreme practical principle for reason could
be found' (4:428). From the principle that 'rational nature exists as an end in
itself' (4:428–9) he derives the Universal Humanity Formula (also known as
the Principle of Humanity)

> So act that you use humanity, whether in your own person or in the per-
> son of any other, always at the same time as an end, never merely as a
> means (4:429).[35]

Germane to this discussion is the important element present in the middle of
the formula, this being 'whether in your own person or in the person of any
other'. By this Kant is alluding to his distinction between duties to oneself and
duties to others, which he raises in the *Groundwork* (4:421) and expands on in
the *Metaphysics of Morals* (6:417). The example that he gives in regards to the
former is that of suicide, which is prohibited based upon the idea that such an
act would involve taking and using the agent's own person merely as a means.
The example he gives for the latter case is that of false promises, which is prohibited as it takes the other person as a mere means (4:430).

At first inspection when an agent lies to another person it may be thought
that they are *only* violating the duty to others. However, Kant believes that
when an agent generally acts contrary to duty (heteronomously), they are not
acting fully rationally, which is thereby a violation of their own humanity.[36]
This can be seen by observing that Kant relates acting according to duty to the
notion of *dignity*

---

35   The Universal Humanity Formula is one of multiple formulations of the Categorical
      Imperative. As Kant states in the *Groundwork* 'The above three ways of representing the
      principle of morality are at bottom only so many formulas of the very same law, and one
      of them of itself unites the other two in it' (4:436). For the purposes of this study it is not
      necessary to explicate this claim.

36   Kant terms this 'humiliation' (*Metaphysics of Morals* 6:435–6). Thus all lies lead to humili-
      ation. The notion of humiliation occurs also in the Second *Critique* (see 5:74–7, 84–5).
      For an expanded discussion of the notion that challenges Kant's idea that humiliation is
      the consequences of a consciousness of not acting according to duty, see P. Saurette, *The
      Kantian Imperative: Humiliation, Common Sense, Politics*, Toronto University Press (2005).

Reason accordingly refers every maxim of the will as giving universal law
to every other will and also to every action toward oneself, and does [...]
from the idea of the dignity of a rational being (*Groundwork* 4:434).

It is thus rational agency that grounds the notion of dignity. This is precisely
what Kant is referring to when he talks of dignity as an inner worth (4:435),
which as noted above, relates naturally to the absolute worth of rational-moral
beings.[37] It can hence be said that lying *generally* (to others and well as to oneself, encompassing duty to oneself and duty to others) violates the dignity of
moral beings. Where lying to others is not to view them with dignity by using
them as a mere means and lying to oneself is undignified because it treats oneself as a mere means (4:430, 423).[38]

In a similar fashion to the discussion in the *Groundwork*, in the *Metaphysics
of Morals* Kant explicates the violation of duty with respect to the dignity of
agents (6:429). He explains that irrespective of to whom the lie is directed
towards (others or to oneself), it must be considered a violation of morality
qua the notion of dignity. Within this context he also introduces the relationship between lying and the 'Doctrine of Right', and the more general concern
of ethics, which he discusses under the remit of the 'Doctrine of Virtue' (6:429).
In the following section I shall briefly explore the relations between lying *qua*
right and lying *qua* virtue. This distinction will then be used to explicate the
difference between internal and external lies.[39] In doing so the final background discussion will be complete. I will then turn to explore the philosophically more controversial claim of an internal lie and the role of conscience in
this conception.

4.4   Lying: Right and Virtue

4.4.1   *Lying* qua *Right*
Kant defines Right as 'every action which by itself or by its maxim enables the
freedom of each to co-exist with the freedom of everyone else in accordance
with a universal law' (*Metaphysics of Morals* 6:230). He then explicates that
the notion of Right is applied to external freedom *alone*, that is to say, actions

---

37   R. Dean discusses how the notion of humanity constitutes a value in the Kantian system
      and how it is that duties can be derived from this value (*The Value of Humanity in Kant's
      Moral Theory*, Chapters 2, 6, 7).

38   See *Metaphysics of Morals* 6:430–1.

39   The distinction between internal and external lies can be found in Baumgarten (Osawa,
      'Perfection and Morality', 231).

which directly or indirectly affect or in any way influence the actions of other agents, where other agents are taken to be free and rational beings. Thus Right concerns 'external and practical' relationships between agents that are considered free subjects (6:230–1). With respect to lying he states explicitly that 'in the doctrine of right an intentional untruth is called a lie only if it violates another's right' (6:429). He makes it clear that duties of Right are distinguished from the duties of Virtue in relation to external lawgiving

> All duties are either duties of Right (*officia iuris*), that is, duties for which external lawgiving is possible, or duties of virtue (*officia virtutis s. ethica*), for which external lawgiving is not possible (6:239).

Hence, with respect to Right Kant explains that an agent is 'authorized to do to others anything that does not in itself diminish what is theirs' (6:238). He explains that in non-juristic contexts 'untrue and insincere' communication is not a violation of Right because 'it is entirely up to [the one being communicated to] whether they want to believe [the said communication] or not' (6:238). Indeed, in a footnote he makes this clear by contrasting examples that involve Right i.e. contracts, courtrooms etc., and circumstances when an agent may simply be stating an opinion that is untrue but does not involve rights (6:238fn).[40] Regarding the latter, in legal-right terms these are not to be considered lying proper.[41] The basic distinction here is between rights and ethics.[42] I will now turn to an explication of lying *qua* virtue.[43]

---

40 See also Second *Critique* 5:44. For a discussion of the legal-right contexts of lies see Wood, *Kantian Ethics*, 240.

41 The distinction here is between communications that bear consequences upon other agents with respect to Right. Thus, Kant's position is far more nuanced than the caricatured picture presented by many commentators hostile to his view on lying (see Introduction to this chapter). For a discussion that deals specifically with the issue of lying *qua* publicity in Kant's political philosophy see O. O'Neill, *Constructions of Reason: Explorations of Kant's Practical Philosophy*, Cambridge University Press (1990), 45. See also *Metaphysics of Morals* 6:260–70.

42 However, as Wood points out, the question does remain as to 'whether the principle of right is based on the principle of morality or is independent of it [...]. Every duty of right, however, in Kant's view also generates an ethical duty, because respecting the innate right to freedom possessed by all persons is an ethical duty grounded on the right of humanity [according to the Formula of Humanity]' (*Kantian Ethics*, 241). An excursion into this issue will take the discussion beyond the remit of this paper and thus this question will be bracketed. See *Metaphysics of Morals* 6:406–7, 220, 237–8, 384–5.

43 Similar to the view of Wood (and also the view I have defended above), Korsgaard argues that unsympathetic readers of Kant attack his supposed rigorous view by ignoring the fact that his discussions are within contexts of his wider theory of human relations i.e.

4.4.2   *Lying* qua *Virtue: Internal and External Lies*

In contrast to the clear definition of Right, Kant does not define virtue as succinctly. For example, in the first paragraph of the introduction to the Doctrine
of Virtue he categorises Virtue *relative* to Right. He states

> The system of the doctrine of Right (*ius*), which deals with duties that
> can be given by external laws, and the system of the doctrine of virtue
> (*Ethica*), which treats of duties that cannot be so given (6:379).[44]

He then explicates the above by firstly outlining that 'the very concept of duty
is already the concept of necessitation (constraint) of free choice through the
law' and then secondly by stating that 'constraint may be an external constraint or a self-constraint' (6:379). When this is coupled with his account of
morally autonomous action, the constraint that is of concern with respect to
virtue is the *self-restraint* that an agent shows towards their propensity to act
heteronomously (6:382).[45] Kant explains that in the case of being constrained
by external laws, say a strong penal code, the constraint is not virtuous because
it is a product of something imposed upon the agent rather than something
that is self-imposed (6:379). As he reiterates, it is the internal determination
of an agent's action i.e. their inner freedom, which is of concern (6:380). Thus
virtuous actions relate to the exhibition of self-constraint, irrespective of any
external laws or empirical circumstances.[46]

Kant's views on lying are situated within particular contexts of action and assumptions
about the particular state of affairs when such acts take place ('The Right to Lie: Kant on
Dealing with Evil', 325–49).

44   Similarly in the Doctrine of Right Kant defines virtue relative to right and negatively, 'All
duties are either duties of Right (*officia iuris*), that is, duties for which external lawgiving
is possible, or duties of virtue (*officia virtutis s. ethica*), for which external lawgiving is not
possible' (6:239).

45   Kant states as much in the following passage, 'The moral imperative makes this constraint
known through the categorical nature of its pronouncement (the unconditional ought).
Such constraint, therefore, does not apply to rational beings as such (there could also be
holy ones) but rather to men, rational natural beings, who are unholy enough that pleasure can induce them to break the moral law, even though they recognize its authority;
and even when they do obey the law, they do it reluctantly (in the face of opposition from
their inclinations), and it is in this that such constraint properly consists.' (6:379–80).

46   See also *Metaphysics of Morals* 6:230, 383. For a discussion of the further nuances that
virtuous actions entail see P. Stratton-Lake, 'Being Virtuous and the Virtues: Two Aspects
of Kant's Doctrine of Virtue', in *Kant's Ethics of Virtue*, ed. M. Betzler, Walter de Gruyter &
Co (2008), 101–22.

Following from the above, Kant's assertion that 'a lie can be an external lie [...] or also an internal lie' (6:429) can be explicated. The key distinguishing factor between internal and external lies relates to the issue of to whom the lie is being communicated to. Kant explains that

> [B]y an external lie a man makes himself an object of contempt in the eyes of others; by an internal lie he does what is still worse: He makes himself contemptible in his own eyes and violates the dignity of humanity in his own person (6:429).

Contrary to the situation of external lies, in the case of internal lies the consequence is that an agent is always contemptible in their own eyes because in some sense the agent must be aware that they have lied to themselves. Indeed, internal lies make an agent contemptible in their own eyes because such lies are communicated *by the agent to the agent*.

An additional difference that can be pointed out between external and internal lies is that the respective courts that may evaluate such lies differ in the nature of their imputation. With respect to external lies that violate the doctrine of Right, a court may be present which has juridical *power*.[47] In contrast to this, in the case of internal lies there is no coercive possibility of reprimand. However, as will be explored below, the metaphorical 'inner court of conscience' can be read analogously with the external court and an account of the judgement of internal lies *qua* conscience can be provided. I will show that it is through the consulting of conscience that internal lies are to be reprimanded and therefore kept in check.

Thus far the discussion has touched upon the notion of lying *qua* duty to others and duty to oneself, and lying *qua* Right and Virtue. It has been shown that although an agent may technically lie, within the context of Right this may not be considered a violation of their duty to others because the nature of that lie may not be one that falls within the remit of the Doctrine of Right. It was also shown that irrespective of a lie not being considered a violation of Right, any lie (external or internal) is to be considered a violation of an agent's dignity. However, external lies (that violate Right) have the possibility of being reprimanded in a court of law with *coercive* capabilities, whereas internal lies are not liable to such coercive reprimand. In the following section I will expand upon the notion that conscience is the mechanism that Kant envisions as a force to keep internal lies in check.

---

47 See *Collins* (27:295), where Kant notes as much.

4.5   Internal Lies and Conscience

Turning now to the relationship between an internal lie and conscience, I will argue below that for Kant the capacity of conscience is an important mechanism by which internal lies are kept in check and thereby self-deception resisted. In order to show this a number of points must be explicated. The first point relates to the conceptual sense in which Kant is employing the notion of an internal lie. The second point is how this notion of an internal lie can be applied to conscience. This will involve a lengthy exegesis of passages found in *Metaphysics of Morals* (6:429–30, 438–9), conducted in light of the treatments of lying found in the preceding sections. The third point is how internal lies are kept in check by conscience. In the following subsections I will explicate these points.

4.5.1   *Self-Deception and Multiple Consciousness*
Kant expands on the notion of an internal lie by exploring how it is even possible for there to be an internal lie (*Metaphysics of Morals*, 6:429). This seems to be motivated by the apparent absurdity of taking to be true something an agent knows to be false, 'for a lie requires a second person whom one intends to deceive, whereas to deceive oneself on purpose seems to contain a contradiction' (6:430).[48] Indeed, the conception of an internal lie carries within it the problematic notion of self-deception.[49] Internal lies are problematic because their status would imply that an agent is lying to themselves about something that they believe is other than that which they hold to be true at a particular time. For example, it would seem to suggest that an agent can choose to act contrary to duty and then lie to themselves that they have acted contrary

---

48   For an in-depth discussion of the paradoxes of self-deception see J. Canfield and P. McNally, 'Paradoxes of Self-Deception', *Analysis*, 21, 6, (1961), 140–44. A first, and albeit rather crude, response to the questioning of the possibility of an internal lie would be to assert that if the notion that agents do not engage in self-deception was denied then paradoxically, the only correct answer would be to respond to the denier that they are in self-denial themselves. Such a paradoxical result is explored by Wood, 'Such paradoxes may point to the fact that self-deception is only partly voluntary, because one reasonable conclusion from them is that it may be impossible for an inner [internal] lie to be entirely conscious and deliberate. At the same time, there is clearly something culpable about the motivated inattention to evidence, or incongruous policies in the weighing of evidence that we see in cases of self-deception', (*Kantian Ethics*, 256). I shall not explore this problem here because it merely avoids the problem rather than addresses it.

49   For a discussion of this problem see M. Johnston, 'Self-Deception and the Nature of Mind', in *Philosophy of Psychology*, ed. C. MacDonald and G. MacDonald, Blackwell (1995).

to duty. Indeed, the notion of an internal lie is problematic philosophically because it represents a conscious attempt at intentionally deceiving oneself regarding a belief that an agent consciously holds. Thus the concept of an internal lie must be explicated further. The core issue that lays at the foundation of internal lies is the subject to which the lying is directed. Indeed, much of the secondary literature on the notion of lying makes it a *sine qua non* that a lie is always directed by one agent to another agent.[50] The reason for this is because deceptiveness requires manipulation of beliefs and, in cases of internal lies, the subject of the lie would be fully conscious of the manipulative actions that are being attempted in the act of deception.[51] In other words, it seems to be a contradiction in terms to assert that an intentional deception could take place when the subject is both doing the deception and is themselves the subject of the deception.[52] Such a scenario seems *prima facia* absurd.[53]

Within the secondary literature there is considerable debate regarding the possibility of self-deception.[54] One approach, which can be broadly outlined

---

50   For example, M. Mothersill writes an entire paper on lying that is premised on this assumption without once stating or arguing for this, see 'Some Questions about Truthfulness and Lying', *Social Research*, 63, 3, (1996), 913–29. See also Kupfer, 'The Moral Presumption Against Lying', 103–26.

51   As Bok succulently points out, "Is there even communication or not? If a person appears to deceive himself, there are not two different human beings of whom one intends to mislead the other. Yet, arguably, two 'parts' of this person are involved in a deceptive relationship. Are there times when the right hand does not know what the left hand is doing? And times when the left hand is in fact deceiving the right hand?" Indeed, Bok defends the possibility of genuine self-deception (*Lying*, 292fn16).

52   As Simpson succinctly puts it, 'without [...] disguise the lie could not succeed, and without the intention that there be this disguise there would be no lie' ('Lying, Liars and Language', 627).

53   Simpson states this condition formally, 'lying is something that is necessarily done to a subject or subjects other than ourselves, or at least, to a consciousness other than our own' ('Lying, Liars and Language', 626). It is interesting to note, however, that despite the seeming absurdity of self-deception, those who deny the possibility are in a minority. As John T. Saunders, a commentator on the self-deception debate, puts it, 'that we engage in self-deception is a datum. How we manage to pull it off is what needs explanation' ('The Paradox of Self-Deception', *Philosophy and Phenomenological Research*, 35, 4, (1975), 559–70). See also H. Fingarette, 'Self-Deception Needs No Explaining', *The Philosophical Quarterly*, 48, 192, (1998), 289–301.

54   As David Kipp states 'the problem still awaits convincing theoretical resolution' ('On Self-Deception', *The Philosophical Quarterly*, 30, 121, (1980), 305–17). See also A. Palmer, 'Characterising Self-deception', *Mind* (*New Series*), 88, 349, (1979), 45–58. An interesting exchange is observed in the literature between an attempt by Gustavson to model

as a separational account of self-deception, functions by asserting that there are separate centres of agency within a single person.[55] An alternative account of self-deception can be broadly outlined as non-seperational, which functions by asserting that agents can hold one belief while keeping at bay another (contradictory) belief.[56] An attempt to model Kant's notion of internal lies upon either the separational or the non-separational models of self-deception would take the discussion beyond the remit of this paper. However these models are instructive insofar as they highlight the fact that in order to understand self-deception, contradictory beliefs as multiple propositions that exist within the mind of an agent are to be considered. Below I will explicate a case in Kant's philosophy that alludes precisely to such a scenario, namely the case of self-conceit.

As a point of departure to understanding Kantian self-deception, it can be pointed out that Kant extensively and forthrightly discusses the notion of self-conceit, which I take to be a form of self-deception. For example, in the Second *Critique* he states

---

self-deception upon interpersonal deception, and Siegler who argues that there are crucial and important differences between self-deception and interpersonal deception, see D. F. Gustavson, 'Self-Deception', *Analysis*, 23, 2, (1962), 32–6 and F. A. Siegler, 'Self-Deception and Other Deception' *The Journal of Philosophy*, 60, 24, (1963), 759–64. See also R. Demos, 'Lying to Oneself', *The Journal of Philosophy*, 57, 18, (1960), 558–95; and for a criticism of Professor Demos's attempt, F. A. Siegler, 'Demos on Lying to Oneself', *The Journal of Philosophy*, 59, 17, (1962), 469–78.

55   See D. Davidson, 'Deception and Division', in *The Multiple Self*, ed. J. Elster, Cambridge University Press (1985), and D. Pears, *Motivated Irrationality*, Oxford University Press (1984). Under the remit of separational theories of self-deception fall also the psychological and psychoanalytical approaches. Such approaches are beyond the purview of this study and hence will not be explored. For an example of one such psychological approach see L. S. Newman, 'Motivated Cognition and Self-Deception', *Psychological Inquiry*, 10, 1, (1999), 59–63. For an example of a psychoanalytical approach see L. Kovar, 'The Pursuit of Self-Deception', *Salmagundi*, 29, (1975), 28–44.

56   As articulated in the work of A. R. Mele in *Irrationality: An Essay on Akrasia, Self-Deception, and Self-Control*, Oxford University Press (1987) and 'Self-Deception', *The Philosophical Quarterly*, 33, 133, (1983), 365–77. An additional approach that is exhibited in the secondary literature incorporates the findings of neuroscience by, for example, taking as a point of departure cases of supposed self-deception in brain damaged patients. For example see W. Hirstein, 'Self-Deception and Confabulation', *Philosophy of Science*, 67, *Supplement. Proceedings of the 1998 Biennial Meetings of the Philosophy of Science Association. Part II: Symposia Papers* (2000), S418–29.

> [The] propensity to make oneself as having subjective determining grounds for choice into the objective determining grounds of the will [...] making itself lawgiving and the unconditional practical principle, [is] called self-conceit (5:74).[57]

Subjective determining grounds are those which are based on inclination and thus self-conceit is an attempt to make such subjective determining grounds into law-like unconditional practical principles and thereby deceive oneself that heteronomous practical principles are autonomously generated. The self-conceit here is, as was highlighted above with respect to lying generally, an act that violates an agent's dignity. Hence self-conceit, considered as a form of self-deception, plays an important role in Kant's account of human behaviour. This is to be considered an internal lie insofar as the deception is directed by the agent to themselves with respect to the agent's self-worth i.e. their dignity as a rational agent (*Groundwork* 4:407).

Kant's account of self-conceit also demonstrates the conceptual sense within which an internal lie is to be conceived. His account of self-conceit falls within the remit of his notion of moral deliberation, which can be summarised as two distinct motivations. The motivation associated with rational action i.e. autonomy, and the motivation associated with inclination i.e. heteronomy. Indeed, Kant relates self-love, via self-conceit, to the notion of humiliation 'in our self-consciousness' (Second *Critique* 5:74). This humiliation in an agent's self-consciousness can be articulated in terms of an agent's consciousness of their rationality i.e. dignity, and the humiliation that is experienced following an awareness of their irrational behaviour in comparison to their rational nature. As such, what can be termed a 'multiple consciousness' account of self-conceit is observed between two consciousnesses that represent the respective competing motivations. This multiple consciousness can also be stated in terms of an agent becoming aware of their dual character as an agent with sensible inclinations and as a rational being who is subject to the moral law. The duality is made apparent by an agent being conscious of their failure to respect the moral law when taking their inclinations as a valid (objective) ground for action. An alternative picture is of an agent acting immorally not due to self-conceit, i.e. an agent choosing to pursue a course of action that they are aware is not objectively grounded. In such cases an agent may still experience humiliation upon realising that in pursing this course of action they would be acting contrary to the moral law. In this case, although

---

57   See also Second *Critique* 5:23, 73, 79, 85, *Groundwork* 4:408.

self-conceit is not a case that is applicable to the particular action, the agent is nonetheless still thought of in terms of multiple consciousness i.e. their experience of humiliation is premised on a consciousness of the demands that morality has placed upon them. This is to say, the agent possess a multiple consciousness in terms of their status as a rational (moral) being *qua* their choice in acting on the sensible motivation. Although this is the case, the analogy of self-conceit with the court of conscience is instructive as the internal lie is a case of an agent possessing multiple consciousness *qua* the internal court. As I will show, consciousness of the internal lie and consciousness of the internal judge represent the aspects of the multiple consciousness associated with conscience.

Kant's account of moral deliberation and self-conceit highlight this notion of a multiplicity of consciousness/dual personality. Below, I will discuss his notion of an internal lie with respect to conscience and employ a similar multiple consciousness explanatory scheme. As will become clear, his notion of an internal court of conscience—with the various constitutive conscious mental states—is vital to understanding the relationship between internal lies and conscience.

4.5.2   *Inner Judge as Ideal Other*
Kant expands upon the relationship between internal lies and conscience in a passage found in *Metaphysics of Morals* (6:429–30). Below, I will explicate this passage in terms of the four criterion of lying that I explicated earlier (namely, i. intention to deceive, ii. belief (particular proposition), iii. background assumptions, beliefs, and context of action, and iv. communicability). For exegetical purposes I have divided this passage into three steps.

> [Step 1] A human being who does not himself believe what he tells another (*even if the other is a merely **ideal** person*) has even less worth than if he were a mere thing; for a thing, because it is something real and given, has the property of being serviceable so that another can put it to some use (bold mine).

Here the concern is with the second criterion of belief and the fourth criterion of communicability. The notion of a person who does not believe what they tell another person is equivalent to saying that a person holds a particular belief but proclaims something else. Crucially this is related to the notion of an internal lie by Kant's qualification that this can take place to an 'other' that may be *ideal*. He makes clear that by this ideal 'other' what he is referring to is the notion of an inner judge of conscience

> [T]o think of a human being who is accused by his conscience as one and the same person as the judge is an absurd way of representing a court, since the prosecutor will always lose—for all duties a human being's conscience will, accordingly, have to think of someone other than himself (i.e. other than the human being as such) as the judge of his actions, if conscience is not to be in contradiction with itself. This other may be an actual or a merely ideal person that reason creates for itself (6:438–9).

As such, the inner judge is this 'ideal other' that is being lied to.[58] Kant's account of the inner judge of conscience playing the role of an idealised 'other' to whom the internal lie is directed can be explicated according to the multiplicity of consciousness picture that rests upon his notion of conscience as an internal court. As was discussed in Chapter 2, he discusses conscience within the metaphor of an internal court: for example he states that 'consciousness of an internal court in man (before which his thoughts accuse or excuse one another) is **conscience**' (6:438). From the above it can be seen that the consciousness before which an agent's 'thoughts accuse or excuse one another' is a reference to the internal judge. That Kant is asserting this picture is made clear in the following sentence where he states 'a man who accuses and judges himself in conscience must think of a dual personality in himself, a doubled self [...]' (6:439fn).[59]

---

58   See also *Vigilantius* 27:572. In *Notes on Moral Philosophy* (1783–4) although Kant does not explicitly speak in terms of the courtroom metaphor he does nonetheless describe conscience in terms of a 'three-fold personality' (18:450).

59   An interesting historical aside is the similarity of Smith's discussion of the impartial spectator as an 'ideal spectator' and his split-personality characterisation of conscience (*The Theory of Moral Sentiments*, 131–86). Smith begins by asserting that when an agent examines their own conduct they 'divide' themselves into 'two persons', in this way there is a 'judge' and 'the person judged of' (ibid., 136). Smith then outlines that there are two ways in which the spectator can be judged: either as a 'partial spectator' or as an 'impartial spectator' (ibid., 137, see also 178). The former relates to an expression of self-love (ibid., 159, 141, 148), the latter relates to the 'real truth' regarding the moral worth of an action, and it is this that is conscience (ibid., 138, 142). Describing the spectator in terms of a 'demigod' which is partly immortal and 'partly too of moral extraction', Smith uses this analogy to point out that in times when an agent is consumed by desires the spectator is closer to the mortal self (the partial), and in times when the judgement transcends these desires the spectator is closer to the 'divine part of his origin' (the impartial) (ibid., 153–4). Indeed Smith describes the spectator as an 'all seeing Judge' (ibid., 144–5) that is 'well-informed', a 'man within the breast, the great judge' (ibid., 152), the 'eyes of a third person', 'the natural eye of the mind' (ibid., 157), 'the respectable judge', the 'ideal man' (ibid., 169). Furthermore, Smith's views on conscience are similar to that of Kant's insofar

With this picture explicated, Kant then goes on to explain that an intentional untruth is being communicated to the inner judge

> [Step 2] But communication of one's thoughts to someone through words that yet (intentionally) contain the contrary of what the speaker thinks on the subject is an end that is directly opposed to the natural purposiveness of the speaker's capacity to communicate his thoughts, and is thus a renunciation by the speaker of his personality, and such a speaker is a mere deceptive appearance of a man, not a man himself.

Here the first criterion of intention to deceive and the third criterion of background beliefs are invoked. The intent to deceive is in regards to being a man. The intention is to convince the 'other' that they are still a man although they are, by the very nature of their communicated thoughts, not being a man. By 'man' Kant is referring to the notion of a person: constitutive of personhood is the rationality which grounds an agent's dignity. This very rationality and dignity is being undermined by the attempt to lie. Lying is prohibited simply as a violation of a duty incumbent upon the agent that is directed to the agent themselves when viewing themselves as a moral being, or in other words, a properly rational agent.[60]

This can be expanded upon by explication of the idea that the speaker's purpose of communication is to realise the end of communicating their thoughts. When a speaker lies they are attempting to communicate the very opposite of what they believe, 'an end that is directly opposed to the natural purposiveness

---

as his view on moral deliberation and the purpose of conscience in the counteracting of self-deception. The former is evidenced when Smith asserts that in moral deliberation an agent is faced with a situation where there are 'separate and distinct' characters existing in the mind of an agent (ibid., 170). The latter is evidenced by Smith's discussion of the role of conscience in countering 'self-deceit' (ibid., 180, 182, 185). For an in-depth discussion of Smith's impartial spectator see D. D. Raphael, *The Impartial Spectator: Adam Smith's Moral Philosophy*, Oxford University Press (2007). For further discussions of the moral views of Smith see C. L. Griswold, *Adam Smith and the Virtues of Enlightenment*, Cambridge University Press (1998), and Schneewind, *The Invention of Autonomy*, 388. For an analysis of Smith's notion of conscience that takes into account the evolution of Smith's thoughts throughout the various amended editions that were published in the lifetime of Smith see Sorabji, *Moral Conscience Through the Ages*, 171–6.

60   See *Metaphysics of Morals* 6:434–40. Kant characterises deception as contrary to a civilised condition (see *Metaphysics of Morals* 6:33–4, 149–53, 332–3) and even goes as far as speaking of deceitfulness as a 'savage' condition that is characterised by 'brutality' (*Religion* 6:33–4). See also Wood, *Kantian Ethics*, 254.

of the speaker's capacity to communicate his thoughts'. Commenting upon the
same passage, Kupfer makes this point with respect to language

> An inherent end of speech is the communication of belief. On this teleo-
> logical view [...] lying runs counter to this natural end of language. [...]
> since the liar necessarily shares in this [use] of language, he opposes
> himself by lying. He opposes himself as a language user and as a thinker
> dependent upon the cogency of his language use. Language is that
> through which we think, with ourselves as well as others. Lying sets lan-
> guage against the linguistic fabric on which the effectiveness of the liar's
> thinking depends. It thereby jeopardizes the coherence of his beliefs and
> his self-knowledge.[61]

The 'fabric' discussed here is equivalent to the criterion of background beliefs.
However, instead of language it is rationality that can be substituted to serve
the same purpose. Rationality provides the background belief that is used
in the attempt to deceive. This may occur in a number of ways. For example,
it may be taken for granted that a rational agent will not behave contrary to
reason, or that the agent who is going to lie may be attempting to deceive the
other by making use of the assumption that the person they are lying to will
rationally evaluate evidence. On this latter point, the liar will be assuming that
the person they are attempting to deceive can weigh up evidence, make relevant and appropriate inferences and various other types of rational actions
that the assumption that an agent is rational begets. In the case of the internal
lie, the object of the deception is the agent's own self and as such the agent
will be 'opposing themselves' and thereby jeopardizing the coherence of their
own beliefs and self-knowledge. Thus internal lies corrupt the very fabric of
rationality leading to the erosion of an agent's personhood. Finally Kant states

> [Step 3] Truthfulness in one's declarations is also called honesty and, if
> the declarations are promises, sincerity; but, more generally, truthfulness
> is called rectitude. Lying [...], need not be harmful to others in order to
> be repudiated [... i.e.] a violation of the rights of others. It may be done
> merely out of frivolity or even good nature; the speaker may even intend
> to achieve a really good end by it. But his way of pursuing this end is, by
> its mere form, *a crime of a man against his own person* and a worthless-
> ness that must make him contemptible in his own eyes (emphasis mine).

---

61   Kupfer, 'The Moral Presumption Against Lying', 118.

This final step falls in to the first criterion of intent to deceive. It provides an example of what is meant by 'regardless of the relative consequences'. The 'mere form' of the intentional untruth (corresponding to the criterion stipulated above) is enough to constitute a crime against one's personhood. This will make an agent contemptible in their own eyes.

The central concern regarding the possibility of internal lies, namely the issue of to whom the lie is communicated to, is fulfilled by the inner judge of conscience (considered as an ideal person). Indeed, with respect to the internal lie what is taking place is an attempt to deceive the inner judge (and thereby the verdict of reason) with respect to the consciousness of what is believed concerning the diligence with which an act was evaluated. This becomes clear when it is noted that Kant tells us 'insincerity is mere lack of conscientiousness, that is, purity in one's professions before one's *inner* judge' and crucially he qualifies this statement by stating that the inner judge is '*thought of as another person when conscientiousness is taken quite strictly* [...]' (emphasis mine, 6:430). The consciousness that is attempting to deceive, i.e. telling the internal lie, is making the subject of their proposed deception the form of consciousness that is the inner judge. Kant calls such attempts to communicate the thoughts of an internal lie an 'inner end' (6:430). Two consciousnesses can be envisioned, the first consciousness of the will attempting to deceive the internal judge and the second consciousness that is the internal judge itself.

An internal lie is possible because it constitutes an *attempt* in the internal tribunal by the practical will to deceive the inner judge.[62] Crucial to understanding this phenomenon is the temporal nature of the internal lie, i.e. it takes place in a telic fashion.[63] The movement is towards the end of attempting to deceive the internal judge and all of this takes place between conscious immediate determinations in the mind of an agent.[64] This also touches

---

62   An additional nuance that can be introduced is the notion asserted by some philosophers that there is a difference between belief (which is dispositional) and thinking (which is occurrent). This distinction is not relevant here because there is no sense in which any of the beliefs that relate to the internal court are 'passive' i.e. not involved in thinking (occurrent). For an exposition of this see K. Bach, 'An Analysis of Self-Deception', *Philosophy and Phenomenological Research*, 41, 3, (1981), 351–70 and J. L. Bermúdez, 'Self-Deception, Intentions, and Contradictory Beliefs', *Analysis*, 60, 4, (2000), 309–19.

63   For a discussion of the relationship between temporality and self-deception see D. Polonoff, 'Reflections on the Self', *Social Research*, 54, 1, (1987), 45–53, see also R. A. Sorensen, 'Self-Deception and Scattered Events' *Mind, New Series*, 94, 373, (1985), 64–9.

64   For a discussion of what is taking place within the consciousness of an agent (when self-deception occurs) see R. Holton, 'What is the Role of the Self in Self-Deception', *Proceedings of the Aristotelian Society*, 101, (2001), 53–69. See also P. Noordhof, 'Self-

upon the relationship between conscience and the notion of 'inner sense'. As Kant explains in the First *Critique*, outer sense is the faculty through which an agent intuits outer appearances, that is to say objects in space (B291), and inner sense is the faculty through which an agent intuit themselves and their own inner states (A33/B49). There is what Kant calls 'subjective' or 'empirical' consciousness. This is the empirical 'I' that concerns space (related to outer sense) and temporality (related to inner sense).[65] The dominate readings of these notions are that inner and outer sense are coextensive.[66] However there are some readings that suggest that temporal consciousness could be taken as primarily inner or subjective. This reading, as summarised by Valaris, has it that 'the application of temporal properties and relations to outer appearances is secondary, and mediated by inner temporality' (see also A34/B50–1).[67] The argument being that some states are intrinsically temporal, that is 'they have durations, temporal parts, beginnings and ends in time'.[68] With respect to conscience there is clearly a parallel here. The inner court of conscience is structurally organised in time: the internal judge is passing judgement upon the immediate awareness that concerns the diligence with which a case has been evaluated. For the present purposes it is unnecessary to make the highly substantive claim that conscience hinges upon a *clear* priority of inner sense over outer sense.[69] It suffices to say that insofar as the judgement of conscience *qua* the internal judge is concerned only inner sense is involved, but insofar as the subsumption of what the various faculties generate (taking into consideration empirical datum) outer sense must be involved. I will refrain from further exploring this point here.[70]

Deception, Interpretation and Consciousness', *Philosophy and Phenomenological Research*, 67, 1, (2003), 75–100.

65   The notion of inner sense *qua* self-consciousness is discussed under the remit of the Transcendental Unity of Apperception (First *Critique* B136–144). Importantly, Kant does not identify the transcendental with the noumenal, as such the assertions I make above should not be read as equivocating the two. In other words the claim here is not that the distinction between the transcendental and empirical I is identical with the I as noumenon and phenomenon.

66   For a detailed discussion see Allison, *Transcendental Idealism*.

67   M. Valaris, 'Inner Sense, Self-Affection, and Temporal Consciousness', *Philosophers' Imprint*, 8, 4, (2008), 11.

68   Ibid., 12.

69   Valaris calls this "a 'radical' account of the interiority of time" (ibid., 13).

70   For a discussion that explores the theme of conscience and practical apperception in the *Lectures on Ethics* see Hoffmann, 'Gewissen als praktische Apperzeption', 424–4.

In the following subsection I will show that although the *attempt* at an internal lie is possible, because the judgement of conscience cannot err *qua* subjective certainty, such attempts *qua* conscience will always fail.

4.5.3   *Truthfulness as Fundamental Duty to Oneself*

In the moral self-reflection that is the consulting of conscience and the corresponding judgement that occurs, an agent is faced with a situation where there is a belief about a particular action that either has, or has not, been diligently examined. As such, with respect to conscience an internal lie is a consciousness that seeks to convince the inner judge that the action has been diligently examined contrary to a (subjectively certain) belief that it has not. For a successful internal lie to have occurred, the case of the internal court of conscience generating a deceived subjective certainty would have to be realised. As explicated in Chapter 3, Kant explicitly denies this possibility. As such, with respect to the judgement of conscience, there can be no equivalent to self-conceit i.e. successful self-deception. The notion of an agent's belief about their own judgement of conscience being subject to manipulation by an agent themselves *viz.* the internal lie, would erode the very possibility of a non-erring conscience, which is grounded on the notion of subjective certainty. Instead of experiencing the pang of conscience upon consulting one's conscience, an agent would simply be able to lie to themselves about the verdict.[71]

---

71   It is on this point that Sticker's analysis is particularly flawed ('When the Reflective Watch-Dog Barks'). Sticker's article relies on an apparent tension, namely, 'there is a tension between Kant's emphasis that self-deception is a pervasive part of human existence and his optimism that conscience can never be fully deceived' (ibid., section 4, similarly Ware also identifies this apparent tension 'The Duty of Self-Knowledge', 685). Such tension is quite adequately dispelled by pointing out the fact that Kant is speaking of different epistemic classes of self-deception; self-deception with respect to the self and one's true motivations (c.f. opacity thesis) and self-deception with respect to subjective certainty (the concern of conscience). Indeed, this is further evidenced by the fact that Sticker speaks of conscience, when properly functioning, as making 'the purity and strictness of the moral law the focal point of [...] deliberation' ('When the Reflective Watch-Dog Barks'): although there are important ways in which the judgement of conscience can indirectly cause the agent to realise things about the way in which they have come to particular first-order moral judgements (as I have explored in the latter sections of Chapter 3, for example with respect to constant conjunction), the immediate concern of conscience is the diligence with which an agent has come to a particular action not the 'purity' of the moral law. A similar criticism can be applied to Ware's account of the role of conscience *qua* self-deception ('The Duty of Self-Knowledge', 690–8).

The point can be illustrated by explicating Kant's two examples of attempted internal lies (*Metaphysics of Morals* 6:430). Both examples can be termed 'religious lies' because in both cases the discussion is in term of a 'future judge', which is a reference to a particular conception of God. Such internal lies are motivated by an attempt to convince the agents themselves that i. by lying to themselves about truly believing in God, if it later turns out there is in fact a God then they will be in 'favour in the case should he exist', and ii. the agent can lie to themselves about acting in a manner that appears to be in accordance with the laws of God, 'through an inward reverence for his law (in a vain act of flattery), when in fact they are acting according to the God's law feeling only fear and seeking to avert punishment' (6:430).[72]

The manner in which such internal lies are supposed to function is that in some way the agent does not believe a particular proposition but nonetheless affirms that they do. Pascal's wager provides a good example because recourse to such a 'reason' concerning the belief in God is premised on a failure to secure the belief in a manner that is fully convincing to the agent.[73] In fact Pascal's wager is *based upon this failure*, for if the agent truly held a belief in God then they would not engage in such machinations.[74] In more generic terms, such internal lies are cases of a proposed proposition being asserted as true by an agent, not because the agent believes in the truth of the proposition

---

72   In similar terms, Wood summarises this type of internal lie by stating, 'The first kind of inner lie includes various styles of religious apologetics, such as Pascal's wager and James's will to believe. We wish to believe something (because we wish it were true, or because it would be flattering to us if it were true), and we satisfy the wish by telling ourselves we believe it, acting as if we believe it and associating with others who are lying to themselves in the same way until eventually we do come to believe it. Whatever advantages (real or imagined) we may acquire in this way are purchased at the cost of our integrity and self-respect' (*Kantian Ethics*, 256).

73   B. Pascal, *Pensees*, part 3, section 233. For a similar discussion see W. James, *The Will to Believe*, (1896). See also P. Gardiner, 'Error, Faith and Self-Deception', *Proceedings of the Aristotelian Society*, 70, (1969–1970), 221–43.

74   J. L. Longeway describes such a situation as one of escapism, which he defines as 'the attempt to avoid awareness of aversive beliefs'. The case explicated above is not strictly 'escapism' because an agent is not avoiding the belief, but rather asserting the contrary belief *despite* believing otherwise. Nonetheless Longeway's discussion provides a host of reasons why an agent would engage in such an act as well as how they may go about doing so pragmatically ('The Rationality of Escapism and Self-Deception', *Behavior and Philosophy*, 18, 2, (1990), 1–20). See also papers by R. Audi, 'Self-Deception and Practical Reasoning', *Canadian Journal of Philosophy*, 19, 2 (1989), 247–66 and 'Self-Deception, Action, and Will', *Erkenntnis*, 18, 2, (1975), 133–58.

i.e. is subjectively certain of it, but rather because the agent believes that some advantage will come about by asserting that this proposition is true.[75]

Notice that both examples can be read as corresponding to the notion of the analogues of conscience. As discussed in Chapter 3, Kant readily acknowledges various phenomena that appear to be the pangs of conscience but are rather the result of a false notion of conscience. The cases that he cites above as religious internal lies correspond to what he terms the 'prudential conscience' (*Herder* 27:25, see also *Collins* 27:355–6).[76] Kant's differentiation of conscience proper from the analogues of conscience is important in this context because it shows that internal lies can be successful only when conscience proper is not consulted. Indeed, as was shown in Chapter 3, according to Kant when conscience proper is consulted then a non-erring judgement will result.[77] As such, his *conception of conscience is an important mechanism to the keeping in check of internal lies*, religious or otherwise, insofar as it is a capacity that when genuinely consulted cannot err in its verdict.[78]

Indeed, Kant's discussion of the need for rigorous examination of beliefs i.e. the consulting of conscience, is derived from his belief that agents are inclined to deceive themselves. In *Vigilantius* he states that

---

75   It may be argued that Pascal's wager is a bad example. The reason for this is because it seems to constitute a case of lacking a belief for or against God rather than disbelieving in God. Perhaps a better example, within the religious theme that Kant is discussing, is the case of Peter denying Christ three times (*The Gospel of Luke* 22:59–62).

76   Kant gives the example of repentance that occurs on a death bed. He denies that this is conscience and maintains that this is due to prudential reasoning. The repentance on the death bed is driven by the impending judgement that will occur before God. In this circumstance the repentance of the agent is not because the agent is remorseful about their 'evil deed' with respect to the moral law i.e. they are not sorry that they have contravened the moral law, but rather they are repenting in order to avoid the punishment that the agent has brought upon themselves. Repenting, feeling remorse, and reproaches are only valid when occurring because of a consciousness regarding the violation of morality, otherwise they are just 'reproaches because of the consequences of imprudence' and thus 'these two things must in no way be confused' (*Collins* 27:353).

77   Furthermore this also corresponds to the case of the Inquisitor that Kant raises in *Religion* 6:187, which I have explicated in Chapter 3.

78   In the *Metaphysics of Morals* Kant expands on the duty to oneself (6:413). Kant makes use of the distinction, which he had explicated in the First *Critique*, between the sensible and intelligible aspects of an agent (6:418) and then tells us that it is only through morally practical relations that an agent becomes aware of the otherwise unattainable aspect of man, namely freedom (6:418). Kant explains that through the consciousness of inner freedom, an agent has an obligation to himself through the humanity in his own person (6:418).

Man is only too readily inclined to persuade himself of something, and conjure up more than the truth. There are tendencies, indeed, in the souls of many, to make no rigorous judgement of themselves—an urge to dispense with conscience. If this lack of conscientiousness is already, in fact, present, we never get that person to deal honestly with himself. We find in such people that they are averse to any close investigation of their actions, and shy away from it, endeavouring, on the contrary, to discover subjective grounds on which to find a thing right or wrong (27:616–7).

Here Kant is highlighting the central role that conscience plays in getting a 'person to deal honestly with [themselves]'. The clear implication is that conscience counters self-deceit (which is of course specifically framed in terms of whether an agent has acted rightly *qua* their conscientious judgement).

When the above is taken into consideration the capacity of conscience can be thought of as a capacity that, if and when consulted, will reveal to the agent whether or not they have lied to themselves regarding the rightfulness of their action. With respect to duty, Kant stresses that in lying to oneself an agent uses oneself as a 'mere means (a speaking machine)' (6:430), and as such, agents are 'under obligation to [oneself] to truthfulness [taken as a duty proper]' (6:430). He relates lying, as insincerity, to conscience and takes the perpetual act of insincerity—which is to assert something that is contrary to what an agent is subjectively certain about, or to knowingly act against the non-erring verdict of conscience—as an erosion of moral worth (6:430).[79] Thereby, the importance of conscience can also be stated in terms of personal integrity, where to consult and act in accordance with one's conscience is to harmonise the moral-rational action of an agent with their rational-self (here in the form of the internal judge).[80] In *Vigilantius* Kant states

The doctrine of conscience is of the greatest importance in morals. *Conscientia*, taken generally, is the consciousness of our self, like *apperceptio; in specie* it involves consciousness of my will, my disposition to do right, or that the action be right, and thus equals a consciousness of what duty is, for itself (24:613–4).

---

79 This also concurs with Kant's description of 'old scoundrels who have been prevaricating for so long, that in time [conscience] is stifled, and a sham version takes over' (*Herder* 27:42).

80 Conscience here being a sufficient but not necessary condition of personal integrity.

Here the centrality of conscience is made clear by the fact that conscience is equated with consciousness of what duty is for itself, which I read in terms of the imperative to act rationally and thereby in accordance with the inner worth and dignity of what it means to be a moral agent. The passage also touches upon the theme of maintaining personal identity insofar as the apperception of an agent in terms of what the agent holds-to-be-true (consciousness of the will) regarding what they believe is the right action and the awareness of what they intend to do (the disposition to do right), is brought forth in the self-consciousness that is conscience.[81]

This also lends credence to the claim that the reason why Kant views truthfulness, (read here as being conscientious) as the 'highest principle' (6:431) is because of the fundamental value that he ascribes to reason. The suggestion here is that the reason why truthfulness is of such value is because Kant's ethical system is grounded on notions such as dignity and humanity that are themselves premised on the value of rational self-governance. It is reason itself (whose capacity resides in humans), which secures objective ethical truth. To engage in self-conceit and self-deception is not only to act contrary to duty by using oneself as a mere thing, it is also to devalue and erode the very foundation of what it means to be a rational being and an agent whose actions have moral worth.[82] Therefore the importance of the capacity of conscience cannot be understated when it is pointed out that Kant considers truthfulness to be of the highest importance.[83] To reiterate the point: the capacity of conscience must be viewed as a capacity that can keep in check the self-deception that is the internal lie and in a roundabout manner facilitate the fundamental duty to oneself, namely to maintain personhood.[84]

---

81   Although I have argued against Moyar's reading of Kantian conscience, his analysis is strong insofar as it highlights the important relationship between conscience and self-consciousness (where conscience is a form of moral self-consciousness), see 'Unstable Autonomy', 347–54.

82   See also Wood, *Kantian Ethics*, 257.

83   For a discussion in the literature of the relationship between self-deception and valuing truth see M. Forrester, 'Self-Deception and Valuing Truth', *American Philosophical Quarterly*, 39, 1, (2002), 31–47.

84   In a discussion regarding a person having to teach something that they themselves do not believe, Leibniz asserts that provided the person does not put themselves in 'great danger' the person should 'frankly declare where he stands and resign from his post', for in this way, he argues, the 'rights of society to prevent something it judges to be bad [can be reconciled with the fact that] the individual can't excuse himself from the duties laid on him by his conscience' (*New Essays on Human Understanding*, 520). Leibniz's position

4.6   Conclusion

Chapter 4 followed as a natural corollary to the discussion of the non-erring judgement of conscience found in Chapter 3. As such it demonstrates the intricate relation between the Absurdity Thesis and the resistance to the notion of internal lies that conscience provides. Indeed, the notion of subjective certainty provides the foundation upon which Kant can present conscience as a mechanism that resists a particular class of self-deception. Notice also that this chapter, in explicating the internal lie, expands upon the theme that conscience is a *turn inwards*. The interiority of the judgement is via the court accessing what an agent holds to be true (i.e. subjective certainty). This is an important step in understanding the Unity Thesis: conscience is not only a higher-order moral judgement, it is also a mechanism that functions in the maintenance of personhood (taken here in terms of rational agency). Nonetheless, the multiple consciousness model that I have provided regarding the internal court of conscience requires further elaboration. I will turn to this task in Chapter 5.

---

appears to both assert the moral primacy of conscience while acknowledging and accommodating for the type of concerns that lead both Hobbes and Locke to their characterisation of conscience. As such, Leibniz, unlike Kant, does not address the issue in terms of internal lies.

The Cultivation of Conscience and Moral Self-Improvement

5.1   Introduction

In the Kantian scheme moral self-improvement is the process of self-correction and the movement towards moral perfection.[1] Moral improvement does not concern the constitutive *capacities of moral agency* (such as rationality), but rather the *correct exercising* of such capacities in morally permissible manners. Kant's views on moral improvement typically involve either a discussion of his views on education or a discussion of his views on the teleological postulate that allows agents to conceive of history as improving.[2] In the former case scholars typically comment on his discussions on education as presented in the Second *Critique*.[3] In the latter case scholars often point to ideas that are present in his political philosophy regarding such things as public reasoning and law,[4] as well as ideas that are present in his moral philosophy such as the notion of an ethical community.[5] An alternative avenue that is explored pays attention to the function of religion.[6] Within the secondary literature Munzel

---

1   See *Metaphysics of Morals* 6:444–6. I will expand upon these passages below.

2   For an overview and analysis of Kant's views on history see Y. Yovel, *Kant and the Philosophy of History*, Princeton University Press (1980). See also P. Kleingeld, 'Kant, History, and the Idea of Moral Development', *The History* of *Philosophy Quarterly*, 16, 1, (1999), 59–80. For a more focused analysis of Kant's views with respect to history and political improvement see O. O'Neill, *Constructions of Reason*, Cambridge University Press (1989), 39–42.

3   See Second *Critique* 'Doctrine of Method' (5:151–63). For examples in the secondary literature that centre on the Second *Critique* see B. Herman, 'Training to Autonomy: Kant and the Questions of Moral Education' in *Philosophers on Education*, ed. A. O. Rorty, Routledge (1998), 255–72 and *The Practice of Moral Judgment*, K. A. Moran 'Can Kant Have a Theory of Moral Education?', *Journal of Philosophy of Education*, 43, 4, (2009), 471–84, and *Kant and Education*, ed. K. Roth and C. W. Surprenant, Routledge (2012).

4   See M. Lucht, 'Toward Lasting Peace, Kant On Law, Public Reasoning and Culture', *American Journal of Economics and Sociology*, 68, 1, (2009), 303–26.

5   See S. R. Stroud, 'Rhetoric and Moral Progress in Kant's Ethical Community', *Philosophy and Rhetoric*, 38, 4, (2005), 328–54.

6   See A. W. Wood, 'Religion, Ethical Community and the Struggle against Evil', *Faith and Philosophy*, 17, 498–511, A.-G. Sharon, 'God and Community: An Inquiry into the Religious

correctly identifies that conscience functions in Kant's conception of practical reason through its role in the notion of 'subjective practicality' (Second *Critique* 5:151), which is the putting into practice of moral principles within an agent's life.[7] As such, Kant's notion of conscience also falls within his notion of moral self-improvement. However, although Munzel mentions that Kant speaks about conscience in religious and non-religious ways he fails to explain why he does so. Rather Munzel merges Kant's treatment into the single concern.[8]

In this chapter I will explicate Kant's account of moral self-improvement with respect to the cultivation of conscience, particularly through religious conceptions. I argue that the reason he employs rational religious notions in his various treatments of conscience is because he believes that such representations present a more effective means, relative to non-religious rational representation, by which conscience is to be cultivated as an indirect duty. I will also argue that Kant's claim is philosophically plausible.

In order to achieve this, I begin by outlining that for Kant moral self-improvement involves three notions of perfection, namely i. 'pragmatic perfection' (concerned with the proper use of an agent's capacities), ii. 'agent perfection' (concerned with attaining a disposition of always choosing to act morally) and iii. 'end perfection' (concerned with the notion of the highest good, which is the notion of an idealised world). I then turn to explicating the cultivation of conscience in terms of Kant's warnings against 'bad conscience' (*Herder* 27:43–4, see also *Collins* 27:356–7, *Vigilantius* 27:619–20), which is a conscience that is deficient in terms of practical action. Following this I then explicate Kant's notion of an agent having an 'indirect duty' (*Metaphysics of Morals* 6:401) to cultivate their conscience. Building upon Timmermann's analysis, which holds that the cultivation of conscience is analogous to the cultivation of happiness, I will show that a limit to this analogy is that unlike happiness the cultivation of reason can never result in an agent having to go

---

Implications of the Highest Good', in *Kant's Philosophy of Religion Reconsidered*, ed. P. J. Rossi and M. Wreeen, Indiana University Press (1991), 113–31.

7   G. F. Munzel, 'What does his Religion Contribute to Kant's Conception of Practical Reason?', in *Kant's Religion within the Boundaries of Mere Reason: A Critical Guide*, ed. G. E. Michalson, Cambridge University Press (2014), 214–32.

8   Although Moyar does discuss Kant's description of the internal judge as God, he does not do so in terms of comparison with the non-religious description of the internal judge as an 'ideal person' ('Unstable Autonomy', 346–7, 353, 356–8). Instead, Moyar discusses the internal judge as God in terms of self-consciousness. Similarly Esser offers no comparative analysis but states that the inner judge can be thought of as analogous to God and that projecting the inner judge as God 'stabilises' the inner court of conscience ('The Inner Court of Conscience', 272, 281–3).

against their conscience.[9] I will then explicate that conscience is cultivated through 'rational representation' (6:400), detailing how the notion of 'holiness' can function as an aspirational ideal that an agent can strive towards. Against Munzel's single treatment of Kant's discussion of conscience in religious and non-religious manners, I will argue that for Kant religious representations can have a greater effect (in comparison to non-religious representations) on the cultivation of conscience and that this claim is philosophically plausible.[10]

5.2   Moral Self-Improvement

In the *Metaphysics of Morals* Kant explicates that the 'First Command of All Duties to Oneself' is to 'know (scrutinize, fathom) thyself' (6:437). He then explains that this moral self-knowledge is 'in terms of your moral perfection in relation to your duty' (6:441). Expanding upon this he asserts

> For in the case of man, the ultimate wisdom, which consists in the harmony of a being's will with its final end, requires him first to remove the obstacle within (an evil will actually present in him) and then to develop the original predisposition to a good will within him, which can never be lost. (Only the descent into the hell of self-knowledge can pave the way to godliness.) (6:441).

Here the duty to scrutinize oneself is related to a 'final end' (the 'ultimate wisdom'), which brings about the 'original predisposition to a good will'. Kant is not claiming that through the scrutinizing of oneself agents can access the moral knowledge of their motivations. In fact he clearly asserts that agents can never know with certainty what their motivations are (*Groundwork* 4:407). Rather by predispositions, Kant is referring to the capacities that the agent possess by virtue of being an agent endowed with reason and freedom. The central claim of concern to the present chapter is the fact that Kant is

---

9   Timmermann, 'Kant on Conscience', 294.

10   Munzel, 'What does his Religion Contribute to Kant's Conception of Practical Reason?', 231. Similarly, Sticker correctly raises the fact that Kant speaks of the ideal other as God, but then fails to explore the full significance of this ('When the Reflective Watch-God Barks', section 3). Again, Ware merely notes Kant's assertions concerning conscience as 'God', and then fails to explore the significance of this at all ('The Duty of Self-Knowledge', 689).

connecting the notion of 'cognising of oneself' and 'moral perfection in relation to [one's] duty'.

Developing on the above, Kant discusses what it is for an agent to 'develop and increase his natural' and 'moral perfection' (6:446–7). With respect to the former he explains that 'a human being has a duty to himself to cultivate (*cultura*) his natural powers [...] as a means to all sorts of possible ends' (6:444). He makes clear that by 'possible ends' what he has in mind is 'a pragmatic purpose', this duty being derived from the fact that 'he owes it to himself (as a rational being) not to leave idle and, as it were, rusting away the natural predispositions and capacities that his reason can someday use' (6:644).[11] Kant is to be read here as referring to the fact that although agents are by definition endowed (predisposed) with various capacities (termed by him as 'powers'), in order for the agent to function properly these capacities must be maintained and developed. Kant provides a list of three powers that are to be developed. The power of the 'spirit' (theoretical reason), the 'soul' (practical reason) and the 'body' (physical health) (6:455). Given that conscience is a particular manifestation of practical reason, germane to the present chapter is the second of these, with respect to which Kant states

> [T]he power of the soul [...] whose [exercises] are at the disposal of understanding and the rule it uses to fulfil whatever purpose one might have, and because of this experience is their guide, [this includes] memory, imagination, and the like, on which [...] furnishes instruments for a variety of purposes (6:455).

He explains that with respect to all the powers an agent possesses, the duty is to 'make these natural perfections his end', which I read as the imperative to develop and maintain them as much as possible. He explains that this is necessary because whatever 'life [one] would choose to lead' (6:445) these powers must be properly functioning for a meaningful choice to be made at all.[12] Due

---

11   See also *Groundwork* 4:423 where Kant discusses the imperfect duty to cultivate one's natural talents.

12   Kant tells us that this duty is an 'imperfect duty' because although 'it does contain a law for the maxim of actions [i.e. maintain and develop one's natural powers], it determines nothing about the kind and extent of actions themselves but allows for a latitude of free choice' (6:446). For the present purposes it suffices to think of imperfect duties simply as duties where an agent has some flexibility in how they fulfil them, which compares to perfect duties where there is no flexibility in how they are fulfilled (for example the duty not to lie).

to the fact that he describes natural perfection in terms of reaching possible ends, I shall term the cultivation described above 'pragmatic perfection'.

Kant then turns to the duty to increase one's moral perfection (which he qualifies by stating 'for a moral purpose only' (6:446)). He states

> *First*, this perfection consists subjectively in the *purity* (*puritas moralis*) of one's disposition to duty, namely, in the law being by itself alone the incentive, even without the admixture of aims derived from sensibility, and in actions being done not only in conformity with duty but also *from duty*. Here the command is "be holy." *Second*, as having to do with one's entire moral end, such perfection consists objectively in fulfilling all one's duties and in attaining completely one's moral end with regard to oneself. Here the command is "be perfect." But man's striving after this end always remains only a progress from *one* perfection to another (6:446).

In the above Kant is speaking about perfection in two distinct manners. In the first case he refers to a purity of disposition, which is to act such that the law alone is the incentive i.e. autonomously. This can be thought of as an agent who is disposed to always acting according to the moral law (being 'holy') and as such I shall term this 'agent perfection'.[13] In the second case he articulates perfection in terms of an agent's 'entire moral end', an ideal world that an agent can hope to realise (I shall expand upon this later) and as such I shall term this 'end perfection'.[14]

These three notions of perfection require further elucidation. In the following sections I will explicate these notions in terms of Kant's theory of conscience. I will briefly flesh out pragmatic perfection in terms of conscience as this is relatively straightforward and then turn to discussing conscience in terms of agent and end perfection with a more extended discussion.

---

13   A similar passage can be found in *Collins* where Kant relates the ideal of holiness to the pursuit of perfection *qua* moral improvement as a philosophical ideal 'The ideal of holiness, as philosophy understands it, is the most perfect ideal for it is an ideal of the greatest purely moral perfection, but because such a thing is unattainable by man, it is based upon a belief in divine assistance. [...] The principles of morality are presented in all their holiness, and now the command is: You are to be holy; but because man is imperfect, this ideal has an adjunct, namely divine assistance' (27:252–3).

14   It should be noted that similarly to pragmatic perfection, Kant also demarcates moral perfection as an imperfect duty 'because of the frailty (*fragilitas*) of human nature' (6:447).

5.3   Pragmatic Perfection

In this section I will firstly discuss the role of conscience in moral improvement with respect to time i.e. conscience before, after and during an action
(*Vigilantius* 27:618). Secondly, I will discuss Kant's notion of a 'bad conscience'
(*Herder* 27:43–4, see also *Collins* 27:356–7, *Vigilantius* 27:619–20), which is a
conscience that is deficient in its practicality. These two discussions will show
that for Kant what is central is the use of conscience to enhance moral practical action and this is related to pragmatic perfection because the enhance-
ment of moral practical action is achieved by the correct use of conscience in
such action.[15]

5.3.1   *Conscience Before, During and After*
Within the historical context there are numerous philosophers who discuss
the operation of conscience with respect to time.[16] For example Shaftesbury,
Hutcheson, Smith and Wolff, all discuss conscience before and after an act.[17]
Of these discussions Smith's account is most detailed with regard to the

---

15   It is likely that Kant is reacting to Baumgarten, who follows his assertion that conscience
      can err with various characterisations of conscience, these being: i. an 'approving con-
      science' (also denoted as a good conscience), concerning legitimate deeds, ii. a 'disap-
      proving conscience' (also denoted as a bad conscience), concerning illegitimate deeds,
      iii. a 'too lax' conscience that approves illegitimacy, and iv. a 'too strict' conscience that
      disapproves legitimacy. Baumgarten asserts that 'straightforward conscience, which
      is to be sought, is neither too lax nor too strict' (Osawa, 'Perfection and Morality', 131),
      which I read as an influence on Kant's own notions of micrological, morbid and nagging
      consciences (explored below). In contrast to Baumgarten's characterisation of bad con-
      science in terms of the disapproving of illegitimate deeds, note that Kant's notion of bad
      conscience refers to consciences that retard practical action.
16   Although I will discuss various thinkers below, it is likely that Kant's talk of antecedent
      and consequential conscience is as a result of the influence of Baumgarten (see Osawa,
      'Perfection and Morality', 131).
17   Shaftesbury speaks of conscience occurring after an action, however he only states this
      in passing and without excluding that it may also occur before an act (*Characteristics
      of Men, Manners, Opinions, Times*, 211). Hutcheson speaks about antecedent conscience
      and subsequent conscience, the former being before an action and the latter being after
      an action (*A Short Introduction to Moral Philosophy*, 101–2, 31). Smith argues that there
      are two occasions when an agent examines their own conduct, namely before an action
      and after an action (*The Theory of Moral Sentiments*, 181). Wolff argues that there are
      'antecedent' and 'consequent' forms of conscience, the former relating to judgements
      before an action is done, the latter when an action has already taken place (*Vernüfftige
      Gedancken*, 339).

differences between the states an agent is in before and after an act. Smith asserts that the passions are most intense before an action and this leads to 'everything being magnified and misrepresented by self-love', which is to be contrasted with the state of an agent after an action when the 'passions have subsided'.[18] In the latter case Smith asserts that 'we can enter more coolly into the sentiments of the indifferent spectator [...] we can identify ourselves, as it were, with the ideal within the breast'.[19] Smith laments this *post facto* judge-ment because it is 'often of little importance [... producing] nothing but vain regret and unavailing repentance; without always securing us from the like errors in time to come'.[20] In this assertion Smith is pointing to the fact that the judgement of conscience has limited practical outcome because although it may sometimes secure one from similar errors in the future, the act has already occurred. The idea is that conscience is more easily consulted after an act than before and this is lamentable because consulting conscience after an act is inconsequential with respect to the particular practical action at hand.[21]

Similarly, Kant also discusses the activity of conscience with respect to time by stressing the importance of consulting conscience before an action. In the *Herder* notes he discusses conscience in three temporal moments: before the deed '*conscientia antecedens* (27:44), after the deed '*conscientia consequens*' (27:44) and during the deed 'in the course of the act' (27:44).[22] He categorises these in terms of the strength of their judgement, ranking them as strongest after an act, then before an act and finally weakest during an act (27:44). He then explicates this ranking by discussion of the relative strength of an agent's 'passions' with respect to time (27:43).[23] Similar to Smith's asser-tions regarding passions before an act, Kant makes the point that inclination is most acute before an act and thus this clouds an agent's moral deliberations

---

18   Smith speaks about 'heat' and 'keenness' (*The Theory of Moral Sentiments*, 181).

19   Ibid.

20   Ibid., 182. Indeed Smith likens agents who do in fact learn and morally improve from con-science after an act to a 'bold surgeon [...] who does not hesitate to pull off the mysteri-ous veil of self-delusion' (ibid.).

21   Indeed, Smith frames his discussion of conscience in terms of moral improvement as it enables agents to enter into the 'great school of self-command'.

22   These three are termed by Kant as '*conscientia consequens*' (27:44) which is expanded on in the translation of Peter Heath to mean 'conscience after and before the act (pang/ qualms)'. However the word *consequens* is ambiguous and as such my taking it to mean simply the consequence of conscience before, during or after an act, is justified.

23   See also *Collins* 27:356.

most intensely as compared to after an action when the passions are no longer there and there is no immediate practical consequence.[24]

Discussion of the temporal activity of conscience is continued in *Vigilantius*
where Kant asserts that

> Cultivation of the *conscientia antecedenti* is thus the primary need; for
> the examination of past actions [is] *conscientia consequens* [...]. A delib-
> erate failure to examine that which is capable of imputation in an action,
> is want of conscience. In *antecedenti* it is present in full, and in *conse-*
> *quenti*, partially so (27:618).

Here he is making a number of points. Firstly he identifies that the primary
need is to cultivate the antecedent conscience. The reason for this is because
a strong antecedent conscience will lead to a lower frequency of conducting
wrong actions. Secondly the consequent conscience must be cultivated in
order to evaluate past actions.[25] This is important in terms of practicality insofar as an agent's appraisal of their past actions may reveal action that was not
right and serve as a lesson not to act in a similar fashion (should the situation
arise once more). As noted earlier (Chapter 3, section 3.5.3), the judgement
of conscience after an act is still a judgement regarding the diligence with
which an agent has acted. Such *post facto* judgements serve as an important
mechanism by which agents can come to know which actions are impermissible. This can function either simply by realising that the evaluation that the
agent thought was appropriate or undertook was insufficient or inappropriate and thereby action evaluated in such ways should not be repeated, or this
can function in the more complex case of constant conjunction. In the case
of the latter, an inference can be made from realising (upon reflection) that
an action cannot be moral because the action *cannot* be examined diligently
and this inference can thereby be transformed into a general rule. Considering

---

24   Kant states 'so long as passion remains, however, the judgement becomes even more par-
      tisan. The fiercer the passions, the more clouded the moral feeling' (27:43).

25   For Smith the cultivation of conscience should result in a situation where an agent is not
      only 'affected' by 'the sentiments of the impartial spectator' but also 'adopts them' (*The
      Theory of Moral Sentiments*, 169). He states that in such agents 'the view of the impartial
      spectator becomes so perfectly habitual to him, that, without any effort, without any exer-
      tion, he never thinks of surveying his misfortune in any other view' (ibid., 171). Indeed,
      Smith explains that conscience can be 'cultivated' so that 'humanity flourishes' because
      'agents are capable of the highest improvement' (ibid., 176) and that 'the abstract and
      ideal spectator of our sentiments and conduct, requires often to be awakened and put in
      the mind of his duty, by the spectator [...]' (ibid., 177).

once more the case of the Inquisitor from *Religion* (6:187), a scenario can be envisioned where an agent who has conducted numerous actions based upon revealed religion realises through *post facto* conscientious judgement that in each particular case the action was unconscientious because of the precariousness of historical texts etc., leading the agent to realise that in each case it is the revealed religion element of the judgement that is rendering the actions unconscientious. Importantly the claim is not that *post facto* conscience is *the*, or *only*, manner in which agents come to know that revealed religion is not a basis for action. More general cases can be thought of where conscience reveals that evidence, say from a particular evaluative procedure, *never* fulfils the criterion of subjective certainty. An agent can infer from this, *via* constant conjunction, that actions based on revealed religion, or the particular precarious evaluative procedure, are always impermissible.[26]

Thirdly he refers to cases where an agent fails to examine an action that *can be put into action* and calls this 'want of conscience'.[27] The suggestion here is that the use of the antecedent conscience is an expression of the agent's desire to fully examine their action in order to act rightfully. The consequent conscience judges the *rightfulness* of the action. In the former case the act has not been realised, whereas in the latter case the act is already done. Hence when Kant states that 'in *antecedent* [,] [conscience] is present in full, and in *consequenti*, partially so' (*Vigilantius* 27:618), he must be read as describing the

---

26   Ware's account of conscience also identifies a role of conscience through action-based inferences, and comparisons between actions that agents have conducted over time ('The Duty of Self-Knowledge'). I think Ware is correct in identifying the indirect manner in which an agent may deduce moral lessons from their judgements of conscience, however I disagree with the emphasis that Ware places on the nature of such 'moral lessons'. For one, although he states explicitly that such inferences do not encroach upon the Opacity Thesis, he nonetheless points to conscience as 'condition[ing] the possibility of self-knowledge' (ibid., 697), which I read sympathetically in relation to the agent reflecting upon their nature as moral beings via conscientious reflection. I will present an argument below that indeed presents Kant's notion of conscientious reflection as a potential facilitator that brings to one's consciousness an agents awareness of their freedom. However, the account I presents differs radically from Ware's insofar as I emphasise the importance of the metaphorical court, whereas Ware argues more directly from the non-erring judgement of conscience (in terms of sincerity and truthfulness) to awareness of ones 'natural perfections' (ibid., 697).

27   It should be noted that the terms 'lack of conscience', 'want of conscience', and 'unconscientiousness' are phrases which are used by translators to render the same German word *Gewissenlosigkeit*. In the discussion provided here I follow the particular translations of each term as these issues of translation do not fundamentally affect the analysis of the issue at hand.

difference between the fact that judgement before an action has an immediately implementable consequence, whereas judgement after an action is lacking in the immediacy of practical action. Clearly the emphasis is on immediate
practical action.[28]

In the following subsection I will explicate the emphasis that Kant places on
practicality *qua* conscience.

5.3.2   *Bad Conscience*

The notion of 'bad conscience' is an important theme within the development of the Lutheran-Protestant tradition.[29] Indeed, the tradition emerges
out of protestations against the Catholic Church's alleged 'terrorisation' of
conscience, which was a label ascribed to Catholic systems of penitence (synonymous with fear and shame) that had developed over time. Common to the
critics of this tradition was the idea that it is through the absolution of a priest,
based upon the Church's claim to be inheritors of the power of 'The Keys' (the
power offered by Christ to Peter of loosening and binding sinners), that an
agent's sins are forgiven.[30] This was criticised because it empowered the insti-
tution of the Church (in the form of the priest) with the power of the Deity
itself. Luther's writings expand on this critique and offer further arguments
against the Catholic notion of conscience. A notable emphasis and point of
difference that Luther forwards is that penitence should be directed directly
to God, that it should be brief and focus on what one is troubled about.[31]
Moreover conscience should not be concerned with matters such as unre-
alistic and elaborate vows and creed, but should be directed towards duties
that concern one's household and neighbours. Significant here is the shift
from what Luther describes as consciences that are 'wretched' and 'tyrannies',

---

28   Another difference between Kant and Baumgarten is that Baumgarten asserts that
      bad conscience (understood as knowledge of what one should not do) should be pri-
      oritised over good conscience (knowledge of what one should do) because the former is
      more 'vivid', whereas Kant prioritises conscience before the act (Osawa, 'Perfection and
      Morality', 131).

29   Richard Sorabji details various approaches to penitence for 'bad conscience' in both
      Pagan and Christian thought and practice between the first and the thirteenth centuries.
      Surveying various sources, Sorabji details debates centring on to whom penitence is made
      (for instance, man or God), for what penitence is to be made (for example beliefs *qua* her-
      etics, and/or actions such as sexual sins and apostasy under duress), and how penitence is
      to be made (for example through confession, public humiliation through labouring etc.)
      (*Moral Conscience Through the Ages*, 73–86).

30   Ibid., 98. Sorabji ascribes this critique to John Wyclif (d. 1384) and Jan Hus (d. 1415).

31   Ibid., 106.

towards a conception of conscience that has more practical concerns.[32] In full rejection of the terrorisation of conscience Luther introduces the notion of a 'joyful conscience', which functions through the knowledge that only God can remit sins and although penitence first generates the fear of God, the process of expiation will ultimately result in a joyful conscience.[33] As will be shown below, Kant discusses these themes albeit within his own notion of conscience and within the Critical framework.

In his pre-Critical Herder notes, Kant refers to the forms of conscience that retard an agent's moral improvement and practical action as 'bad conscience' (27:43–4). An example of a bad conscience is a conscience that has not been cultivated such that it informs and motivates an agent sufficiently *before* an act takes place.[34] In this case Kant tells us that the optimal functioning of conscience is when it 'speaks long before hand' as this stops an agent doing the wrong thing in the first place (27:44). This notion is expanded upon in *Collins* and *Vigilantius* where Kant details examples of bad conscience, referring to them as 'micrological conscience' (*Collins* 27:356), 'morbid conscience' (27:356–7) and 'nagging conscience' (*Vigilantius* 27:619). I shall survey these below in order to flesh out the claim that the 'preoccupation with conscience must always be practical' (*Vigilantius* 27:620), which is what Kant also refers to as a 'lively conscience' in *Collins* (27:356).

There are a number of ways in which the pangs of conscience become progressively weaker or morally debilitating. One is through continuously failing to consult the capacity of conscience. As Kant states 'conscience eventually loses all respect, and then, too, the accusation ceases, having become superfluous, since nothing is any longer decided or carried out in the courtroom' (*Collins* 27:356). Another way in which the voice of conscience can become less acute is when conscience becomes 'micrological', which is the case when 'conscience is burdened with many small scruples on matters of indifference' (27:356).[35] Here he is referring to something akin to a pedantic and paralysing conscience which occupies itself with the minutia of 'trivial matters' relating to apparent moral behaviour. As he states 'the more micrological and subtle

---

32   Ibid., 102–6.

33   Ibid., 104.

34   As Kant states 'the *conscientia consequens* is thus the strongest, but bad when the *conscientia antecedens* does not precede it; to be sorry afterwards is no reparation […] who is caught with dagger in hand is not punished with death' (27:43–4).

35   Kant states 'the questions laid before it are the subject of casuistry, e.g., whether one should tell lies to a person, to make an April fool of him? Whether in certain rituals one should perform this action or that?' (27:356).

the conscience is over such trivialities, the worse it is in practical matters' (27:356).[36] Another form of conscience that he warns against is the 'morbid conscience' (27:356–7). These are cases where an agent seeks to 'impute evil in his actions, when there is really no ground for it' (27:356–7). He explains that such a conscience also produces an excess of feelings that 'torment' an agent, and thereby conscience becomes a 'tyrant within us',[37] the result being that 'those who have a tormenting conscience eventually grow weary of it entirely and finally send it on vacation' (27:356–7), i.e. the agent eventually disregards their conscience.[38]

Elsewhere, in *Vigilantius* Kant speaks of a 'nagging conscience' that differs from the normal pangs of conscience by the 'degree of reproach' (27:619). The nagging conscience is to be silenced not by

> [S]elf-anguish, but a bettering of the action's consequences (so far as this may be), or an endeavour to hold off the worst consequences, and an effort to make them good (27:619).

By self-anguish he is referring to exuberance in the level of 'remorse' an agent experiences. If conscience leads to paralysis, mediated by extreme guilt or self-lamentation, then it is a conscience that is to be avoided.

The above examples of bad conscience can be grouped together in terms of the retardation of practical action. Indeed, as is stated by Kant's student

---

36 Similarly Hutcheson refers to a 'scrupulous conscience' (*A Short Introduction to Moral Philosophy*, 101–2).

37 Both Locke and Hutcheson employ similar terminology to Kant, however, contrastingly to Kant they both employ the notion in a positive light. For Locke a criminal can be motivated through a 'terrified conscience' to act morally by the thought of hell (*An Essay Concerning Human Understanding*, 147–8, see also Ojakangas, *The Voice of Conscience*, n8, Schneewind, *The Invention of Autonomy*, 146–9). Similarly Hutcheson thinks that sometimes it is only the 'terror of the most formidable evils which enforces us [to follow conscience]', (*A Short Introduction to Moral Philosophy*, 104–5). It must also be noted that Rousseau believes that conscience can be experienced as a positive and a negative feeling. When an agent is cognisant of their conscience i.e. when the voice of conscience is being heard, upon seeing immoral acts or intending to/conducting immoral acts themselves, the experience is of 'reproach' or can even be 'tyrannical' (*Emile*, 309, 288). Whereas, when an agent behaves or intends to behave in a manner that is conducive to the positive evaluation of conscience an agent can said to have a 'good conscience'.

38 Similarly, in *Brauer* Kant is observed as stating 'tormenting consciences in the long run become dulled and ultimately cease to function' (134–5). For an interesting aside that has Kant taking about a tormenting conscience in terms of Stoicism see *Mrongovius* 29:623.

Vigilantius, 'Professor Kant holds the preoccupation of conscience to be **always practical**' (bold mine, 27:620). This emphasis on practicality is compounded by what Kant denotes as the best form of conscience, the 'lively conscience' (*Collins* 27:356). The lively conscience 'exists when the agent can reproach himself for his misdeeds' (27:356) such that the result is a type of moral evaluation leading to improvement in practical action rather than some form of impractical asceticism.[39] This is the proper functioning of conscience.[40]

Importantly, improvement in the use of conscience occurs via reflection upon the above mentioned notions. An agent can reflect on past experiences by asking: were there cases when I thought I was being conscientious but really it was a case of a bad conscience i.e. a micrological conscience, a morbid and tormenting conscience, a nagging conscience? An agent can reflect on their tendency to be conscientious: did I forget to consult my conscience in the particular case? By engaging with, and reflecting upon, past experiences an agent may make it less likely that they will repeat incidents of bad conscience. In this way an agent's conscience can be improved. These are cases of cultivating conscience *qua* pragmatic perfection because they are primarily concerned with the appropriate use of the capacity of conscience.

In the following sections I will turn to Kant's account of moral improvement with respect to the cultivation of conscience *qua* agent perfection and end perfection. This will entail explicating how through 'rational representation' (*Metaphysics of Morals* 6:400) conscience can be cultivated.

5.4   The Cultivation of Conscience as an Indirect Duty

In the *Metaphysics of Morals* Kant makes it very clear that an agent's conscience can be cultivated through rational representations. He states

> [O]bligation with regard to moral feeling can only be to *cultivate* it and to strengthen it through wonder at its inscrutable source. This comes about by its being shown how it is [...] induced most intensely in its purity by merely rational representation (6:400).

---

39   Elsewhere, in similar terms, Kant explicates how the morbid and tyrant forms of conscience are to be avoided (27:576–7).

40   See also 27:354, where Kant expressly states that simply expressing remorse upon a guilty verdict of conscience does not suffice; rather agents must make 'payment' i.e. some practical effect. See also Wood, *Kantian Ethics*, 190–1.

He supplements this by stating

> The duty here is only to cultivate one's conscience, to sharpen one's atten-
> tiveness to the voice of the inner judge, and to use every means to obtain
> a hearing for it (hence the duty is only indirect) (6:401).

In the above Kant specifies two things regarding the purpose of the cultivation of conscience: his talk of 'sharpening one's attentiveness' should be taken
as a reference to hearkening to the verdict of conscience, and 'obtain[ing] a
hearing for conscience' should be taken as a reference to the consulting of the
capacity of conscience.[41] With respect to the former, the phenomenological
concern can be stated in terms such that although the voice of the inner judge
is simply present, the level to which an agent can pay attention to the voice
of the inner judge is variable. Using a sound analogy it can be said that the
volume of the voice of the internal judge, although only proclaiming two notes
(either acquittal or guilt), *can vary*.

In contrast to pragmatic perfection (where the concern is the proper functioning of conscience), here the issue concerns the attitude an agent possess
towards conscience i.e. things like how likely they are to consult conscience or
follow its verdict. However, although for analytical purposes I have presented
these notions of perfection in three distinct ways they are nonetheless highly
interrelated. For example, as shown in the previous section, if an agent uses
their conscience in a micrological or morbid manner this makes them more
susceptible to not consulting their conscience in the long run. Before turning
to the manner in which the cultivation of conscience can take place, it is first
necessary to explicate what Kant means by 'the duty to cultivate one's conscience [...] is only indirect' (6:401). I shall do so below.

In the *Groundwork* Kant makes a number of distinctions regarding the types
of duty that an agent may possess.[42] With respect to this chapter the relevant
distinction is between direct duties and indirect duties. Direct duty refers to
the necessity of an action from respect for the moral law (4:403–4), whereas
an indirect duty is an obligation regarding the means by which an agent may
achieve or promote the end that is obeying the moral law. Indirect duties
relate to things that may aid an agent in behaving morally. Timmermann presents an account of the indirect duty to cultivate conscience as analogous to

---

41   In *Miscarriage* Kant argues that conscience is to be cultivated because 'human beings are
      gladly passive with their conscience' (8:268fn).

42   For example Kant distinguishes between duties to oneself and duties to others as well as
      perfect and imperfect duties (*Groundwork* 4:421, 429).

the indirect duty for an agent to pursue happiness (*Groundwork* 4:399, 415).[43]
Kant explains that when an agent is 'under pressure from many anxieties' the
temptation to choose an action contrary to duty is greater than when the agent
is free from such anxieties. The point can be illustrated by thinking about
the acquisition of prosperity as an indirect duty that may fend off the temptations that poverty confers.[44] Indirect duties are not 'real duties' in strictly
Kantian terms because an agent could remain moral even if they did not cultivate or perform such indirect duties. Timmermann argues that indirect duties
may be thought of as akin to 'technical imperatives' (*Groundwork* 4:416–7)
that are a type of hypothetical imperative (4:414).[45] Hypothetical imperatives
relate to the means by which an end that an agent is committed to can be
achieved. Kant calls these 'imperatives of skill' (4:415) or 'rules of skill' (4:416).
An example of a hypothetical imperative could be 'I must exercise in order
to become fit'. The end that is sought is fitness and the means that will be
employed to achieve this is exercising. Technical imperatives draw upon an
agent's experience with the workings of the world in order to realise the particular end skilfully.[46]

For Timmermann there is no philosophical difference between cultivating the voice of conscience and things such as fending off poverty 'to prevent
being overpowered by the temptations of need' or learning how to swim in
order to jump into the water to save a drowning child.[47] The assertion is that
such technical imperatives are equivalent because they all help an agent to
do their duty. Technical imperatives are only a 'matter of means no more than
that; and means *per se* possess instrumental, not moral worth'.[48] Indeed, like
the ability to swim, the ability to utilise ones conscience is to be considered a
technical skill. By cultivating conscience, an agent is enhancing a mechanism
that they have within them to improve in the dispensation of moral demands
in the form of duties. By being effective in their use of conscience, when
presented with moral judgements an agent will be able to execute their duty

---

43   Timmermann, 'Kant on Conscience', 294.

44   As Timmermann states, "The acquisition of wealth [...] is not an end that we have a duty
      to respect or further. This is borne out by the fact that if you are sufficiently wealthy not
      to be unduly tempted by material things, there is no duty for you to pursue wealth any
      further, not even an 'indirect' one [...] This specific 'indirect' duty is part of the general
      'indirect' duty to facilitate the performance of morally good action" (ibid., 299).

45   Ibid., 301.

46   Ibid., 302.

47   Ibid.

48   Ibid.

with greater diligence. However Timmermann's use of the analogies of happiness and prosperity are limited. The limitation is derived from the difference in the nature of conscience to that of happiness or the acquirement of wealth. To wit: there are some cases where an agent in following the moral law may have to go against their own happiness, whereas there are no cases where an agent would have to go against conscience.

The central reason for the difference is due to the rational nature of conscience. Conscience, considered within the remit of a *feeling of reason*, requires cultivations that relate to an agent's rationality, which is the very thing that (positive) morality is rooted in. When discussing 'the true vocation of reason' as the production of a 'will that is good' Kant states that 'it is entirely consistent with the wisdom of nature if we perceive that the cultivation of reason [...] limits in many ways [...the attainment of] happiness' (4:396).⁴⁹ Thus conscience as a feeling of reason, contrary to happiness (which 'rests upon empirical grounds') can never be *limited* via the cultivation of reason because conscience is a particular manifestation of reason. In fact the opposite assertion is to be made: the cultivation of reason can only lead to the cultivation of conscience because the latter is a particular manifestation of the former.

In the above I have sketched out what Kant means by the indirect duty to cultivate conscience. In the following sections I will flesh out how such cultivations actually function through rational representation. In order to achieve this I will first explicate the manner in which rational representation of the highest good (moral ideal world) can play a role in Kant's account of morality. Secondly, I will explicate how the cultivation of reason, in the case of the moral feeling of respect (which is closely related to conscience) is achieved through the notion of perfection (referred to as 'holiness' (*Groundwork* 4:435)). Drawing upon these I will then turn to discuss the cultivation of conscience as analogous to the cultivation of respect. This will allow for the explication of agent perfection and end perfection *qua* the cultivation of conscience in subsequent sections.

---

49   Kant makes clear that, 'all the elements that belong to the concept of happiness are without exception empirical [...] they must be borrowed from experience'. Indeed, Kant makes clear that an agent should act according to duty even when it goes against an agent's happiness (*Groundwork* 4:418, 442).

5.5   Moral Ideals: The Moral World and the Ideal of Holiness

i.   The Moral/Ideal World

Kant's conception of happiness and its role in his ethical system is nuanced and debated by scholars.[50] What is agreed upon is that happiness is not a concern that encroaches upon the moral worth of an action, which means happiness can never be a determining ground for moral action.[51] A rather simple manner in which to explain the cultivation of happiness within the context of indirect duties is to point out that a concern for happiness has moral value only insofar as the promotion of happiness may reduce the temptation that an agent has to behaving immorally. However, Kant's views on the notion of happiness go far beyond this assertion and exhibit claims that sit within his wider views of moral improvement.

Kant explains that reason directs agents towards the 'highest good' which is the union of virtue and the happiness that a virtuous person deserves (Second Critique 5:21–6, 108). Here Kant is not claiming that happiness is an appropriate end in itself in moral deliberation. Rather, the highest good is only valuable when it results from the pursuit of an agent's duty. He asserts that it is 'absolutely false' to claim that 'happiness produces a ground for a virtuous disposition', but that it is not absolutely false to claim that a 'virtuous disposition necessarily produces happiness' (5:114). Kant's claim here, and the Second Critique as a whole, is rooted within the results of the First Critique and thereby his doctrine of Transcendental Idealism. That it is not absolutely false to claim that a virtuous disposition necessarily produces happiness rests on the possibility that some such connection exists in the realm of things in themselves.[52]

---

50   Kant speaks about happiness in a number of ways. He sometimes refers to it as a form of 'welfare' or 'well-being' (Groundwork 4:395, Metaphysics of Morals 6:389), other times as an unattainable goal (Groundwork 4:399), also as 'contentment' (Metaphysics of Morals 6:398, Second Critique 5:22) and as getting all that an agent 'desires' (Groundwork 4:405, 399). These various definitions present a considerable ambiguity regarding exactly what Kant takes happiness to be before even attempting to interpret the role of happiness in his ethical system. I will not enter into this debate as it will present a digression to the present discussion. For discussion on the definition of happiness see Hill, Human Welfare, 168 and Hills, 'Kant on Happiness and Reason', 245.

51   See Groundwork 4:398 and Second Critique 5:21–6. See also Hill, Human Welfare, 169, Moran, 'Can Kant Have a Theory of Moral Education?', 472–5, Hills, 'Kant on Happiness and Reason', 243–61 and Timmermann, 'Kant On Conscience', 298.

52   See E. Watkin, 'The Antimony of Practical Reason: Reason, the Unconditioned and the Highest Good', Kant's Critique of Practical Reason: A Critical Guide, 145–68.

As such it is not rationally incoherent for an agent to hope that by acting virtuously this may ultimately result in their happiness.[53] In this way happiness is not a motive upon which practical reason is directed but is nonetheless a postulate of pure practical reason.[54]

However, simply asserting that something is *possible* does not secure a reason for its promotion. In order to address this issue it is necessary to point out that in the First *Critique* Kant explicates the notion of the highest good as the idea of a 'moral world' (A808/B836).[55] Such a world is one that is in 'conformity with all moral laws', which is a world where the 'freedom of all rational beings' is in accordance with the 'necessary laws of morality' (A808/B836). This is a world of universal virtue. Kant argues that this idea comes about when agents abstract 'all conditions (ends) and all the special difficulties to which morality is exposed (weakness or depravity of human nature)' and thereby conceives of a world of agents whose actions are always those that obey the moral law (A808/B836). Such a world is conceived of as an 'intelligible world' because the world of sensible agents is one of 'weakness or impurity of human nature' (A808/B836). He explains that

> [The idea of a moral world] is therefore a mere, yet practical, idea, which really can and should have its influence on the sensible world, in order to make it agree as far as possible with this idea (A808/B836).

By asserting that the concept can and should have an influence on the world that agents inhabit, Kant is arguing that agents should promote and seek this end in the world that they occupy. As Kleingeld succinctly puts it

> The only way to bring the sensible world into conformity with the moral world is through obeying the moral law. The idea of a moral world is *not* presented here as an attractive goal independent of the moral law, for which we subsequently have to figure out the most expedient means to attain it. Rather, the idea of a moral world is constructed on the basis

---

53   See P. Kleingeld, 'What Do the Virtuous Hope For: Re-Reading Kant's Doctrine of the Highest Good', in *Proceedings for the Eighth International Kant Congress*, ed. H. Robinson, Marquette University Press (1995), 91–112.

54   For a discussion that address this point see M. Willaschek, 'The Primacy of Practical Reason and the Idea of a Practical Postulate', *Kant's Critique of Practical Reason: A Critical Guide*, 168–96.

55   Here I follow the work of Kleingeld, 'What Do the Virtuous Hope For: Re-Reading Kant's Doctrine of the Highest Good', 93–5.

of the question what a world would look like in which everyone would always obey the moral law from duty.[56]

Following the introduction of the notion of a moral world Kant then explicates that such a world would be characterised by general happiness. He makes this claim by asserting that in the moral world 'a system of happiness proportionately to morality and mortality can also be thought as necessary, since freedom, partly moved and partly restricted to moral laws, would itself be the cause of general happiness' (A809/B837). He then goes on to argue that the connection is a 'necessary [and causal] connection of the hope of being happy with the unremitting effort to make oneself worthy of happiness' (A810/B838).[57] Such an idea is one of 'self-rewarding morality' (A809/B837). When this is connected to his treatment of happiness in the Second *Critique*, the pure practical postulate concerning the relation of happiness to virtue serves as an ideal that agents can hope for i.e. an *aspirational ideal* rather than a motive that in itself may ground their actions.[58]

ii.   Holiness: The Voice of Reason and Rational Representation

Within Kant's discussion of the ideal of the moral world ('the ideal of the highest good') he talks of 'the idea of [...] an intelligence, in which the morally most perfect will [is] combined with the highest blessedness' (A810/B839), which I read to be a reference to a perfectly virtuous agent. In this subsection I will expand upon Kant's connection of the notion of 'the most perfect will' with the ideal of the highest good. I will firstly show that through the notion of a 'holy will' (*Groundwork* 4:439), a will constitutionally incapable of acting against the moral law, Kant represents a thought experiment that highlights the moral stature of an agent by highlighting the status of human agents as endowed with the freedom to *choose* moral action. In other words, the idea of a holy will is not to serve as an aspirational ideal because it is fundamentally deficient given its lack of choice. Following this, in contrast to the notion of a holy will I will show that 'holiness' is a notion which relates to cases of an agent endowed with freedom continually *choosing* to act autonomously and as such

---

56   Ibid., 93.

57   See also *Religion* 6:6–8, where there is a strong parallel with the above mentioned.

58   How, and the success with which, Kant argues for the connection between happiness and virtue is beyond the remit of this chapter. For discussions see Kleingeld, 'What Do the Virtuous Hope For', 94 and S. Engstrom, 'The Concept of the Highest Good in Kant's Moral Theory', *Philosophy and Phenomenological Research*, 52, 4, (1992), 747–80.

holiness is a concept that can function as an aspirational ideal that fits into Kant's views of cultivation i.e. moral improvement through postulates of pure practical reason.

Within the context of the notion of the cultivation of reason, Kant's language when talking about respect is particularly germane. In the *Groundwork* he states

> [I]t could be objected that I only seek refuge, behind the word *respect*, [...]. But though respect is a feeling, it is not one *received* by means of influence; it is, instead, a feeling *self-wrought* by means of a rational concept and therefore specifically different from all feelings of the first kind, which can be reduced to inclination or fear (4:401fn).

Here he is establishing that there are *feelings of reason* that can be brought about in themselves through a rational concept functioning as a representation. Due to the fact that both respect and conscience are feelings of reason, a natural analogy can be made between the cultivation of respect and the cultivation of conscience through rational representation. As such, it will be fruitful to expand into more detail on the manner in which respect is cultivated through rational representation before turning to how this occurs with respect to the cultivation of conscience.[59]

Kant connects the notion of acting out of respect for the moral law (with dignity) with the notion of the 'purity of origin' of moral concepts (*Groundwork* 4:411). He asserts that the consciousness of reason's dignity *qua* purity of origins secures 'moral instruction' able to bring about a 'pure moral disposition' that is attained by 'engrafting' moral principles onto an agent's mind (4:412). Such agents are said to have moral 'dispositions' (4:435). Interestingly he then introduces theological terminology by stating that these moral dispositions represent a 'holiness' insofar as an agent has a

> [W]ill that practices them as the object of an immediate respect, and nothing but reason is required to *impose* them upon the will, not to *coax* them from it, [...]. This estimation therefore lets the worth of such a cast of mind be cognized as dignity and puts it infinitely above all price [i.e.] *holiness* (emphasis mine, 4:435).

This passage occurs at the end of a discussion where he has discussed, amongst other things, the moral worth of an action done out of 'basic principles (not

---

59   See *Groundwork* 4:403, 405.

from instinct)' (4:435), which he asserts is the expression of an agent's 'inner worth'. As such Kant's employment of the term 'holiness' in the above passage is to be read as being descriptive (in some sense) of an agent who is *choosing* to will autonomously. This element of choice is thus central to the notion of holiness. Notice also that this corresponds to his talk in the *Metaphysics of Morals* regarding agent perfection discussed earlier in terms of being 'holy' (6:446).

In contrast to the notion of holiness is the notion of a 'holy will' (*Groundwork* 4:439). Kant explicates what he means by a holy will by stating that 'a will whose maxims necessarily harmonize with the laws of autonomy is a *holy*, [an] absolutely good will' (4:439).[60] The introduction of this concept functions as a kind of thought experiment that invites the reader to conceive of an agent who cannot will other than in accordance with the moral law. The holy will can be thought of as possessed by a purely rational being that lacks any sensible self, and thereby any desire or inclination. Making this clear in the *Metaphysics of Morals* he fleshes the term out by explaining that the notion of the holy will is not to be taken as a will that an agent possess simply when willing rationally (6:379–80). Rather the holy will is a category that is not applied to 'natural beings' who possess 'pleasures' (read: inclinations) that 'can induce them to break the moral law', which is a reference to human agents. Kant's purpose is to highlight that such a being would lack any notion of choice.[61] From this he then explicates that it is the very act of choosing that grounds the notion of obligation and thereby duty (*Groundwork* 4:439).[62] This crucially allows him to make the point that a holy will is in a fundamental way deficient because it does not exhibit self-legislation in terms of the moral law, but is rather subordinated to it by virtue of its very constitution.[63] The central notion that he is inviting agents to reflect upon is the freedom that agents possess as moral beings, and how it is this freedom that grounds the worth of an autonomous

---

60   For discussions of Kant's conception of the holy will see J. J. Callanan, 'The Role of the Holy Will', *Hegel Bulletin*, 35, 2, (2014), 163–84, and H. E. Allison, *Kant's Groundwork for the Metaphysics of Morals: A Commentary*, Oxford University Press (2011), 275–6.

61   Callanan explicates this point in terms of Augustine's distinction between *libertas minor*, indicating the power of free choice that is available to subjects capable of failing to obey morality and thereby falling prey to sin, and *libertas major*, indicating that perfection of our power of free choice whereby the representation of the good is so evident to the subject that it is constitutionally incapable of freely choosing otherwise. The holy will is to be thought of in terms of the latter category ('The Role of the Holy Will', 168).

62   Indeed, Kant ascribes the notion of sublimity only to agents who have this choice (4:439).

63   See Callanan, 'The Role of the Holy Will', 172.

action. It is thus important that the notions of holiness and a holy will are not confused.[64]

The notion of holiness is to be thought of as functioning as a rational representation of a perfect and pure will, where such a representation may lead to moral improvement. At the outset it is necessary to note that Kant's talk of holiness (idealised perfection) as an 'incentive' (4:439) cannot be read as the rational representation providing a ground for the agent to act morally. Such a case would constitute heteronomy as the act would have incorporated a principle other than pure reason.[65] The term 'incentives' [*Triebfedern*] is employed by Kant in the Second *Critique*'s Doctrine of Method where he explores 'the way in which one can make objectively practical reason *subjectively* practical as well' (5:151). Within this context by 'subjectively practical' he is referring to the putting into practice of moral principles.[66] He explicitly states that his purpose is to find a method for the 'cultivating of genuine moral dispositions' (5:153). An aim of Kant's discussion is to move away from mere 'legality of action' towards a morality where these dispositions are cultivated (5:151).[67]

---

64   Indeed Kant makes this clear when, after stating that "'ought' is strictly speaking a 'will' that holds for every rational being under the condition that reason in him is practical without hindrance", he qualifies this by asserting that this claim is to be understood as applying to 'beings like us—who are also affected by sensibility' (4:449). The conceivable ideal that Kant is referring to is one of an agent who continually chooses to will in accordance with the moral law i.e. the form of holiness, rather than to aspire to be a holy will which would be impossible given an agent's sensible self, and also undesirable given the lack of freedom that such a will would represent. For a broader discussion of the moral law see F. Rauscher, 'Pure Reason and the Moral Law: A Source of Kant's Critical Philosophy', *History of Philosophy Quarterly*, 13, 2, (1996), 255–71, and for a discussion of the 'ought' to do (*Groundwork* 4:413–4, 439–40, 406–8) see D. Jacquette, 'Moral Dilemmas, Disjunctive Obligations, and Kant's Principle That 'Ought' Implies 'Can'', Synthese, 88, 1, (1991), 43–55.

65   Indeed at the very outset of *Religion* Kant makes it clear that 'on its own behalf morality in no way needs religion [. . .] but is rather self-sufficient by virtue of pure practical reason' (6:3). Here I take Kant's employment of 'religion' in a wide sense to include theological terminology such as 'holy will'. Below I will explicate what exactly he means by 'religion'.

66   Explicated by S. Bacin as '[the] connecting [of] philosophical inquiry to its outcome in the life of moral subjects', 'The Doctrine of Method of Pure Practical Reason', (*Kant's Critique of Practical Reason*, 200). Indeed within the very context where he introduces the notion of holiness in the *Groundwork* Kant makes the same distinction between subjectively and objectively practical (4:436).

67   Kant employs the same terminology in the *Groundwork*'s discussion of holiness (4:412). An account of the notion of a moral disposition as a Kantian theory of 'moral character' that is more than simply maxim-making acts, which draws primarily on *Religion* is

Importantly he explains that a 'morality of dispositions' can only take place if 'the immediate representation of the law and the objectively necessary observance of it [become] the proper incentives to action' (5:151).[68] This clarification functions as an important reconciliation with the pure rationalistic ethical project of the *Groundwork*.[69]

Kant goes on to talk about a moral disposition being a 'receptivity to pure moral interest' that has a counterpart in the fact that the 'pure representation of virtue [...] is the most powerful incentive to the moral good' (5:152). He details educational techniques that can be employed to achieve the end of representing virtue (5:154–7) and explains that 'morality must have more power over the human heart the more purely it is presented', which he refers to as 'the image of holiness' (5:156). Kant argues that the nature of the representations of virtue must be appropriate to the end of creating 'veneration and a lively wish that he himself could be such a man' (5:156), i.e. it is not a way to ground action but rather to bring about what he refers to as a 'progress in goodness' (5:157).[70] Crucially he then explains that for this end to be achieved

---

       explored by Alison Hills, 'Gesinnung: Responsibility, Moral worth, and Character', *Kant's Religion within the Boundaries of Mere Reason: A Critical Guide*, 79–97.

68   Bacin, 'The Doctrine of Method of Pure Practical Reason', 202.

69   As expressed in the *Groundwork*, Kant asserts that it is not extremely difficult but rather that it is *impossible to know* through the introspective means of self-examination whether an agent has acted according to the moral law or according to self-love (4:407). This claim is characteristic of Kant's account of the Self as fundamentally inaccessible or opaque (generally referred to as the 'Opacity Thesis'). This thesis maintains that an agent's motivations and dispositions are not, by their very nature, accessible as objects of knowledge (he asserts that agents can never know the 'real determining cause of the will'). Indeed Kant further asserts that the tendency for self-deception is a part of the human condition where agents like to 'flatter' themselves by falsely attributing to themselves a 'nobler motive'. In fact Kant's theory of moral fallibility can be read as grounding moral improvement. The relationship here is between the possibility of acting morally and the impossibility of moral self-knowledge. Striving to act according to the moral law is characterised as 'because an agent can never know their true motivations they must always strive to improve them'. Nonetheless a full exposition of the relationship between the Opacity Thesis and Kant's command that an agent should 'know thyself' requires further discussion that will take the discussion beyond the immediate concern of this chapter. On this point see C. Kelly, 'Kant's Dynamic Theory of Character', *Kantian Review*, 7, (2003), 38–71. For a discussion of the claim that moral fallibility grounds moral improvement see H. E. Allison, *Kant's Groundwork for the Metaphysics of Morals: A Commentary*, Oxford University Press (2011), 102fn and *Kant's Theory of Freedom*, 176–9.

70   As Kant explains, the Doctrine of Method does not show the way to 'moral progress' (5:84). See also *Metaphysics of Morals* 6:409.

the agent must become conscious of the connection between the humanity
i.e. the virtue/goodness that constitutes the representations of the moral law
and their own 'individuality' (5:157).[71] He explains that such 'consciousness of
one's moral disposition and of a character of this kind [is] *the highest good in
human beings*' (emphasis mine, 5:157). This comes about, in part, by the fact
that agents are conscious of their ability to 'raise oneself altogether above the
sensible world [and become] consciou[s] of a power ruling over sensibility,
even if not always with effect' (5:159), and this 'lets us feel our own cognitive
powers' (5:160). He asserts that representations through examples of the 'purity
of will' work by bringing to realisation the 'negative perfection of the will insofar as in an action from duty no incentives of inclination have any influence
on it as determining grounds [for action]'. Following this the agent who is con-
templating on the representation will fix their attention to their own freedom
(5:160). This consciousness is of an 'inner freedom to release [oneself from the
determinations of] inclination' (5:161). In this way the notion of holiness, similarly to the notion of the holy will, brings to the consciousness of an agent an
awareness of the value of being endowed with freedom (where holiness functions via a positive example of a will that always chooses the good and a holy
will functions via a negative example of a will that has no choice).[72]

The notion of holiness serves as a particularly powerful ideal by which reason can be cultivated because it relates to a state of moral perfection (here
taken in terms of the highest good).[73] The concept of holiness can be applied
to an agent in the form of a postulate of pure practical reason (Second *Critique*
5:122). The idea is that although human agents as 'rational beings of the sensible
world' will never attain 'complete conformity of the will with the moral law',
it is 'nevertheless required as practically necessary [and] it can only be found
in an *endless progress* toward that complete conformity' (5:122), where endless progress is secured by the teleological postulate of pure practical reason

---

71   See G. F. Munzel, *Kant's Conception of Moral Character*, University of Chicago Press
     (1999), 246.

72   Kant also discusses the difference between holiness ('the absolute or unlimited moral
     perfection of the will') and the contrasting notion of God as 'holy' in *Lectures on Religion*
     (28:1075).

73   In the Second *Critique* Kant discusses the relationship between the notion of perfection
     as an ideal and moral improvement (5:84–5, 123–5). In a particularly pertinent footnote
     he describes the idea of perfection as a 'moral idea' that serves as an 'archetype of practi-
     cal perfection' and as a 'standard of comparison' (5:127n). See also Callanan, 'The Role of
     the Holy Will', 163–84.

(concerning end perfection).[74] It is important to note that in the *Metaphysics of Morals* section where Kant outlines the notions of perfection (pragmatic, agent and end perfection), similarly to his treatment of holiness as an 'endless progress' in the Second *Critique*, he states that 'it is a human beings duty to strive for this perfection, but not to reach it **(in this life)**, and his compliance with this duty can, accordingly, consist only in **continual progress**' (bold mine, 6:446). The stipulation of 'not to reach it in this life' is crucial insofar as it introduces the pure practical postulate of God: here functioning as a postulate that renders belief in the endless progress reaching the ideal end (the moral/ideal world where happiness is in proportion to morality) possible. Indeed, aside from this passage there is plenty of evidence throughout Kant's corpus that he takes the pure practical postulate of God and an afterlife as central to his notion of the highest good.[75] Notice two things: firstly, that holiness as an aspirational ideal of moral perfection i.e. always choosing to act according to the moral law, relates to agent perfection, and that endless progress, whose 'end' is the moral ideal world, relates to end perfection. Secondly, in the *Metaphysics of Morals* Kant first differentiates these two concerns of perfection and then treats them together when he explains that perfection cannot be achieved (in this life) but rather consists in continual progress. The important point here is that agent and end perfection are intricately related.

Drawing upon the above, in the following sections I will explicate the mechanism that Kant provides for the cultivation of conscience. I will pursue this aim by fleshing out Kant's recourse to religious terminology with respect to conscience. I will highlight the mechanism by which the representation of the moral law as 'divine' ties in with his encouragement that agents think

---

74   Exposition of this account will require recourse into Kant's teleological philosophy thereby taking the discussion beyond the remit of this chapter. In this case the teleological postulate that is intricately related to the notion of endless progress is that of the immortality of the soul (Second *Critique* 5:122). For discussion of Kant's views on the immortality of the soul within his discussion of the practical postulates in the Second *Critique* see C. W. Surprenant, 'Kant's Postulate of the Immortality of the Soul', *International Philosophical Quarterly*, 48, 1, (2008), 85–98. Typically discussions in the secondary literature focus on teleological postulates in political-historical and aesthetic terms. For studies that address teleology primarily in terms of morality see T. Auxter, *Kant's Moral Teleology*, Mercer University Press (1982) and K. Ameriks, 'Kant, Miracles, and Religion, Parts One and Two', *Kant's Religion within the Boundaries of Mere Reason: A Critical Guide*, 137–55.

75   For examples see Second *Critique* 5:114–5 and *Religion* 6:88, 89fn. For an exposition of Kant's argument for faith in the existence of God in terms of the highest good see A. W. Wood, *Kant's Moral Religion*, Cornell University Press (1970), 25–34, 100–53.

of the 'inner judge' of conscience as 'God' and the 'voice of conscience' as the 'voice of God'.

5.6   The Rational Religious Representation of the Internal Court of Conscience

Within the secondary literature Munzel correctly identifies that conscience plays a role in Kant's conception of practical reason through its role in the notion of subjective practicality.[76] However, although Munzel mentions that Kant talks about conscience in religious and non-religious ways he fails to explain why Kant discusses conscience in these manners. Rather, Munzel merges Kant's treatment into a single concern.[77] This is peculiar as the context within which Munzel addresses conscience is one where he is arguing that Kant's views in *Religion* are such that it 'serves an integral role in completing [the] moral account'.[78] Indeed, Munzel's treatment of conscience is as a *religious concept* rather than, as I will present here, a concept that can be supplanted by religious notions. This is an important distinction between Munzel and I; although I will argue that religious notions can certainly cultivate conscience, I do not claim that conscience functions via religious conceptualisations. In other words, Kantian conscience is not inherently a religious notion.

As a first step, it is necessary to differentiate the relationship between conscience and the cultivation of conscience for the purposes of moral self-improvement. The former relates to the role that conscience plays in regard to practical action (explicated in section 5.2). This is the context within which Kant can speak of 'conscience as practical reason' (*Metaphysics of Morals* 6:400). The latter relates to the means by which an agent can pursue perfection in their moral disposition. It is within this context that Kant's talk of conscience in theological terms is to be understood.

As such, a further differentiation is to be introduced, namely between religious and non-religious rational representations as mechanisms for moral cultivation. Examples of the latter are cases where Kant talks about conscience in relation to simply an 'ideal person' (*Metaphysics of Morals* 6:439–40). Indeed, one notable place where Kant does not utilise rational religious representations is *Miscarriage*. Although he does say that if a God figure is conceived as

---

76   Munzel, 'What does his Religion Contribute to Kant's Conception of Practical Reason?', 230–32.

77   See ibid., 231.

78   Ibid., 232.

the internal judge of conscience lying becomes absurd because it is 'before a reader of hearts' (8:269), when he turns specifically to discussing the cultivation of conscience he simply specifies that an agent should reflect upon 'the depiction of a character which is sincere, and distant from all falsehood and deliberate dissemblance' (8:270). Examples of the former are when he talks of 'the image of God in conscience' (*Herder* 27:19) and conscience as a 'divine tribunal' (*Collins* 27:296). Importantly, while discussing conscience as a 'divine court' (a phrase I explicate below) Kant makes the point that

> [T]his much is certain, that even in a man with no belief in God, a conscience can still be presumed if he possesses moral principles as such; for otherwise it would have to be supposed that he had lost all belief whatsoever, and that it would thus be possible for him to assail the right of another (*Vigilantius* 27:575).

What exactly Kant means in this passage will be fleshed out below. For the present it suffices to say that although the focus of his discussions regarding the cultivation of conscience are primarily through rational religious representations, the claim is not that *only* through rational religious conceptualisations is the cultivation of conscience possible.

Nonetheless, it is clear that when Kant does shift from talking about conscience as practical reason to talking about conscience in terms of cultivation through rational representations he does so overwhelmingly in religious terms. Three reasons can be given as to why this is the case. The first is because of the historical context. A second reason is that his talk of conscience in such terms can be read as an extension of his general employment of theological terminology with respect to moral improvement (the notion of holiness explored above being an example of this). As a corollary to this second reason, a third reason is because Kant envisions rational religious conceptualisations as more effective than non-religious conceptions.

In the remainder of this section I will explore these reasons. I shall do so by firstly providing a brief survey of religious language regarding conscience in the historical context and secondly by explicating exactly what Kant means by the notion of 'rational religion'. In the following section I turn to explicating how and why Kant utilises religious language with respect to the cultivation of conscience.

5.6.1   *Religion and Conscience in the Historical Context*

Within the historical context there are numerous examples of philosophers who connect their discussions of law and conscience with theological concepts.

Rather surprisingly, in *De Cive* Hobbes argues that natural law lies in reason and that this engenders an obligation to follow the internal court (*in foro interno*) of conscience.[79] Indeed, in various places in *Levitation* Hobbes argues similarly to the aforementioned, talking of an 'internal tribunal' and conscience as a 'judge' where 'God raigneth'.[80] What is important to this discussion is to point out that Hobbes merely challenges the authority of private conscience in the grounding of a public action. Thus, Hobbes can talk of sovereigns ordaining and 'doing many things [...] contrary to their [own] conscience'.[81] Both Rousseau and Crusius intimately connect conscience with God, with the former talking of conscience as the 'voice of God' and the latter asserting that to act in accordance with conscience is to 'do what is in accordance with the perfection of God'.[82] In *A System of Moral Philosophy* Hutcheson claims that God has instituted conscience into an agent's nature, and through corruption conscience loses its 'dominion over bodily appetites' and must thereby be 'reinstated on her throne'.[83] He makes it clear that conscience is to be considered a 'judicious spectator' that condemns when agents act against the 'divine

---

79   T. Hobbes, *On the Citizen*, Cambridge University Press (1998), 54, 59. See also Darwall,
       British Moralists, 56, Ojakangas, *The Voice of Conscience*, 117. See also Hobbes, *On the
       Citizen*, 132.

80   Hobbes, *Leviathan*, 110, 231, 244.

81   Ibid., 172. See also Ojakangas, *The Voice of Conscience*, 117–8.

82   Within the context of discussing natural religion, Rousseau refers to conscience as 'the
       holy voice of nature' (*Emile*, 288) and as 'celestial voice [...] making man like unto God'
       (ibid., 290). He argues that agents should engage in the 'cultivations' of 'God-given facul-
       ties' in order to fully utilise their conscience (ibid., 307, see also 259). See Crusius, *A Guide
       to Rational Living*, 576. In a similar vein, Pufendorf argues that in order to 'give force' to
       natural law, 'it is necessary to presuppose that God exists', (*The Duty of Man and Citizen*,
       163). He states elsewhere that 'we have evidence that the social life has been enjoined
       upon men by God's authority, in the fact that in no other creature do we find the religious
       sentiment or fear of the Deity—a feeling which seems inconceivable in a lawless animal'
       (ibid., 164), a sentiment which he discusses also in terms of conscience (ibid., see also
       ibid., 170, 172, 177 and Schneewind, *The Invention of Autonomy*, 120–2). Leibniz explains
       that conscience relates to theology, which 'treats of eternal happiness, and of everything
       that bears on that in so far as it depends on the soul and the conscience', and this is a kind
       of "jurisprudence that has to do with the matters that are said to concern the 'inner tribu-
       nal' of conscience, and that brings in invisible substances and minds". He contrasts this
       with 'jurisprudence [that] is concerned with government and with laws, whose goal is the
       happiness of men in so far as it can be furthered by what is outer and sensible' (Leibniz,
       New Essays on Human Understanding, 526).

83   Hutcheson, *A System of Moral Philosophy*, 132. For discussion see Darwall, *British Moralists*,
       215 and Schneewind, *The Invention of Autonomy*, 330–9.

law'.[84] In fact he makes this claim just after explaining that an agent should follow God and his laws, thereby equating the 'spectator' with the 'Deity' itself.[85] Contrastingly, Shaftesbury, Smith and Wolff talk of the non-necessary but nonetheless morally beneficial conceptualisation of conscience in theological terms (akin to a kind of theological instrumentilisation).[86] For example, although Wolff argues that man would still be obligated by the moral law if God did not exist, he nonetheless connects following the law with God.[87] He argues that through the 'representation of [His i.e. God's] perfection' an agent can be motivated to act with 'what the law of nature requires' and 'in this way simultaneously, natural obligation is divine obligation, and the law of nature is a divine law'.[88] Indeed Wolff states that in this way an agent becomes 'like God'.[89] As I will detail below, Kant's employment of such terms is also instrumentalist. However, it is idiosyncratic and thus differs from the historical

---

84   Ibid., 234–5.

85   Ibid. Elsewhere he talks of the 'matter of conscience' being the need to 'obtain the approbation of God and our own hearts' (ibid., 257). Indeed Hutcheson talks of conscience as a 'divine senate' (*A Short Introduction to Moral Philosophy*, 41). Elsewhere in the same text he talks about natural conscience resulting in the 'most excellent' of action, namely the fulfilling of the 'duty of loving God with the highest veneration' (ibid. 50). For further evidence of Hutcheson's connecting of God to conscience see ibid., 111, 115, 216.

86   Shaftesbury argues that conscience is thought of as 'religious conscience' (*Characteristics of Men, Manners, Opinions, Times*, 209) when 'moral deformity and odiousness of any act with respect purely to the divine presence and the natural veneration due to such a supposed being' (ibid.). Smith connects conscience to the 'hope and expectation of a life to come' (*The Theory of Moral Sentiments*, 154) by making the analogy between the judgement of God to the judgement of the impartial spectator (ibid., 155). He explains that 'it is from [the impartial spectator] only that we learn the real littleness of ourselves, [...] and the natural misrepresentations of self-love can be corrected only by the eye of this impartial spectator' (ibid., 159). Sorabji also discusses Smith's appeal to God in the notion of an impartial spectator (*Moral Conscience Through the Ages*, 174). Hutcheson argues that conscience is to be cultivated (*On Human Nature*, 132, 138–9, 142, 147). Within the context of discussing conscience he states 'Cultivate virtue [...] follow nature and God as your guide' (ibid., 142). Although Hutcheson is speaking of the cultivation of conscience and the taking of 'God as your guide' within the same vein, he merely mentions this hence I have chosen not to categorise Hutcheson's position within the notion of theological instrumentilisation.

87   Wolff claims that the law comes from nature, and is validated through nature alone hence Wolff argues that atheists too are obligated by the law (*Vernüfftige Gedancken*, 336, 337).

88   Ibid. Wolff completes this assertion by stating 'it follows at once from this that God can give men no other law than the law of nature, and never a law that conflicts with the law of nature' (ibid).

89   Ibid.

context in this way. Below I shall explicate this idiosyncrasy by exploring what Kant means by 'religion'.

5.6.2   Revealed and Natural Rational Religion

As has been noted above, Kant uses theological terminology in various places throughout the post-Critical corpus (*Groundwork* 4:434, 439, Second *Critique* 5:128–9, *Collins* 27:295) and more specifically in various discussions of conscience. Before turning to explicate the theological instrumentalisation present in such discussions of conscience it is first necessary to note the difference between revealed and natural religion and thereby explicate what Kant means by 'religion' and 'God'. What Kant is referring to by 'religion' and more generally his theological terms such as 'God' and 'divine laws', is clarified in *Religion* where he explicates the claim that 'Religion is [...] the recognition of all our duties as divine commands' (6:153–4)

> Religion, in which I must first know that something is a divine command in order that I recognise it as my duty, is *revealed religion* (or a religion that requires revelation); by contrast, the religion in which I must first know that something is duty before I can acknowledge it as a divine command is natural religion (6:154).

There is therefore an important distinction between revealed and natural religion. The former takes the form of *firstly* recognising divine commands and *then* taking these divine commands as duty. The latter takes the form of *firstly* recognising duty and *then* taking duty as divine commands. The difference here is between the grounding that moral action is based upon. In the case of revealed religion the grounding is revelation, which would entail a subjective determining ground i.e. historical contingency, making it 'merely based on facts' (6:104). This makes it subjective insofar as the historical validity can always be questioned. In the rationalistic Kantian picture of morality an agent will generate duty according to the Categorical Imperative. This is sufficient for morality. However this rationalistic-duty can be supplemented and become religious when such duty is *thought of* as divine commands.[90]

---

90   Compare this to Grotius's argument that natural law can be thought of as the command-
     ment of God, so long as 'true law of nature' is understood in relation to the law of God
     only when 'we carefully distinguish between the law of God, which God sometimes exe-
     cutes through men, and the law of men in their relations with one another' (*On the Law of
     War and Peace*, 95). In fact Grotius argues that the holy law is a higher degree of perfection

Kant further clarifies the difference between revealed and natural-rational religion by explaining the role of God in considering religion as the recognition of duties as divine commands. He first explicates that God is to be taken as an assumption that is a 'presupposed assertoric faith' not 'assertoric knowledge' (6:154). The latter would relate to claims that are impermissible in the Kantian system because it would be a knowledge claim about something that is 'supersensible' i.e. non-experienceable (a claim that he denies in the First *Critique*). The former relates simply to a belief in God that has been secured merely as a possibility in the First *Critique*; one that is *presupposed* and 'promises a result for the final aim of religion' (6:154). As Kant states, 'this faith needs only *the idea of God* which must occur to every morally earnest (and therefore religious) pursuit of the good, without pretending to be able to secure objective reality for it through theoretical cognition' (6:154). In this conception God is not a knowledge claim at all but rather it is the '*minimum* of cognition (it is possible that there is a God)' which 'must alone suffice for what can be made the duty of every human being' (6:154). In this sense God is an assumed and presupposed faith that is secured by the possibility that there *could* be a God and *instrumentalised* as an aid towards moral behaviour.[91] He states 'there are no particular duties toward God in a universal [i.e. rational, natural] religion' (6:154).[92] The point here is that ultimately it is the duty that is grounded in reason that matters and that all other considerations (such as public laws, revealed religion, clerical opinion etc.) are to be assessed according to this criterion.[93]

---

than natural law requires (ibid., 96). See also Leites (ed.), *Conscience and Casuistry in Early Modern Europe*, 3–4, 10, 117.

91   Indeed Kant argues that the fact that a proof of God's existence cannot be given proves crucial to moral behaviour because if such a clear proof existed agents would find themselves standing before the eyes of God and thereby they would act out of fear rather than out respect for the moral law. See Second *Critique* 5:147 and Callanan, 'The Role of the Holy Will', 175.

92   Hence Kant states "Even when it is said: 'One ought to obey God before human beings', this only means that whenever statutory commands, regarding which human beings can be both legislators and judges, conflict with duties which reason prescribes unconditionally—and God alone can judge whether they are observed or transgressed—the former must yield precedence to the latter" (6:154). For a further explication of Kant's distinction between revealed and rational-natural religion see S. R. Palmquist, *Kant's Critical Religion*, Ashgate (2000).

93   An area of Kant's discussion of religion that I shall not enter is his views on Christianity. He states in *Religion* that revealed and historical religion can be important to morality as a 'vehicle' (symbolic or pictorial guide) to moral improvement i.e. as an advancement of moral ends (see *Religion* 6:106, 115, 118, 123fn). For a discussion that address this see O. Hoffe, 'Holy Scriptures within the Boundaries of Mere Reason: Kant's Reflections', in

In the above I have provided the necessary background from which to explore Kant's rational religious talk with respect to the cultivation of conscience. This will involve explaining why he discusses conscience in such rational religious notions when non-religious notions are available to him.[94]

5.7   Why Have Religious Representations at All?

In Chapter 4, I presented a multiple consciousness model of the internal court of conscience. In doing so I showed that Kant's account of an internal lie is coherent once it is understood that the subject to which the lie is directed to is the internal judge. Although the internal judge was discussed under the remit of the 'ideal other', the notion was not fully fleshed out at that stage. I believe that it is only through the discussions presented thus far in this chapter that the notion can now be fully explored (albeit within the context of the cultivation of conscience). This will involve exploration and evaluation of Kant's assertions regarding conscience and the conception of divinity, a task I turn to below.

I noted earlier that when Kant talks about the cultivation of conscience he does so predominantly in rational religious terms. This raises a central question: why, when the non-religious representations are available does he delve into rational religion? One reason could be that he is obliged to discuss conscience in this manner given his historical context (section 5.6). However, such a reason is both philosophically unexplanatory and fails to explain both the consistency and extensiveness with which Kant expresses the cultivation of conscience through religious notions. An alternative reason could be that he is committed to the position that rational religious notions are more effective in comparison to non-religious ones. Questions that arise from this are, is there textual evidence that supports this claim and is there anything philosophically to be said regarding this notion? In this section I will show that Kant does

---

Kant's Religion within the Boundaries of Mere Reason: A Critical Guide, 10–30. For a discussion of Kant's view of Jesus as a 'personified idea of the good principle' see M. Kuehn, 'Kant's Jesus', in *Kant's Religion within the Boundaries of Mere Reason: A Critical Guide*, 156–74 and *Kant: A Biography*, Cambridge University Press (2002), 24–60 (for a discussion of Kant's religious upbringing). For a more general discussion of Kant's relationship with Christianity see Schneewind, *The Invention of Autonomy*, 536–40.

94   It is also interesting to note that at two points in *Conflict of Faculties* Kant's comparisons between rational faith and ecclesiastical religion involve remarks on the (negative) impact that the latter has on the conception of conscience (7:51, 7:61fn).

indeed believe that the religious is more effective than the non-religious and
that this is a philosophically plausible claim.

Beginning by considering the notion of agent perfection, it is clear that there
is no obvious reason why the religious would be more effective in comparison
to the non-religious. Agent perfection relates to an aspirational ideal of always
choosing to act according to the moral law (explicated above as holiness). The
non-religious aspirational ideal is perfectly capable of fulfilling the role of cultivation. The 'ideal person' (*Metaphysics of Morals* 6:439) that represents the
inner judge could simply be the thought of a perfect human who always judges
impartially (rather than the God figure that Kant also suggests). Indeed, when
Kant states that agent perfection is to 'be holy' (6:446), although the term holy
does strike one as invoking a theological notion, in effect it just means always
acting according to the moral law. In fact, given Kant's emphasis that a holy
will (constitutionally incapable of not acting according to the moral law) is not
an aspirational model, the burden now rests on showing why at all he would
employ the more explicit theological language (albeit within his rational religious framework) with respect to conscience. Taking agent perfection alone, it
is difficult to see why he would have spoken in such a religious manner other
than because of the historical precedent.[95]

Turning to end perfection (a process of endless progress towards the ideal,
perfectly moral world), it is clearer why Kant would have employed rational
religious notions. The first point to note is that I have referred to evidence
earlier that Kant envisions end perfection as 'not to be reached (in this life)'
(*Metaphysics of Morals* 6:446). Taken as such, Kant's talk of rational religion
becomes central to the notion of end perfection: the endless progress that an
agent must strive towards is secured by the belief that such perfection is possible in an afterlife. However, Kant's theory of the morally idealised highest
good is complicated by the fact that at a number of points he seems to envi-
sion that the ideal world is, and can be, in reference to the sensible world.[96] In
'Two Conceptions of the Highest Good in Kant', Reath surveys Kant's writings
on the highest good and argues that two notions are present:[97] a 'theological
interpretation' that relies on notions such as the existence or activity of God,
or such concepts as that of an afterlife or another world, and contrastingly a

---

95   It is interesting to note that in a particular passage in *Conflict of Faculties* Kant can be read
      to be alluding to the belief in God as a practical postulate that allows an agent to coher-
      ently hope, and strive towards, achieving such a state (7:44).

96   See Third *Critique* 5:450–1, 453, 469, *Religion* 6:5, and Second *Critique* 5:120.

97   A. Reath, 'Two Conceptions of the Highest Good in Kant', *Journal of the History of
      Philosophy*, 26, 4, (1998), 593–619.

'secular interpretation' that can describe the highest good in entirely natural-istic terms 'as a state of affairs to be achieved in this world, though *human activity*'.[98] Reath elucidates his thesis by asserting that: i. both conceptions are present throughout Kant's work (an assertion that is supported by ample textual evidence), and ii. that the secular and theological interpretations have irreducible differences.[99] On the latter point Reath states that 'the theological version [...,] could not result from human conduct under any circumstances [...] we cannot even say what [it] would involve, or be like, without bringing in some theological notions (such as the activity of God). But we can say what the Highest Good would be like in its secular form—what ends it would involve, and how, within that state of affairs, they would be achieved—by referring only to human actions'.[100] The central irreducibility is that the secular refers to the sensible world and the theological to 'another' world.

Reath argues that the secular conception is preferable in comparison to the theological notion. Firstly, Reath explicates that the motivation to adopt the theological version rests on 'our inability to imagine the Highest Good occurring in this world lead[ing] us to posit its possibility in another', which he argues is problematic given the fact that 'one could construct the idea of a historical state of affairs in which social institutions were arranged to promote happiness in proportion to virtue [...] which individuals in the present [seek] to promote as the final end of moral conduct'.[101] Secondly, he explains that whereas the secular version is an ideal by which to guide conduct in order to 'bring about a world in which individuals can develop a morally good char-acter, and have the ability and means to achieve these ends', the theological conception is a not a state of affairs that an agent can adopt as an end for their concept.[102] This is problematic because 'it makes no sense to adopt a state of affairs as an end unless we can see ourselves as the agents who would bring it about'.[103] Reath's point here is that the role of human agency would be lim-ited. This leads him to assert that the secular conception provides a superior response to the problem of the imperfect world that agents live within. This is because the secular proposes 'a social ideal in which moral conduct is effec-tive in achieving certain ends, to be advanced by a restructuring of the exist-ing social environment', which is preferable to the theological version which

---

98   Ibid., 601.

99   Ibid., 593–4.

100   Ibid., 602.

101   Ibid., 602–3.

102   Ibid., 608.

103   Ibid., 609.

'might suggest the response that, while it is true that good conduct often does not lead to the results for which one hopes, that should not be a matter of great concern. The injustices of this world will be corrected in another, so that all moral agents eventually receive their due', i.e. a form of deferred justice.[104]

I believe that both of Reath's assertions are correct. Firstly it is clearly true that an agent can generate an idealised social world in the manner that Reath explicates, and posit this social world as some future state that an agent can continually progress towards. Secondly, I believe a stronger motivation for supporting Reath's thesis is that the secular is preferable because of the emphasis Kant places upon practical orientation in his vision of morality. Indeed, assuming that both views are available within the framework of what ideal the notion of end perfection should be like, the secular reading would be preferred to the theological for precisely this pragmatic/practical concern. However, there is a crucial ambiguity present with respect to the role of God at hand. The notion of end perfection is not only one that concerns what the end would be like i.e. a social ideal vs. ideal other world, but, more importantly it involves the very *securing of the possibility* that such ideals can even be coherently thought of and presumed. In fact, specifically with regard to this issue Reath makes it clear that

> Kant thought that, ultimately, we cannot fully understand how even the secular version of the Highest Good would be possible without the postulate of a moral author of the world, who orders the laws of history in a certain way.[105]

---

104   Ibid., 619. Reath also argues that the theological version seems to render itself susceptible to the charge of heteronomy in a manner that does not affect the secular version. Reath makes this point by asserting that the theological version reads as a kind of 'system of rewards and punishments' (ibid., 610), whereas in the secular version 'happiness of all would be a consequence of the proper functioning of [the ideal social] system. [...] Individuals [would not] promote the realization of this state of affairs by aiming at a connection between virtue and happiness. They would seek to establish social conditions that support moral conduct and the realization of various moral ends; once these conditions existed, the happiness of all would be the natural result' (ibid., 615). I cannot analyse this argument here.

105   Ibid., 601. Reath asserts this point again elsewhere, 'Even where Kant has a secular version in mind, he thought that we could not meaningfully conceive of it as a real possibility without adopting a belief in a moral author of the world, who ordered the laws of history so as to support progress towards this end in time' (ibid., 602).

Curiously, Reath makes this assertion without commenting upon the philo-sophical plausibility or consequence of this upon his two conceptions thesis. Rational religious notions cannot simply be reduced to the theological notion of another world. Rather, the secular view can be maintained alongside a more streamlined rational religious notion (that excludes the highest good being located in another world) so long as the latter is read as referring only to the possibility and utilisation of the pure practical postulate of God (thought of here as the 'moral author of the world' (Second *Critique* 5:145)).

I believe that this is a crucial point because although in the secular notion of the highest good the concept of God is present, it is vague, highly abstract and does not do much work, whereas with respect to conscience Kant's talk of God is in much more active forms.[106] Within this vein Davidovich explains that '[in order to] protect the practice of morality we must cultivate trust in a divine being who will assist in the realization of the ultimate moral end'.[107] This is of course only a limited role for God, which shows that faith can be rational but not rationally necessitated. An example of where Kant holds such a position is in his discussion of the concept of justice,[108] the central idea being that if an agent assumes that a supersensible moral being (suitably empow-ered) exists, then such a being would consider the suffering and injustices of the world unacceptable.[109] Notice that this does not invoke the notion of another world where justice will be realised. Rather, emphasis is on the postu-lation of God as a response to the imperfection of this world, not only to secure the possibility of a social ideal end but also to respond to the agent's embod-ied condition. Indeed there are no historical examples that an agent can draw upon as a social ideal and there are plenty of times that acting morally may

---

106 Here I draw upon A. Davidovich's treatment of the role of God as a richer concept (which she refers to as 'constructivism') that is more than simply an abstract pure practical pos-tulate, 'Kant's Theological Constructivism', *The Harvard Theological Review*, 86, 3, (1993), 323–51. Her study is particularly germane given the fact that she case studies conscience within her discussions.

107 Ibid., 326.

108 Kant speaks in terms of postulating 'divine assistance', that 'Every wish is impermissible, insofar as there is a lack of any rational ground for anticipating its fulfilment in accor-dance with the divine wisdom; so the only allowable wish is the moral one, i.e., that the petitioner's actions to the desired end be so constituted, that his own conscience may grant him approval, and that, insofar as he may think himself incapable of achieving it by his own powers, he may hope that God's assistance will be vouchsafed to him. This wish is good in itself, and conformable to morality' (27:728–9). See also *Collins* 27:251–2 and Second *Critique* 5:111.

109 See Davidovich, 'Kant's Theological Constructivism', 335fn38.

actually result in an agent becoming unhappy and/or suffering. This may lead to a kind of moral paralysis, where although an agent can know that the possibility of realising the social ideal of the highest good is rationally possible and therefore a permissible belief to hold, the agent nonetheless is psychologically incapable (in a practical sense) of utilising this abstract permissible belief.[110] This concept of God is far richer in its psychological dimension than that of Reath's theological minimalism. The role of God is not simply in being a postulate that secures possibility of the highest good being realised. Rather, what Kant is also alluding to is, as Davidovich puts it, '[the] psychological necessity of *trust* in God' (emphasis mine).[111]

The above is connected to the role of God in Kant's discussion of the role of conscience in the process of moral deliberation. Firstly, in terms of end perfection the belief in God can be thought of as an abstract postulate that secures the possibility that an agent may realise the morally idealised end of becoming an agent (or a world of such agents) whose conscience is always consulted, who judges impartially and whose judgment is always heeded, and that the happiness of such an agent will be in proportion to morality. Secondly, concerning a richer notion of God, Kant's discussion of conscience in the *Metaphysics of Morals* (6:438) is such that when an agent conceives of conscience they do so as a distinct person that they cannot escape. Indeed, it is within this context that he refers to conscience as 'peculiar' given the fact that 'its business is a business of a human being with himself', which is 'one constrained by his reason sees himself constrained to carry it out as the bidding of *another person*' (6:438). Kant justifies the solution of the positing of another person because of the peculiar complication of conscience in having the one agent act as defendant, prosecutor and judge all at once. He argues that to function the judge must be represented as 'someone other than himself', otherwise the 'prosecutor would always lose' i.e. the agent would always acquit themselves. He then states that this 'other may be an actual person or merely an ideal person that

---

110   Kant alludes to this in the Second *Critique* in a section titled 'On Assent from a Need of Pure Reason' where he discusses the 'subjective effect' of the pure practical postulates derived as possibilities from 'speculative reason' (5:142). Kant explains that in order to 'promote the *practically possible* highest good' an agent must 'presuppose at least' its practical possibility, otherwise 'it would be *practically impossible* to strive for the object of a concept that would be [...] empty and without on object' (emphasis mine, 5:143). Immediately following this Kant explains that the 'postulates concern only the physical and metaphysical [...] possibility of the highest good', suggesting that practical possibility is in reference to the envisioned highest good, standing in contrast to contentless/highly abstracted postulates.

111   Davidovich, 'Kant's Theological Constructivism', 336.

reason creates itself' (6:439), in other words in order for conscience to fulfil its role it must project itself as an outwardly image. Expanding on this Kant states that

> Such an **ideal person** (the **authorised judge of conscience**) must be a scrutinizer of hearts, [...] he must also impose all obligation, that is, he must be thought as, a person in relation to whom all duties whatsoever are to be regarded as also his commands; for **conscience is the inner judge of all free actions**—Now since such a moral being must also have all power (in heaven and earth) in order to give effect to his laws (as is necessarily required for the office of judge), and since such an omnipotent moral being is called God, **conscience must be thought of as the subjective principle of being accountable to God** for all one's deeds. In fact the latter concept is always contained **(even if only in an obscure way)** in the **moral self-awareness of conscience** (bold mine, 6:439).

He then explains that although an agent's conscience 'unavoidably guides him, to assume such a supreme being actually exists outside himself' an agent is not 'bound by his conscience' to assume such an idea, which he goes on to say is given to the agent 'only subjectively, by practical reason' (6:439). After stressing that this imaginative projection does not entitle agents to suppose that God exists, Kant goes on to assert that

> [I]n following out the analogy with a lawgiver for all rational beings in the world, human beings are merely pointed in the **direction of thinking of conscientiousness** (which is also called *relgio*) as accountability to a holy being (morally lawgiving reason) distinct from us yet present in our inmost being, and of submitting to the will of this being, as the rule of justice. The concept of religion is here for us only "a principle of estimating all our duties as divine commands" (bold mine, 6:439–40).[112]

---

112   Ware provides an analysis of the internal court such that the 'otherness' of the internal judge is limited i.e. the internal judge must be viewed as an ideal of one's self. Ware does so in order to counter the apparent problem that envisioning the inner judge as genuinely 'other' would make it more liable to an attempted deception ('The Duty of Self-Knowledge', 690, 95). Two problems arise from this reading. The first problem involves the ample textual evidence that shows that Kant speaks of conscience in the projected manner outlined above (Ware fails to survey these texts). The second problem involves the discussions in Chapter 4, namely, for the court of conscience to be coherent, *in order for the agent not to engage in flippant acquittal of oneself*, the otherness of the internal judge must be *emphasised*.

As explicated in the previous section, he employs the terms religion and divine command in the rational religious sense of instrumentalised aids towards moral behaviour. Crucial to the present discussion is noticing how far Kant strays from the notion of positing God merely as an abstract postulate that secures the possibility of a moral ideal. In the above he is talking about a 'direction of thinking' *qua* God as present in the moral self-awareness of conscience 'if only in an obscure way'. A few pages later, in a passage that reads as though directly following the above quote, he argues that the utilisation of

> [t]he Idea of God, [...] is not consciousness of a duty *to God*. For this Idea proceeds entirely from our own reason and *we ourselves make it, whether for the theoretical purpose of explaining to ourselves the purposiveness in the universe as a whole or also for the purpose of serving as the incentive in our conduct.* [...] it is a duty of man to himself to apply this Idea [...] where it is of the greatest moral fruitfulness. In this **(practical)** sense it can therefore be said that to have religion is a duty of man to himself (emphasis mine, 6:443–4).

In the above Kant is arguing that the idea of God should be judged by its fruitfulness, which clearly suggests that there can be more to the concept of God than simply its employment as an abstract practical postulate. In fact, as I have emphasised in the quote above, he explicates that an agent can make use of the idea 'for theoretical purpose' in explaining the 'purposiveness' of the universe as a whole *or* for the purpose of incentivising conduct.[113] It is this latter form of the utilisation of God that Kant's discussions of God and conscience touch upon.[114]

---

113   An example of this can be found in Kant's discussions of anthropomorphism. In the *Prolegomena* Kant explains that the dogmatic form of anthropomorphism, which attributes human properties to God, is to be avoided for reasons of transcendental idealism however agents can 'allow themselves a *symbolic* anthropomorphism, which in fact concerns only language and not the object itself' (4:357). Similarly in *Religion* Kant stresses that any conception of God cannot be one of 'an anthropomorphic servile faith' (6:141) because this notion is contrary not only to transcendental idealism but is also contrary to moral improvement (6:142). In fact, following the explication of how an agent can think of God in a permissibly construed anthropomorphism Kant then moves on to employ the example of where an agent can find themselves summoned to account before a judge in conscience (6:145). Clearly Kant is here explaining that a concept richer than the abstract postulate of God—the symbolic notion of God—can be utilised by an agent without falling foul to modes of thought deemed impermissible.

114   In the late text *The End of All Things* (1794) Kant discusses conscience precisely within the context of the belief in God and a future moral world (8:329–30). His discussion fits neatly

Throughout Kant's various discussions of conscience there is certainly evidence that he does indeed believe that the richer conception of God has greater moral fruitfulness than the use of God merely as a theoretical postulate. Beginning with the pre-Critical *Herder* notes, the preoccupation of conscience with God *qua* moral self-improvement is clear. For example, in a highly suggestive and somewhat mystical passage Kant talks of the 'image of God [...] in conscience'

> Perhaps the image of God consisted in the immediately clear sensation of the divine presence—not symbolic, but intuitive; not from inference but from sensation; and in that case, how vivid the effect upon morality and the ground of blessedness. With us, perhaps, the broadest and vaguest concept thereof still resides, even now, in conscience (27:19).

Although the preceding passage to the above quote does not provide any indication as to what Kant is referring to by 'consisted', given the manner with which he is talking about a false sensation of God it is highly likely that he is referring to 'enthusiasm' (the idea that agents can have direct sensation of God).[115] In the above, although Kant denies that the sensation of God is possible he nonetheless asserts that something may still be salvaged in the imagery associated with such a conception of God.[116] The purpose of pointing this out is directly related to self-improvement.[117] This becomes clear when he states (in the second half of the above passage)

> If we directly improve our moral feeling, we approach the divine presence in sensation; so maybe such people again develop the image, although their spiritual utterances sound fanatical; and religion elevates us to the highest degree of such sensation (27:19).

---

into the above analysis as he first makes it clear that the remit for such beliefs is 'practical' and not 'dogma', and then follows this by relating these beliefs to conscience as the judger of the agent in terms of how they have lived their lives. Admittedly Kant's remarks here are only cursory and require further explication, a task which I shall refrain from.

115 See Second *Critique* 5:86.

116 Kant situates this within a discussion where he surveys various false notions of religion, namely 'enthusiasm' (27:22) and 'pietism' (27:23). He explains that the 'image of God' can still serve a purpose in 'true morality', which 'partly already precedes all religion, but a part is greatly enhanced by religion, and since religion enhances the whole summa of morality' (27:19).

117 Indeed Kant sets up the discussion by pointing out 'God as a means is when we utilize the divine will as a means to the betterment of our own morality' (27:18).

The central point here is that it is by thinking with rational religious notions that agents are 'elevated' to such high degrees of sensation (divine presence), which may lead to moral improvement. Indeed elsewhere in *Herder*, when discussing the judge of conscience as an 'ideal man' who would judge impartially, Kant then moves on to invite agents to reflect upon the notion of an agent passing judgement upon themselves after they have passed away, 'debarred from passion after death, we are then impartial judges upon ourselves, and on our morality; the judgment upon our life will then be far more vivid and truthful [...]' (27:43). Here Kant is clearly invoking the thought of a kind of God's-eye-view identifying an idealised case of impartiality in comparison to embodied judgement.

Turning to the Critical period, *Collins* presents perhaps the best example of where rational religious notions are to be utilised as more than abstract practical postulates: Kant asserts that religious representations are relatively superior to non-religious representations via an analogy between the court of conscience, the external court of law and the divine court (27:295–7).[118] Kant explains that the appropriate way of thinking of the internal court is as analogous to the divine court, the reason being that external courts invoke the notion of being tried according to 'external universal law', whereas the divine court invokes the notion of being compelled to stand before something that has 'in fact [...] already occurred within him', in order to be 'punishable within himself' (27:298). Elsewhere, on the same point he compares the 'inner tribunal of conscience' with an external court and then immediately outlines that this comparison is lacking insofar as the court of conscience contains a 'law that we can in no way corrupt, nor dispute the rights and wrongs of' (27:354). He then shifts to exemplifying the comparison via an assertion that 'this moral law underlies humanity as a holy and inviolable law' (27:354).[119]

Kant actually outlines three reasons why 'conscience represents the divine tribunal' within agents

---

118   Pufendorf explicates the difference between natural and divine law in terms of legal forums, where natural law relates to the 'human forum' and divine law relates to 'the divine forum' (*The Duty of Man and Citizen*, 159). Where the former concerns 'only the external actions of man' and the latter 'is concerned chiefly with [...] the mind and its internal movements be[ing] fashioned after the will of the deity' (ibid.). Pufendorf's discussion of law in terms of both theological and secular terminology presents him as a synthesis between modern and classical natural law. For a discussion on his point see Schneewind, *The Invention of Autonomy*, 118–140.

119   See also *Collins* 27:433, *Vigilantius* 27:572.

[F]irst, because it judges our dispositions and actions according to the purity of the law; second, because we cannot deceive it; and last, because we cannot escape it, since, like the divine omnipresence, it is always with us. It is thus the representative within us of the divine justice, and hence must on no account be injured (27:355).

Presented in this form the relative superiority of rational religious notions becomes apparent. In terms of the first reason, the ideal man (however impartial his judgement may be) can only judge according to the best estimate of the law, which is in contrast to the purity with which the divine courts judge. With respect to the second and third reasons, however ideal the external judge may be such a judge is still susceptible to being deceived because its judgement is passed upon an evaluation of an agent from 'outside' rather than the inescapable evaluation of the inner judge which judges from the 'inside'. The inner (divine) judge has manifestly before itself an agent's inner beliefs (analogously to how the deity would be able to judge).[120] The very fact that Kant makes this distinction clearly shows the emphasis he places upon the difference between representations of secular and religious perfectionist models.[121]

Further evidence is to be found in *Lectures on Religion* where Kant states

[R]etributive punishments will become obvious only when our whole existence is considered, [...] *It is from this we get the majestic idea of a*

---

120   Elsewhere in *Collins* Kant explains that to not act against one's own conscience 'must be holy to me' (27:335). In explication of this he asserts 'to discern God's perfection is a necessary part of religion, which is meant to strengthen and reinforce our will to live according to the holy will of God. [...] We praise God only when we employ His perfections, and the glorification of them, as a motivating ground to awaken good dispositions of a practical kind in ourselves. [...] [The] usefulness [His perfections] is therefore merely subjective, and objective indirectly, by means of that.[...] in order for us to feel within us the greatness of God, we must be able to intuit it [...]' (emphasis mine, 27:336).

121   In *Lectures on Anthology* Kant makes the clearest statement of what is being presented in the above discussion of conscience in rational religious terms. In a discussion of the 'character of humanity in general' Kant refers to conscience as the 'Deity's Vicar' (a reference to Rousseau?) and asserts that the 'final constraint' is the 'constraint of conscience, where everyone would judge in accordance with his conscience about his actions' (25:695). Such a scenario would be 'the dominance of conscience [...] the kingdom of God on Earth' (ibid.). Kant states that the constraint of conscience 'cannot be achieved without religion, but religion cannot have any effect without morality; hence religion aims at the highest perfection of human beings'. See also 25:695–6 and, for a discussion of these passages see Munzel, 'What does his Religion Contribute to Kant's Conception of Practical Reason?', 219–20.

universal judgment of the world. There it is to be made well known before
all the world how far the human race has made itself *worthy* of a determinate happiness or unworthy of it through transgression of holy moral
laws. At the same time, the conscience, that judge in us which is not
to be bribed, will place before the eyes of each one the whole world of
his earthly life and convince him himself of the justice of the verdict
(28:1087).

Here, Kant's use of language (in particular his talk of a 'majestic idea') is particularly strong in evoking a connection between a God-like divine judgement
and the notion of conscience. More precisely, in describing conscience as
convincing an agent of the justice of such God-judgements the *priority* of conscience becomes apparent (it is conscience that is ultimately *authoritative* for
an agent and as such *it can* and *must confirm* such judgements to the agent
themselves).[122]

As an evaluation and response to the above an argument may be put forth
that although the religious model of conscience introduces a richer notion
of God, it nonetheless falls foul to a number of criticisms. The first is that
it is difficult to assess an argument that relies on psychological assumptions
regarding the need to invoke theological notions in the face of suffering
and injustice.[123] The second is that although Kant is introducing the religious
notions and, as I have argued, is asserting that they present greater moral
fruitfulness (more effective) than the secular notions, suitable secular notions
can be generated that dissolve the apparent superiority of the religious representations. For example, in response to Kant's assertion that it is better to
think of the inner judge as a God-like figure rather than as a perfectly impartial judge (because however impartial the latter is it cannot judge 'hearts'),
perhaps a thought experiment could be invoked where judges are thought of
as employing machine-like devices which function as advanced polygraphs
that are infallible. The third is that rather than suggesting Kant's religious talk
has anything to do with its relative superiority over the non-religious, a more
simple explanation would be that religious notions of conscience present but
one example of his greater project of 'making room for faith' (First *Critique*
Bxxx). In other words, he should be read as simply providing an intellectually
permissible option for the religiously inclined.

---

122   See also *Lectures on Religion* 28:1120.
123   For example, one only needs to compare the atheistic existentialism of Camus to that of
      the theistic existentialism of Dostoyevsky.

These are certainly strong retorts to the claim that philosophically the religious model can be defended as superior relative to the non-religious (in terms of moral self-improvement), however in the particular case of having to represent an ideal other in the internal court there is a strong reason that the religious notion should be affirmed as comparatively superior. The philosophical concern is one that centres on the fact that the very functioning of conscience as an internal court rests upon the ability of an agent to project the judge as distinct from themselves. Recall that for Kant although conscience is an internal voice it needs nonetheless to be considered as distinct from oneself (otherwise the absurdity of being the defendant, prosecutor and judge all at the same time would occur (*Metaphysics of Morals* 6:438)).[124] The religious is still to be considered superior because how the subject characterises the inner voice (what the agent *imagines* is going on) is what is crucial. If an agent imagines a secular judge, the agent may think that all they have to do is convince this judge, i.e. I need to convince this other person. When the judge is thought of as God, because God knows the thoughts of an agent as they think them ('all seeing'), although God is a distinct mind there is no equivalent gap as there would be between the agent's thoughts and that of a secular judge. In other words, with respect to God there is an immediacy which is not present with respect to the secular judge. Whereas there is no negotiating with God, there is at least the possibility to do so with the secular judge. This distinction is still applied to the notion of an infallible polygraph because although the polygraph may reveal the honesty of an agent, an agent can still imagine that there is some way in which they can navigate the judge who utilises the results of the polygraph.[125] It may be construed that the secular judge is infallible in *all senses*, and hence also infallible in the interpretation of the polygraph. However such a stipulation would make the secular judge equivalent to the notion of God and thereby itself be in essence a religious example. As such, I believe that

---

124   Here I put aside the concerns regarding this claim, such as why it cannot simply be the case that the various representations are not just different aspects of the self (rather than the judge as a distinct person).

125   In making use of the polygraph, the judge of conscience must of course also be thought of as enforcing its judgement, see *Metaphysics of Morals* 6:439, and *Collins* 27:355. Moreover, in the case of conscience the thought of a holy will can even be introduced. Recall that the holy will is deemed as undesirable by Kant because it fails to exhibit free choice. However, in the case of conscience such a notion would be thought of as an ideal model i.e. the thought of an internal judge that judges the heart being constitutionally incapable of judging partially would actually be the most distant idealised 'other' possible. Here the religious is providing an exemplar which does not appear to have a non-religious (read: embodied) equivalent.

Kant's claim that a religious notion may be more effective in the cultivation of conscience compared to a non-religious notion is philosophically plausible.

5.8   Conclusion

Concerning the Unity Thesis, Chapter 5 showed that Kant's views on conscience are firmly situated within his views on moral self-improvement, and that conscience must be cultivated in such a manner as to sustain the viability of the internal court that an agent is to take authoritatively. Indeed, this highlighted that the concept of conscience may contain the notion of divinity, a point that cannot be understood by simply looking at the judgement of conscience (Chapter 2), or the non-erring nature of conscience (Chapter 3), or the fact that conscience resists self-deception (Chapter 4). A central element in understanding the role of conscience in turning inwards *qua* morality was also explicated here. In the cultivating of conscience Kant envisions a movement towards perfection. Indeed, conscience proves to be an important mechanism by which an agent may reflect on their character as a rational being, and within a moral teleology.

CHAPTER 6

Conclusion

This study provides both a descriptive account of Kant's theory of conscience and philosophically explores issues that his theory raises from the position of contemporary (analytical) philosophy. With respect to the Unity Thesis, this study followed the following line: Chapter 2, constituted the first stage in the presentation of the Unity Thesis by outlining the fundamental nature and function of conscience *qua* the judgement of conscience. I did this by arguing that Kant takes conscience to be a particular manifestation of practical reason, which results in a feeling that is produced as a result of its determination viz. a judgement with respect to whether or not an agent has been diligent in the examination of their actions. However, at various points I bracketed certain issues that arose. Most importantly, I did not fully explore the function that conscientious reflection plays in revealing a bindingness of duty to *oneself.* In order to fully explicate this point, it was necessary to delve deeper into the nature of the judgement of conscience. Chapter 3 provided an important step in the defence of the Unity Thesis as it built upon the explication of the judgement of conscience presented in Chapter 2. Indeed, by discussing the non-erring judgment of conscience, and the extent and nature of Kant's notion of subjective certainty within this context, the importance of conscience is elevated from merely a higher-order judgement to one where an agent can gain 'certainty' in their actions (an element vital for Kantian moral practice). Crucially, by demonstrating the importance of the notion of subjective certainty, and how this relates to conscientiousness, the emphasis of conscience with respect to the first-personal perspective was shown. Conscience concerns actions that 'I must undertake'. It involves a fundamental turn to oneself in light of one's held beliefs regarding propositions (c.f. formal conscientiousness) and actions more generally (c.f. material conscientiousness). This turn towards the 'I', that is central to the understanding of conscience, is paradoxically facilitated by the notion of an internal court—a court that is premised on the notion of an 'other' that is represented by the inner judge. Chapter 4 followed as a natural corollary to the discussion of the non-erring judgement of conscience found in Chapter 3. As such it demonstrates the intricate relation between the Absurdity Thesis and the resistance to the notion of internal lies that conscience provides. Indeed, the notion of subjective certainty provides the foundation upon which Kant can present conscience as a mechanism that resists a particular class of self-deception. Notice also that this chapter,

© KONINKLIJKE BRILL NV, LEIDEN, 2017 | DOI 10.1163/9789004340664_007 in explicating the internal lie, expands upon the theme that conscience is a *turn inwards*. The interiority of the judgement is via the court accessing what an agent holds to be true (i.e. subjective certainty). This is an important step in the understanding of the Unity Thesis: conscience is not only a higher-order moral judgement; it is also a mechanism that functions to preserve personhood (taken here in terms of rational agency). Nonetheless, the multiple consciousness model that I had provided regarding the internal court of conscience required further elaboration. I turned to this task in Chapter 5. Concerning the Unity Thesis, Chapter 5 showed that Kant's views on conscience are firmly situated within his views on moral self-improvement, and that conscience must be cultivated in such a manner as to sustain the viability of the internal court that an agent is to take authoritatively. Indeed, this highlighted that the concept of conscience may contain the notion of divinity, a point that cannot be understood by simply looking at the judgement of conscience (Chapter 2), or the non-erring nature of conscience (Chapter 3), or the fact that conscience resists self-deception (Chapter 4). A central element in understanding the role of conscience in turning inwards *qua* morality was also explicated here. In the cultivating of conscience Kant envisions a movement towards perfection. Indeed, conscience proves to be an important mechanism by which an agent may reflect on their character as a rational being, and within a moral teleology.

In defending the Unity Thesis, I believe I have not only bought to the fore the richness of Kant's theory of conscience, but also highlighted the concern that Kant himself has for this concept. Indeed, I believe I have shown that the concept not only reveals aspects of Kant's thoughts regarding various issues, but have also shown that conscience itself—its function, activity and cultivation—provides a perspective on the nature of moral practice in Kant generally. Conscience demonstrates a double movement. Firstly, by providing a direct aide in the advancement of moral action through its higher-order moral judgement. Through conscience agents may improve the moral success (in term of acting in accordance with utmost diligence) of their moral-practical action. Secondly, conscience provides an important *turn inwards*. It directs an agent to take concern for actions that 'I' must undertake. Indeed, *via* rational reflection *qua* the cultivation of conscience, agents have a mechanism by which they maintain their personhood, come to a heightened awareness of their status as free, rational beings, and thereby the incumbency of acting morally. Importantly, this double movement can be read as occurring together. Kantian morality is about the practical orientation, and conscience certainly functions in this role via the higher-order judgement, but concurrently to this is also the concern for morality itself which conscience provides via the very nature of its functioning as an internal court (with the presence of the ideal other i.e. the internal judge). Crucially, this is important insofar as a correct understanding of Kant's account of conscience sheds light on his ethical thought. Conscience brings together the (external) practical action with the (internal) concern for morality itself: I must act morally, and such moral actions must be conducted veraciously.

More directly, Kantian conscience helps us better understand the ethics as a whole when it is pointed out that it completes the moral picture. Conscience functions at the higher, reflective level of morality. When Kant discusses conscience, he can be read as doing so after laying the foundations of this ethical thought in the *Groundwork* and the Second *Critique*. As discussed in Chapter 2, in these texts Kant presents the basic concepts of morality and moral action. It is following these that Kant can then discuss moral practice more generally. It is in this broader sense, in explication of the full vocation of moral life that conscience can be observed as central, and as such, in order to fully appreciate Kant's ethics his notion of conscience must be understood. In other words, conscience completes Kant's account of a fully functioning moral agent (hence why it touches on such disparate notions as higher-order moral judgement, subjective certitude, and moral cultivation).

On the descriptive side of this study, I have shown that despite the fact that Kant refers to conscience in disparate manners—within the contexts of feelings, as a power, as a judgement, as a capacity, as a court, as the voice of God, etc.—it is nonetheless still possible to read him as referring to one underlying concept. I have been able to demonstrate this by treating his assertions thematically and by showing that in each seemingly disparate description of conscience he is referring to a particular aspect of the notion of conscience. As a result of this analysis it is clear how Kant can coherently speak of conscience as practical reason and as the voice of God i.e. internal consistency. To reiterate, the Unity Thesis is not an assertion that Kant's notion of conscience remained the same throughout the Critical period: indeed, that he amends, adds to and changes the emphasis on particular aspects of conscience is entirely compatible with the Unity Thesis. One example of where Kant provides inconsistent accounts of an aspect of conscience is in the two versions of the Absurdity Thesis (as presented in Chapter 3). Although I showed that Kant has two (inconsistent) expressions of the Absurdity Thesis, ascribing the Absurdity Thesis claim itself to conscience does not contradict the analysis regarding the cultivation of conscience viz. rational religious representation. Indeed, I have shown how the characterisation of conscience as practical reason is congruent with the cultivation of conscience as the voice of God by demonstration of what particular aspect of conscience is in play.

Philosophically, I believe the work presented here brings to the fore and sheds light on various aspects of the practice of morality in Kant. Indeed, I have attempted to evaluate issues raised by the notion of conscience. In Chapter 2 I fleshed out the notion of conscientious higher-order moral judgement. This is important in terms of moral practice as it presents a more holistic picture of moral judgements (in comparison to the highly commented upon first-order moral judgement). In Chapter 3 I attempted to read the Absurdity Thesis from the perspective of assertive statements and epistemological justification. I believe Kant's notion of subjective certainty is a rich concept whose application in the context of conscientiousness was particularly fruitful. I also believe that this contributes to understanding an aspect of the relationship between Kant's ethics and his epistemology of moral commitment. In Chapter 4 I provided an account of Kantian moral deliberation within the context of conscience and have provided a model (multiple consciousness) by which to explicate the possibility of internal lies. I believe that this is an important and novel contribution to the literature on Kantian self-deception. In Chapter 5 I fleshed out Kant's account of an indirect duty to cultivate conscience and explicated his religious language in this context. It is my belief that this has highlighted an important element in his religious philosophy and more broadly contributes to questions that concern the relationship between religious and non-religious notions of conscience in the relevant historical context.

Admittedly, the study provided here has been limited specifically to an explication of Kant's notion of conscience and has not fully explored the relationship between conscience and other themes. As such, the work provided here can be expanded upon or utilised to inform a number of other studies. For example, given the fact that the judgement that comes from the inner judge of conscience seems to be an expression of a unified self-consciousness—the 'I' as ideal other, which seems to be a paradigmatic case in Kant's practical philosophy—the relationship between conscience and apperception can be explored further (or more broadly, Kant's philosophy of mind). Moreover, the exploration of conscience *qua* indirect duty that I have provided here can be expanded upon to categorise and explore conscience *qua* different types of duty (perfect/imperfect, Right/Virtue and oneself/others). A further study can be conducted on Kantian conscience and his aesthetics. Here I see two potentially fruitful studies: i. modelling the feeling of conscience on the sublime. This comes from the fact that conscience can be read as having two moments; a negative moment in the form of a pang, followed by the potentially positive moment of realising that this is derived from an agent's rational capacity. And, ii. a more general exploration that attempts to read conscience in terms of the

Third *Critique*. An alternative avenue that can be explored is the relationship between conscience and the political philosophy. Here an investigation can be conducted into the potential conflict, or reconciliation, between Kant's assertion that one must always follow ones conscience and his conservative political philosophy.

Bibliography

Allison, H. E. *Kant's Transcendental Idealism: An Interpretation and Defence*, Yale University Press (2004).

Allison, H. E. 'Morality and Freedom: Kant's Reciprocity Thesis', *The Philosophical Review*, 95, 3, (1986), 393–425.

Allison, H. E. *Kant's Groundwork for the Metaphysics of Morals: A Commentary*, Oxford University Press (2011).

Allison, H. E. *Kant's Theory of Freedom*, Cambridge University Press (1990).

Allison, H. E. *Kant's Groundwork for the Metaphysics of Morals: A Commentary*, Oxford University Press (2011), 275–6.

Allport, G. W. and Postman, L. *Psychology of Rumor*, Henry Hold & Co. (1947).

Ameriks, K. 'Kant, Miracles, and Religion, Parts One and Two', in *Kant's Religion within the Boundaries of Mere Reason: A Critical Guide*, ed. G. E. Michalson, Cambridge University Press (2014), 137–55.

Anderson, D. J. 'Knowledge and Conviction', *Synthese*, 187, 2 (2012), 377–92.

Atwell, J. E. *Ends and Principles in Kant's Moral Thought*, Nijhoff Publishers (1986).

Audi, R. 'Self-Deception, Action, and Will', *Erkenntnis*, 18, 2, (1975), 133–58.

Audi, R. 'Self-Deception and Practical Reasoning', *Canadian Journal of Philosophy*, 19, 2, (1989), 247–66.

Augustine. *Treaties on Various Subjects*, ed. R. J. Deferrari, Catholic University of America Press (1952).

Auxter, T. *Kant's Moral Teleology*, Mercer University Press (1982).

Ayers, M. *Locke*, Routledge (1996).

Bach, K. 'An Analysis of Self-Deception', *Philosophy and Phenomenological Research*, 41, 3, (1981), 351–70.

Bagnoli, C. 'Self-deception: a Constructivist Account', *HumanaMente* 20, (2012), 93–116.

Banham, G. 'Kantian Respect', *Kant Studies Online*, (2008), 1–14.

Barnes, J. 'Belief is up to Us', *Proceedings of the Aristotelian Society*, 106, (2006), 189–206.

Barnes, W. H. F. 'Knowing', *The Philosophical Review*, 72, 1 (1963), 3–16.

Beets, M. G. J. *Reality and Freedom: Reflections on Kant's Moral Philosophy*, Eburon Press (1988).

Benton, R. J. 'Political Expediency and Lying: Kant vs Benjamin Constant', *Journal of the History of Ideas*, 43, 1, (1982), 135–44.

Bermúdez, J. L. 'Self-Deception, Intentions, and Contradictory Beliefs', *Analysis*, 60, 4, (2000), 309–19.

Bielefeldt, H. *Symbolic Representation in Kant's Practical Philosophy*, Cambridge University Press (2003).

Bok, S. *Lying: Moral Choice in Public and Private Life*, Pantheon Books (1978).

Bratman, M. 'Practical Reasoning and Acceptance in a Context', *Mind*, 101, 401, (1992), 1–15.

Buckareff, A. A. 'Acceptance and Deciding to Believe', *Journal of Philosophical Research*, 29, (2004), 173–90.

Buckareff, A. A. 'Doxastic Decisions and Controlling Belief', *Acta Analytica*, 21, (2006), 102–14.

Callanan, J. J. 'The Role of the Holy Will', *Hegel Bulletin*, 35, 2, (2014), 163–84.

Canfield, J., and McNally, P. 'Paradoxes of Self-Deception', *Analysis*, 21, 6, (1961), 140–4.

Carmichael, P. A. 'Knowing', *The Journal of Philosophy*, 56, 8, (1959), 341–51.

Carson, T. L. 'The Definition of Lying', *Nous*, 40, 2, (2006), 284–306.

Carson, T. L. *Lying and Deception: Theory and Practice* Oxford University Press (2010).

Chignell, A. 'Belief in Kant', *The Philosophical Review*, 116, 3, (2007), 323–60.

Chignell, A. 'Kant's Concepts of Justification', *Nous*, 41, 1, (2007), 33–63.

Chisholm R. M., and Feehan, T. D. 'The Intent to Deceive', *Journal of Philosophy*, 74, (1977), 143–59.

Cohen, J. *An Essay on Belief and Acceptance*, Oxford University Press (1992).

Cohen, J. 'Belief and Acceptance', *Mind*, 98, (1989), 367–89.

Cousin, D. R. 'Probability', *The Philosophical Quarterly*, 4, 14, (1954), 82–4.

Cummiskey, D. *Kantian Consequentialism, Ethics*, 100, 3 (1990), 586–615.

Darwall, S. L. 'Kantian Practical Reason Defended', *Ethics*, 96, 1 (1985), 89–99.

Darwall, S. L. *The British Moralists and the Internal 'Ought' 1640–1740*, Cambridge University Press (1995).

Davidovich, A. 'Kant's Theological Constructivism', *The Harvard Theological Review*, 86, 3, (1993), 323–51.

Davidson, D. 'Deception and Division', in *The Multiple Self*, ed. J. Elster, Cambridge University Press (1985), 79–92.

de Pierris, G. 'Subjective Justification', *Canadian Journal of Philosophy*, 19, 3, (1989), 363–82.

Dean, R. *The Value of Humanity in Kant's Moral Theory*, Oxford University Press (2006).

Demos, R. 'Lying to Oneself', *The Journal of Philosophy*, 57, 18, (1960), 558–95.

Denis, L. 'Kant's Ethics and Duties to Oneself', *Pacific Philosophical Quarterly*, 78, 4, (1997), 321–48.

Denis, L. *Moral Self-Regard. Duties to Oneself in Kant's Moral Theory*, Garland Publishing (2001).

Desideri, F. *L'ascolto della coscienza: una ricerca filosofica*, Feltrinelli Editore (1998).

Despland, M. 'Can Conscience Be Hypocritical? The Contrasting Analyses of Kant and Hegel', *The Harvard Theological Review*, 68, ¾, (1975), 357–70.

Dewey, J. *Leibniz's New Essays Concerning the Human Understanding: A Critical Exposition*, Nabu Press (2011).

DeWitt, J. 'Respect for the Moral Law: the Emotional Side of Reason', *Philosophy*, 89, 1, (2014), 31–62.

Edward, G. 'Hobbes on Conscience within the Law and without', *Canadian Journal of Political Science*, 32, 2, (1999), 203–25.

Eells, E. 'Objective Probability Theory', *Synthese*, 57, 3, (1983), 387–442.

Engstrom, S. 'Deriving Duties to Oneself: Comments on Andrews Reath's 'Self-Legislation and Duties to Oneself', *The Southern Journal of Philosophy*, 36, (1997), 125–30.

Engstrom, S. 'The Concept of the Highest Good in Kant's Moral' Theory', *Philosophy and Phenomenological Research*, 52, 4, (1992), 747–80.

Engstrom, S. 'The *Triebfeder* of pure practical reason', in *Kant's Critique of Practical Reason: A Critical Guide*, ed. A. Reath and J. Timmermann, Cambridge University Press (2010), 90–118.

Esser, A. M. 'The Inner Court of Conscience, Moral Self-Knowledge, and the Proper Object of Duty (TL 6:437–444)', in *Kant's "Tugendlehre". A Comprehensive Commentary*, ed. O. Sensen, J. Timmermann and A. Trampota, Walter de Gruyter (2013), 269–91.

Feldman, K. S. 'Conscience and the Concealment of Metaphor in Hobbes's Leviathan', *Philosophy and Rhetoric*, 34, 1, (2001), 21–37.

Feldman, R. 'Voluntary Belief and Epistemic Evaluation', in *Knowledge, Truth, and Duty*, ed. M. Steup, Oxford University Press (2001), 77–92.

Fingarette, H. 'Self-Deception Needs No Explaining', *The Philosophical Quarterly*, 48, 192, (1998), 289–301.

Firestone, C. L., and Jacobs, N. *In Defense of Kant's Religion*, Indiana University Press (2008).

Formose, P. 'Is Kant a Moral Constructivist or a Moral Realist?', *European Journal of Philosophy*, 21, 2, (2013), 170–96.

Forrester, M. 'Self-Deception and Valuing Truth', *American Philosophical Quarterly*, 39, 1, (2002), 31–47.

Franks, P. W. *All or Nothing: Systematicity, Transcendental Arguments, and Skepticism in German Idealism*, Harvard University Press (2005), 260–336.

Fulton, R. 'Pierre Bayle and Human Rights', *Fifth Annual History Graduate Student Association Conference, Northern Illinois University Selected Conference Papers*, (2012), 60–93.

Funke, G. 'Gutes Gewissen, falsches Bewußtsein, richtende Vernunft', *Zeitschrift für Philosophische Forschung*, 25, (1971), 226–51.

Gardiner, P. 'Error, Faith and Self-Deception', *Proceedings of the Aristotelian Society*, 70, (1969–1970), 221–43.

Gilbert, P. 'Immediate Experience', *Proceedings of the Aristotelian Society*, 92, (1992), 233–50.

Gill, M. B. 'Ethics and Sentiment', in *Routledge Companion to Ethics*, ed. J. Skorupski, Routledge (2010), 111–22.

Gill, M. B. *The British Moralists on Human Nature and the Birth of Secular Ethics*, Cambridge University Press (2006).

Grenberg, J. *Kant's Defense of Common Moral Experience: A Phenomenological Account*, Cambridge University Press (2013).

Griswold, C. L. *Adam Smith and the Virtues of Enlightenment*, Cambridge University Press (1998).

Grotius, H. *On the Law of War and Peace*, trans. A. C. Campbell, Wildside Press (2011).

Guevara, D. *Kant's Theory of Moral Motivation*, Westview Press (2000).

Gustavson, D. F. 'Self-Deception', *Analysis*, 23, 2, (1962), 32–6.

Guyer, P. 'Moral Feelings in the Metaphysics of Morals', in *Kant's Metaphysics of Morals: A Critical Guide*, ed. L. Denis, Cambridge University Press (2010), 143–52.

Guyer, P. *Kant and the Claims of Knowledge*, Cambridge University Press (1987), 333–70.

Guyer, P. *Kant on Freedom, Law, and Happiness*, Cambridge University Press (2000), 292–305.

Haakonssen, K. 'Early Modern Natural Law', in *Routledge Companion to Ethics*, ed. J. Skorupski, Routledge (2010), 76–87.

Haakonssen, K. *Natural Law and Moral Philosophy*, Cambridge University Press (1996).

Hampton, J. *Hobbes and the Social Contract Tradition*, Cambridge University Press (1986).

Henige, D. 'The Implausibility of Plausibility/The Plausibility of Implausibility', *Historical Reflections*, 30, 2, (2004), 311–35.

Henrich, D. 'The Proof-Structure of Kant's Transcendental Deduction', *Review of Metaphysics*, 22, 4, (1969), 640–65.

Herman, B. 'Training to Autonomy: Kant and the Questions of Moral Education', in *Philosophers on Education*, ed. A. O. Rorty, Routledge (1998), 255–72.

Herman, B. *The Practice of Moral Judgment*, Harvard University Press (1993).

Hernandez, J. G. 'Impremisibility and Kantian Moral Worth', *Ethical Theory and Moral Practice*, 13, 4 (2010), 403–19.

Heubült, W. 'Gewissen bei Kant', *Kant-Studien*, 71, (1980), 445–54.

Hill, T. E. *Human Welfare and Moral Worth*, Oxford University Press (2002), 279–307.

Hill, T. E. 'Kant's Theory of Practical Reason', *The Monist*, 72, 3, (1989), 363–83.

Hills, A. 'Duties and Duties to the Self', *American Philosophical Quarterly*, 40, 2, (2003), 131–42.

Hills, A. 'Gesinnung: Responsibility, Moral worth, and Character', *Kant's Religion within the Boundaries of Mere Reason: A Critical Guide*, ed. G. E. Michalson, Cambridge University Press (2014), 79–97.

Hills, A. 'Kant on Happiness and Reason', *History of Philosophy Quarterly*, 23, 3, (2006), 243–61.

Hirst, R. J. *Problems of Perception*, Routledge (2013).

Hirstein, W. 'Self-Deception and Confabulation', *Philosophy of Science*, 67, *Supplement. Proceedings of the 1998 Biennial Meetings of the Philosophy of Science Association. Part II: Symposia Papers* (2000), S418–29.

Hobbes, T. *Leviathan*, Cambridge University Press (2012).

Hobbes, T. *On the Citizen*, Cambridge University Press (1998).

Hochstrasser, T. *Natural Law Theories in the Early Enlightenment*, Cambridge University Press (2000).

Hoffe, O. 'Holy Scriptures within the Boundaries of Mere Reason: Kant's Reflections', in *Kant's Religion within the Boundaries of Mere Reason: A Critical Guide*, ed. G. E. Michalson, Cambridge University Press (2014), 10–30.

Hoffmann, T. S. 'Gewissen als praktische Apperzeption: Zur Lehre vom Gewissen in Kants Ethik-Vorlesungen', *Kant-Studien*, 93, (2002), 424–4.

Hofmeister, H. E. M. 'The Ethical Problem of the Lie in Kant', *Kant-Studien*, 63, (1972), 353–68.

Hofmeister, H. E. M. 'Truth and Truthfulness: A Reply to Dr. Schwars', *Ethics*, 82, (1972), 262–7.

Hohlrabe, W. *Kants Lehre vom Gewissen; historisch-kritisch dargestellt*, Inaugural Dissertation, Leipzig, (1880).

Holton, R. 'What is the Role of the Self in Self-Deception', *Proceedings of the Aristotelian Society*, 101, (2001), 53–69.

Howard, J. J. 'Kant and Moral Imputation: Conscience and the Riddle of the Given', *American Catholic Philosophical Quarterly*, 78, 4, 609–27.

Hume, D. *A Treatise of Human Nature (Second Edition)*, Oxford University Press (1978).

Hunter, I. *Rival Enlightenments: Civil and Metaphysical Philosophy in Early Modern German*, Cambridge University Press (2001).

Hutcheson, F. *A Short Introduction to Moral Philosophy*, The University of Glasgow (1787).

Hutcheson, F. *A System of Moral Philosophy*, R. and A. Foulis (1755).

Hutcheson, F. *On Human Nature*, ed. T. Mautner, Cambridge University Press (1993).

Irwin, T. *The Development of Ethics, Vol II*, Oxford University Press (2011).

Ishikawa, F. 'Das Gerichtshof-Modell des Gewissens', *Aufklärung*, 7, 1, (1993), 43–55.

Jacquette, D. 'Moral Dilemmas, Disjunctive Obligations, and Kant's Principle That "Ought" Implies "Can" ', Synthese, 88, 1, (1991), 43–55.

Jeffrey, R. *Subjective Probability*, Cambridge University Press (2004).

Johnson, R. N. 'Value and Autonomy in Kantian Ethics', in *Oxford Studies in Metaethics: Volume II, Volume 2*, ed. R. Shafer-Landau, Oxford University Press (2007), 133–47.

Johnston, M. 'Self-Deception and the Nature of Mind', in *Philosophy of Psychology*, ed. C. MacDonald and G. MacDonald, Blackwell (1995).

Johnstone, H. W. 'The Logical Powerfulness of Philosophical Arguments', *Mind*, 64, 256, (1955), 539–41.

Kahn, S. 'Kant's Theory of Conscience', in, *Rethinking Kant*, ed. P. Muchnik, O. Thorndike, Cambridge Scholars Publishing, (forthcoming).

Keith, P. *Certainty*, University of Minnesota Press (1981).

Kelly, C. 'Kant's Dynamic Theory of Character', *Kantian Review*, 7, (2003), 38–71.

Kilcullen, J. *Sincerity and Truth: Essays on Arnauld, Bayle and Toleration*, Oxford University Press (1988).

Kipp, D. 'On Self-Deception', *The Philosophical Quarterly*, 30, 121, (1980), 305–17.

Kirwan, C. A. 'Truth and Universal Assent', *Canadian Journal of Philosophy*, 11, 3, (1981), 377–94.

Kitcher, P. 'Kant's Argument for the Categorical Imperative', *Nous*, 38, 4 (2004), 555–84.

Kitcher, P. 'Kant on Self-Identity', *Philosophical Review*, 91, 1, (1982), 515–47.

Kittsteiner, H. D. 'Casuistry and Character', in *Conscience and Casuistry in Early Modern Europe*, ed. E. Leites, Cambridge University Press (1988), 185–213.

Kleingeld, P. 'Kant, History, and the Idea of Moral Development', *The History* of *Philosophy Quarterly*, 16, 1, (1999), 59–80.

Kleingeld, P. 'Moral consciousness and the "fact of reason"', in Kant's Critique of Practical Reason: A Critical Guide, ed. A. Reath and J. Timmermann, Cambridge University Press (2010), 73–89.

Kleingeld, P. 'What Do the Virtuous Hope For: Re-Reading Kant's Doctrine of the Highest Good', in *Proceedings for the Eighth International Kant Congress*, ed. H. Robinson, Marquette University Press (1995), 91–112.

Klemme, H. F. 'The Origin and Aim of Kant's Critique of Practical Reason' in *Kant's Critique of Practical Reason*, ed. A. Reath and J. Timmermann, Cambridge University Press (2010).

Knapp, M. L. *Lying and deception in human interaction*, Pearson Education/Penguin Academics, (2008).

Korsgaard, C. 'Kant's formula of universal law', *Pacific Philosophical Quarterly*, 66, 1–2, (1985), 24–47.

Korsgaard, C. 'Realism and Constructivism in Twentieth-Century Moral Philosophy', *The Journal of Philosophical Research*, 28, (2003), 99–122.

Korsgaard, C. 'The Right to lie: Kant on Dealing with Evil', *Philosophy and Public Affairs* 15, 4, (1986), 325–49.

Kovar, L. 'The Pursuit of Self-Deception', *Salmagundi*, 29, (1975), 28–44.

Kuehn, M. *Kant: A Biography*, Cambridge University Press (2002).

Kuehn, M. 'Kant's Jesus', in *Kant's Religion within the Boundaries of Mere Reason: A Critical Guide*, ed. G. E. Michalson, Cambridge University Press (2014), 156–174.

Kupfer, J. 'The Moral Presumption Against Lying', *The Review of Metaphysics*, 36, 1, (1982), 103–26.

Kvanvig, J. L. 'Subjective Justification', *Mind*, 93, 369, (1984), 71–84.

Lehmann, G. *Kants Tugenden: Neue Beitr ge zur Geschichte und Interpretation der Philosophie Kants*, Walter de Gruyter (1980).

Leibniz, G. W. *New Essays on Human Understanding*, trans. and ed. B. Remmant and J. Bennet, Cambridge University Press (1998).

Lennon, T. M. *Reading Bayle*, Toronto University Press (1999).

Locke, J. *An Essay Concerning Human Understanding*, ed. A. S. Pringle-Pattison, Oxford University Press (1947).

Locke, J. *A Letter Concerning Toleration*, Hackett (1983).

Locke, J. *Essay Concerning Human Understanding*, ed. P. H. Nidditch, Clarendon (1979).

Longeway, J. L. 'The Rationality of Escapism and Self-Deception', *Behavior and Philosophy*, 18, 2, (1990), 1–20.

Longuenesse, B. *Kant and the Capacity to Judge*, Princeton University Press (1998).

Lucht, M. 'Toward Lasting Peace, Kant On Law, Public Reasoning and Culture', *American Journal of Economics and Sociology*, 68, 1, (2009), 303–26.

MacBeath, M. 'Kant on Moral Feeling', *Kant-Studien*, 74, (1973), 283–314.

Mahon, J. E. 'A Definition of Deceiving', *International Journal of Applied Philosophy*, 21, (2007), 181–94.

Mahon, J. E. 'Kant and the Perfect Duty to Others Not to Lie, *British Journal for the History of Philosophy*, 14, 4, (2006), 653–85.

Mahon, J. E. 'The Truth about Kant on Lies', in *The Philosophy of Deception*, ed. C. Martin, Oxford University Press (2009).

Mahon, J. E. 'Two Definitions of Lying', *International Journal of Applied Philosophy*, 22, (2008), 211–30.

Markie, P. J. 'Justification and Awareness', *Philosophical Studies: An International Journal for Philosophy in the Analytic Tradition*, 146, 3, (2009), 361–77.

Marks, J. *Perfection and Disharmony in the Thought of Jean-Jacques Rousseau*, Cambridge University Press (2011).

Marks, J. 'The Divine Instinct? Rousseau and Conscience', *The Review of Politics*, 68, (2006), 564–85.

Marques, A. 'Imputation Judgement in Kant's Practical Philosophy', in *Kant und die Philosophie in Weltbürgerlicher Absicht. Akten des XI. Internationalen Kant-Kongress, Bacin, Ferrarin*, Walter De Gruyter, (2013), 385–93.

Marshall, J. *'John Locke'*, Cambridge University Press (1994).

Matson, W. I. 'Kant as Casuist', *Journal of Philosophy*, 51, (1954), 855–60.

Mayes, B. T. G. *Counsel and Conscience, Lutheran Casuistry and Moral Reasoning after the Reformation*, Vandenhoeck & Ruprecht (2011).

McCarty, R. R. 'Kantian Motivation and the Feeling of Respect', *Journal of the History of Philosophy*, 31, 3, (1993), 421–35.

Mele, A. R. *Irrationality: An Essay on Akrasia, Self-Deception, and Self-Control*, Oxford University Press (1987) and, 'Self-Deception', *The Philosophical Quarterly*, 33, 133, (1983), 365–77.

Mele, A. R. *Self-Deception Unmasked*, Princeton University Press (2001).

Melzer, A. M. *The Natural Goodness of Man: On the System of Rousseau's Thought*, University of Chicago Press (1990).

Moore, G. E. 'A Reply to My Critics', in *The Philosophy of G. E. Moore*, ed. P. A. Schlipp, Northwestern University Press (1942), 544–45.

Moran, K. A. 'Can Kant Have a Theory of Moral Education?', *Journal of Philosophy of Education*, 43, 4, (2009), 471–84.

Mori, G. 'Pierre Bayle, the Rights of the Conscience, the Remedy of Toleration', *Ratio Juris*, 10, 1, (1997), 45–60.

Morrisson, I. P. D. *Kant and the Role of Pleasure in Moral Action*, Ohio University Press (2008).

Mothersill, M. 'Some Questions about Truthfulness and Lying', *Social Research*, 63, 3, (1996), 913–29.

Moyar, D. 'Unstable Autonomy: Conscience and Judgment in Kant's Moral Philosophy', *Journal of Moral Philosophy*, 5, (2008), 327–60.

Munzel, G. F. *Kant's Conception of Moral Character*, University of Chicago Press (1999).

Munzel, G. F. 'Kant on Moral Education, or "Enlightenment" and the Liberal Art', *The Review of Metaphysics*, 57, 1 (2003), 43–73.

Munzel, G. F. 'What does his Religion Contribute to Kant's Conception of Practical Reason?', *Kant's Religion within the Boundaries of Mere Reason: A Critical Guide*, ed. G. E. Michalson, Cambridge University Press (2014), 214–32.

Newman, L. S. 'Motivated Cognition and Self-Deception', *Psychological Inquiry*, 10, 1 (1999), 59–63.

Noordhof, P. 'Self-Deception, Interpretation and Consciousness', *Philosophy and Phenomenological Research*, 67, 1, (2003), 75–100.

O'Neill, O. *Acting on Principle*, Columbia University Press (1974).

O'Neill, O. *Constructions of Reason*, Cambridge University Press (1989).

O'Neill, O. *Constructions of Reason: Explorations of Kant's Practical Philosophy*, Cambridge University Press (1990).

Ojakangas, M. *The Voice of Conscience: A Political Genealogy of Western Ethical Experience*, Bloomsbury Academic Press (2013), 143–63.

Osawa, T. 'Perfection and Morality: A Commentary on Baumgarten's *Ethica Philosophica* and its Relevance to Kantian Ethics', (PhD Diss. Macquarie University 2014).

Palmer, A. 'Characterising Self-deception', *Mind* (*New Series*), 88, 349, (1979), 45–58.

Palmquist, S. R. *Kant's Critical Religion*, Ashgate (2000).

Pascal, B. *Pensees*, Penguin Classics (1995).

Paton, H. J. 'An alleged Right to Lie, A problem with Kantian Ethics', *Kant-Studien*, 45, (1953), 190–203.

Paton, H. J. 'Conscience and Kant', *Kant-Studien*, 70, (1979), 239–51.

Paton, H. J. *Categorical Imperative: A Study of Kant's Moral Philosophy*, University of Pennsylvania Press (1971).

Paton, M. 'A Reconsideration of Kant's Treatment of Duties to Oneself', *Philosophical Quarterly*, 40, 159, (1990), 222–33.

Pears, D. *Motivated Irrationality*, Oxford University Press (1984).

Pepperell, K. C. 'Religious Conscience and Civic Conscience in Thomas Hobbes's Civic Philosophy', *Educational Theory*, 39, 1, (1989), 17–25.

Pereboom, D. 'Kant on Justification in Transcendental Philosophy', *Synthese*, 85, (1990), 25–54.

Pfisterer, C. C. 'Ryle on Perception' in *Ryle on Mind and Language*, ed. D. Dolby, Palgrave Macmillan (2015), 146–64.

Plantinga, A. 'Epistemic Justification', *Nous*, 20, 1, (1986), 3–18.

Pollock, J. 'Epistemology and Probability', *Synthese*, 55, 2, (1983), 231–52.

Polonoff, D. 'Reflections on the Self', *Social Research*, 54, 1, (1987), 45–53.

Proops, I. 'Kant's Legal Metaphor and the Nature of a Deduction', *Journal of the History of Philosophy*, 41, 2, (2003), 209–29.

Pufendorf, S. *On the Duty of Man and Citizen According to Natural Law*, ed. J. Tully, Cambridge University Press (1991).

Quinton, A. 'Ryle on Perception', in *Ryle*, ed. O. P. Wood, G. Pitcher, Palgrave Macmillan (1971).

Raphael, D. D. *The Impartial Spectator: Adam Smith's Moral Philosophy*, Oxford University Press (2007).

Rauscher, F. 'Pure Reason and the Moral Law: A Source of Kant's Critical Philosophy', *History of Philosophy Quarterly*, 13, 2, (1996), 255–71.

Reath, A. 'Legislating the Moral Law', *Nous*, 28, 4, (1994), 435–64.

Reath, A. 'Two Conceptions of the Highest Good in Kant', *Journal of the History of Philosophy*, 26, 4, (1998), 593–619.

Reath, A. *Agency and Autonomy in Kant's Moral Theory*, Oxford University Press (2006).

Reath, A. 'Agency and the Imputation of Consequences in Kant's Ethics', Annual Review of Law and Ethics, 2, (1994), 259–281.

Reath, A. 'Self-Legislation and Duties to Oneself', *The Southern Journal of Philosophy*, 36, (1997), 103–24; reprinted in *Kant's Metaphysics of Morals: Interpretive Essays*, ed. M. Timmons, Oxford University Press (2002), 349–70.

Robinson, R. 'Necessary Propositions', *Mind*, 67, 267, (1958), 289–304.

Rorty, A. O. University of California Press (1988).

Rousseau, J. J. *Emile, or On Education*, trans. A. Bloom, Basic Books (1979).

Rutherford, D. *Leibniz and the Rational Order of Nature*, Cambridge University Press (1995).

Ryle, G. *The Concept of Mind*, Routledge (2009).

Sargentis, K. 'Moral Motivation in Kant', *Kant Studies Online*, (2012), 93–121.

Saul, J. M. *Lying, Misleading, and What is Said: An Exploration in Philosophy of Language and Ethics*, Oxford University Press (2012).

Saunders, J. T. 'The Paradox of Self-Deception', *Philosophy and Phenomenological Research*, 35, 4, (1975), 559–70.

Saurette, P. *The Kantian Imperative: Humiliation, Common Sense, Politics*, Toronto University Press (2005).

Schmidt, E., Schönecker, D. 'Kants Philosophie des Gewissens. Skizze für eine kommentarische Interpretation', in M. Egger (ed.), *Philosophie nach Kant. Neue Wege zum Verständnis von Kants Transzendental- und Moralphilosophie*, Berlin/Boston: de Gruyter, (2014), 279–312.

Schmidt, E., Schönecker, D. 'Vernunft, Herz und Gewissen. Kants Theorie der Urteilskraft zweiter Stufe als Modell für die Medizinische Ethik', in *Gewissen. Dimensionen eines Grundbegriffs medizinischer Ethik*, ed. F-J. Bormann, V. Wetzstein, Berlin/Boston: de Gruyter, (2014), 229–50.

Schneewind, J. B. *Moral Philosophy from Montaigne to Kant*, Cambridge University Press (2003).

Schneewind, J. B. *The Invention of Autonomy*, Cambridge University Press (1998).

Schollmeier, P. 'Practical Reason and Empirical Principles', *The Pluralist*, 2, 3, (2007), 120–33.

Schonecker, D. 'Kant's Moral Intuitionism: The Fact of Reason and Moral Dispositions', *Kant Studies Online* (2013), 1–38.

Schrader, G. A. 'Autonomy, Heteronomy, and Moral Imperatives', *The Journal of Philosophy*, 60, 3 (1963), 65–77.

Schwarz, W. 'Kant Refutation of Charitable Lies', *Ethics*, 81, (1970), 62–7.

Schwarz, W. 'Truth and Truthfulness: A Rejoinder', *Ethics*, 83, (1972–73), 173–5.

Sedgwick, S. *Kant's Groundwork of the Metaphysics of Morals*, Cambridge University Press (2008).

Sedgwick, S. 'On Lying and the Role of Content in Kant's Ethics', *Kant-Studien*, 82, (1991), 42–62.

Sensen, O. *Kant on Human Dignity*, Walter de Gruyter Press (2011).

Sensen, O. 'Kants Begriff des Gewissens', in *Gewissen zwischen Gefühl und Vernunft*, ed. S. Bunke, K. Mihaylova, Würzburg: Königshausen und Neumann, (2015), 126–38.

Senser, A. Kant und das Gewissen (Phd diss. University of Bern 1997).

Sharon, A.-G. 'God and Community: An Inquiry into the Religious Implications of the Highest Good', *Kant's Philosophy of Religion Reconsidered*, ed. P. J. Rossi and M. Wreen, Indiana University Press (1991), 113–31.

Shell, S. M. *Kant and the Limits of Autonomy*, Harvard University Press (2009).

Shell, S. M. *The Embodiment of Reason*, University of Chicago Press (1995).

Shklar, J. N. *Men and Citizens: A Study of Rousseau's Social Theory*, Cambridge University Press (1969).

Shuger, S. 'Knowledge and its Consequences', *American Philosophical Quarterly*, 20, 2 (1983), 217–25.

Siegler, F. A. 'Demos on Lying to Oneself', *The Journal of Philosophy*, 59, 17, (1962), 469–78.

Siegler, F. A. 'Self-Deception and Other Deception' *The Journal of Philosophy*, 60, 24, (1963), 759–64.

Siegler, F. A. 'Voluntary and Involuntary', *The Monist*, 52, 2, (1968), 268–87.

Simmons, K. 'Kant on Moral Worth', *History of Philosophy Quarterly*, 6, 1, (1989), 85–100.

Simpson, D. 'Lying, Liars and Language', *Philosophy and Phenomenological Research*, 52, 3, (1992), 623–40.

Smith, A. *The Theory of Moral Sentiments*, Penguin Books (2009).

Soldati, G. 'Direct Realism and Immediate Justification', *Proceedings of the Aristotelian Society*, 112, (2012), 29–44.

Sorabji, R. *Moral Conscience Through the Ages*, Oxford University Press (2014), 178–83.

Sorensen, R. A. 'Lying with Conditionals', *The Philosophical Quarterly*, 62, 249, (2012), 820–32.

Sorensen, R. A. 'Self-Deception and Scattered Events' *Mind*, New Series, 94, 373, (1985), 64–9.

Sorensen, R. A. 'What Lies Behind Misspeaking', *American Philosophical Quarterly*, 48, 4, (2011), 399–409.

Sosa, E. 'Knowledge in Context, Skepticism in Doubt: The Virtue of Our Faculties', *Philosophical Perspectives*, 2, (1988), 139–55.

Stalnaker, R. *Inquiry*, MIT University Press (1984).

Statton-Lake, P. *Kant, Duty and Moral Worth*, Routledge (2000).

Stevens, R. P. *Kant on Moral Practice: A Study of Moral Success and Failure*, Mercer University Press (1981).

Stevenson, L. 'Opinion, Belief or Faith, and Knowledge', Kantian Review, 7, (2003), 72–101.

Sticker, M. 'When the Reflective Watch-Dog Barks: Conscience and Self-Deception in Kant', *Journal of Value Inquiry*, (forthcoming), 1–20.

Stratton-Lake, P. 'Being virtuous and the virtues: two aspects of Kant's doctrine of virtue', in *Kant's Ethics of Virtue*, ed. M. Betzler, Walter de Gruyter & Co (2008), 101–22.

Stroud, B. 'Epistemological Reflection on Knowledge of the External World', *Philosophy and Phenomenological Research*, 56, 2, (1996), 345–58.

Stroud, S. R. 'Rhetoric and Moral Progress in Kant's Ethical Community', *Philosophy and Rhetoric*, 38, 4, (2005), 328–54.

Sullivan, R. *Immanuel Kant's Moral Theory*, Cambridge University Press (1989).

Surprenant, C. W. 'Kant's Postulate of the Immortality of the Soul', *International Philosophical Quarterly*, 48, 1, (2008), 85–98.

Third Earl of Shaftesbury, Anthony Ashley Cooper. *Characteristics of Men, Manners, Opinions, Times*, Cambridge University Press (2000).

Timmermann, J. 'Kantian Duties to the Self, Explained and Defended', *Philosophy*, 81, 317, (2006), 505–30.

Timmermann, J. *Kant's Groundwork of the Metaphysics of Morals: A Commentary*, Cambridge University Press (2007).

Timmermann, J. 'Kant on Conscience, "Indirect" Duty, and Moral Error', *International Philosophical Quarterly*, 46, 3, (2006), 293–308.

Timmermann, J. *Kant's Groundwork of the Metaphysics of Morals: A Commentary*, Cambridge University Press (2007).

Timmermann, J. 'Agency and Imputation: Comments on Reath', *Philosophical Books*, 49, 2, (2008), 114–124.

Timmons, M. 'Kant on the Possibility of Moral Motivation', *Southern Journal of Philosophy*, 23, (1984), 377–98.

Timmons, M. 'Evil and Imputation in Kant's Ethics', *Jahrbuch für Recht und Ethik*, 2, (1994), 113–141.

Tuck, R. *The Rights of War and Peace: Political Thought and the International Order from Grotius to Kant*, Oxford University Press (1999).

Valaris, M. 'Inner Sense, Self-Affection, and Temporal Consciousness', *Philosophers' Imprint*, 8, 4, (2008), 1–17.

van Fraassen, B. C. 'Belief and the Will', *The Journal of Philosophy*, 81, (1984), 235–256.

Velleman, D. 'The Voice of Conscience', *Proceedings of the Aristotelian Society*, 99, (1999), 57–76.

Vogt, K. M. 'Duties to Others: Demands and Limits', in *Kant's Ethics of Virtue*, ed. M. Betzler, De Gruyter, (2008), 219–44.

Voitle, R. B. 'Shaftesbury's Moral Sense', *Studies in Philology*, 52, 1, (1955), 17–38.

von der Pfordten, D. 'On the Dignity of Man in Kant', *Philosophy*, 84, 329, (2009), 371–91.

Vujosevic, M. 'The Judge in the Mirror: Kant on Conscience', *Kantian Review*, 19, 3, (2014), 449–74.

Walker, R. C. S. *Kant*, Routledge & Kegan Paul (1978).

Ware, O. 'Kant, Skepticism, and Moral Sensibility' (PhD diss. University of Toronto 2010).

Ware, O. 'The Duty of Self-Knowledge', *Philosophy and Phenomenological Research*, 79, (2009), 671–98.

Watkin, E. 'The Antimony of Practical Reason: Reason, the Unconditioned and the Highest Good', in *Kant's Critique of Practical Reason: A Critical Guide*, ed. A. Reath and J. Timmermann, Cambridge University Press (2010), 145–68.

Webb, M. O. 'Natural Theology and the Concept of Perfection in Descartes, Spinoza and Leibniz', *Religious Studies*, 25, 4, (1989), 459–75.

Wellmon, C. 'Kant and the Feelings of Reason', *Eighteenth-Century Studies*, 42, 4, (2009), 557–80.

Wilhelmus, T. 'Knowing', *The Hudson Review*, 41, 3, (1988), 548–56.

Willaschek, M. 'The Primacy of Practical Reason and the Idea of a Practical Postulate' *Kant's Critique of Practical Reason: A Critical Guide*, ed. A. Reath and J. Timmermann, Cambridge University Press (2010), 168–96.

Williams, B. *Truth and Truthfulness: An Essay in Genealogy*, Princeton University Press (2002).

Wolff, R. *The Autonomy of Reason*, Harper and Row (1973).

Wood, A. W. 'Religion, Ethical Community and the Struggle against Evil', *Faith and Philosophy*, 17, 498–511.

Wood, A. W. 'The Final Form of Kant's Practical Philosophy', in *Kant's Metaphysics of Morals: Interpretive Essays*, ed. M. Timmons, Cambridge University Press (2004), 1–21.

Wood, A. W. *Kant's Ethical Thought*, Cambridge University Press (1999).

Wood, A. W. *Kantian Ethics*, Cambridge University Press (2008), 182–92.

Wood, A. W. *Kant's Moral Religion*, Cornell University Press (1970).

Xie, S. S. 'What Is Kant: A Compatibilist Or An Incompatibilist? A New Interpretation of Kant's Solution to the Free Will Problem', *Kant-Studien*, 100, 1, 53–76.

Yovel, Y. *Kant and the Philosophy of History*, Princeton University Press (1980).

Zinkin, M. 'Respect for the Law and the Use of Dynamical Terms in Kant's Theory of Moral Motivation', *Archiv für Geschichte der Philosophie*, 88, 1, (2006), 31–53.

Edited Collections

Conscience and Casuistry in Early Modern Europe, ed. E. Leites, Cambridge University Press (1988).

Kant and Education, ed. K. Roth and C. W. Surprenant, Routledge (2012).

Kant on Emotion and Value, ed. A. Cohen, Palgrave Macmillan (2014).

Kant's Critique of Practical Reason and Other Works on the Theory of Ethics, trans. L. W. Beck, The University of Chicago Press (1949).

Kant's Critique of Practical Reason: A Critical Guide, ed. A. Reath and J. Timmermann, Cambridge University Press (2010).

Kant's Metaphysics of Morals: A Critical Guide, ed. L. Denis, Cambridge University Press (2010).

Kant's Metaphysics of Morals: Interpretive Essays, ed. M. Timmons, Cambridge University Press (2004).

Kant's Religion within the Boundaries of Mere Reason: A Critical Guide, ed. G. E. Michalson,
    Cambridge University Press (2014).
Moore's Paradox: New Essays on Belief, Rationality, and the First Person, ed. M. S. Green
    and J. N. Williams, Oxford University Press (2007).

Translated Anthologies

Locke: Political Essays, ed. M. Goldie, Cambridge University Press (2002).
Rousseau, The Discourses and other Early Political Writings, ed. V. Gourevitch, Cambridge
    University Press (1997).
Schneewind, J. B. *Moral Philosophy from Montaigne to Kant*, Cambridge University
    Press (2003). Specifically, the following selections were used:
    Crusius, C. A. *A Guide to Rational Living, translations from Schneewind, Moral
        Philosophy from Montaigne to Kant*, 568–85.
    Grotius, H. *On the Law of War and Peace*, 88–100.
    The Political Writings of Samuel Pufendorf, ed. C. L. Carr, Oxford University Press
        (1994).
    Pufendorf, S. *The Duty of Man and Citizen*, 156–82.
    Wolff, C. *Vernüfftige Gedancken von der enschen Thun und Lassen zu Beförderung
        ihrer Glückseeligkeit*, 331–50.

Index